THEORY AND INTERPRETATION OF NARRATIVE

James Phelan, Peter J. Rabinowitz, and Robyn Warhol, Series Editors

The Reader as Peeping Tom

Nonreciprocal Gazing in Narrative Fiction and Film

Jeremy Hawthorn

THE OHIO STATE UNIVERSITY PRESS

COLUMBUS

Copyright © 2014 by The Ohio State University.
All rights reserved.

Library of Congress Cataloging-in-Publication Control Number
2013042396
ISBN-13: 978-0-8142-1257-8 (cloth : alk. paper)
ISBN-13: 978-0-8142-9360-7 (cd-rom)

Cover design by Janna Thompson-Chordas
Text design by Juliet Williams
Type set in Adobe Sabon
Printed by Thomson-Shore, Inc.

♾ The paper used in this publication meets the minimum requirements of the American
National Standard for Information Sciences—Permanence of Paper for Printed Library
Materials. ANSI Z.39-1992.

9 8 7 6 5 4 3 2 1

CONTENTS

ACKNOWLEDGMENTS

I OWE a large debt of thanks to friends and colleagues who have helped me in the writing of this book. Domhnall Mitchell and Paul Goring have commented on draft chapters, opening my eyes to many weaknesses and suggesting improvements. Katrine Antonsen, for whom I have acted as academic supervisor at master's and doctoral level, has made me think much more about the human impulse *not* to violate the private lives of our fellows, but to respect their right to privacy. I owe an especial debt to Jakob Lothe, who has provided detailed comments both on early versions of chapters and on the whole book in draft form, with a meticulous attention to details of the argument and to problems relating to matters of theory and terminology. Two readers for The Ohio State University Press, James Phelan and an anonymous reviewer, also made very valuable and, in James Phelan's case, extensive, suggestions for improving the text. My excellent copyeditor, Kristen Ebert-Wagner, has removed many infelicities, inconsistencies, and unnecessary words from my text, and has brought order to my references and bibliography. I am deeply grateful to all of these individuals. All inadequacies that remain are, of course, solely my own responsibility.

I am, again, deeply grateful to my wife, Bjørg, for her support during the many years that this book has been in the making. The reciprocity of our relationship has remained a valuable reference point as I have investigated the often disturbing depths of various kinds of non-reciprocity.

This book could not have been written without the support of my late employer, the Norwegian University of Science and Technology. A generous provision of research leave and support for travel and other research costs was consistent during my time of employment. Since retirement I have been granted a workspace and computer facilities by the university. I am most grateful for this support.

I would also like to express my thanks to the unpaid experts who offer help on the WordPerfect® Universe site <www.wpuniverse.com>, who have solved problems for me quickly and courteously for over two decades.

Some of the chapters in this book consist of revised versions of previously published articles. An earlier version of the chapter on *Oliver Twist* was published as "Seeing Is Believing: Power and the Gaze in Charles Dickens's *The Adventures of Oliver Twist*" in *Nordic Journal of English Studies* 1, no. 1 (2002): 107–32. An earlier version of the chapter on *Typee* was published as "Herman Melville's *Typee*: The Voyeur and the Imperial Gaze" in Jakob Lothe, Anne Holden Rønning, and Peter Young, eds., *Identities and Masks: Colonial and Postcolonial Studies* (Kristiansand: Norwegian Academic Press, 2001), 33–50. An earlier version of the chapter on "In the Cage" was published as "Class, Voyeurism and Sadism: Henry James's 'In the Cage'" in Ulf Lie and Anne Holden Rønning, eds., *Dialoguing on Genres* (Oslo: Novus Press, 2001), 181–97. An earlier version of the chapter on *Peeping Tom* was published as "Morality, Voyeurism, and 'Point of View': Michael Powell's *Peeping Tom*" in *Nordic Journal of English Studies* 2, no. 2 (2003): 303–24. I am grateful to the editors concerned for their help and encouragement in the writing of these articles.

INTRODUCTION

IN MY LEISURE TIME I like to spy on people. I enjoy watching them as they live their lives, especially in their most private and intimate moments. Personal letters, private conversations, secret emotions: these are some of the things I find most fascinating. And the best of it is that they do not know that I am spying on them. They, after all, are fictional characters, and I am a reader of books or a member of the cinema audience. In the world of the fiction these characters interact with one another, but they do not interact with me. If it were known that I spied on my fellow human beings in the way that I do on the lives of the fictional characters that I meet in books and films, I would become a social outcast. As it is, none of my friends object to my voyeuristic behavior: after all, most of them are doing the same thing. It appears, then, that while one set of ethical rules operates within our everyday world, and also within the worlds created and portrayed in works of fiction, a different set of ethical rules appears to govern my behavior as a real-life individual who observes characters and events in these fictional worlds. This contrast between two sets of ethical rules both puzzles and intrigues me. And it is this contrast that I attempt to explore in the pages that follow.

This book is, then, about reciprocity, and the denial or prevention of reciprocity, on a number of levels and in a variety of contexts. On a thematic level it focuses on a selection of narratives that depict a range of non-reciprocal human relationships: spying, surveillance, voyeurism, and gender- or racially based objectification. On a formal level it explores the implications of the fact that as readers and viewers we have relationships with fictional narratives, their narrators, and their characters, that are non-reciprocal—thus producing the paradox that we may engage with critiques of non-reciprocal relationships through forms that are themselves fundamentally non-reciprocal. It is almost as if those enemies of the theater, the Puritans, had put on plays to make their case. Finally, at the points where the thematic and the formal intersect, I attempt to investigate the varied ways in which different narratives deal with this paradoxical state of affairs: for example by concealing or denying the non-interactive nature of our engagement with fiction, or alternatively by using the reader's or viewer's experience of non-reciprocity to illustrate and explore one-way communication at the thematic level.

Reciprocity: "a state or relationship," the *OED* informs us, "in which there is mutual action, influence, giving and taking, correspondence, etc., between two parties or things." Reciprocity does not necessarily entail full equality between different parties, but it does require some form of mutual recognition on the part of two people or entities, some verification of the other's existence through an exchange of mutually significant information. In Joseph Conrad's *Lord Jim* (2012), the character-narrator Marlow makes reference to "the mysterious power of the human glance that can awaken the feelings of remorse and pity" (106), and in the same writer's novella *Heart of Darkness* (2010b), it is the gaze of the dying helmsman that moves Marlow from a view of him as "a savage who was no more account than a grain of sand in a black Sahara" to one of him as a fellow human being: "the intimate profundity of that look he gave me when he received his hurt remains to this day in my memory—like a claim of distant kinship affirmed in a supreme moment" (96). Intimacy, note, is something that emerges in interaction between at least two individuals: surveying the private details of another person's life without their knowledge or consent does not create genuine intimacy, although, as we shall see, it may create an illusion of intimacy, what some commentators have termed pseudo intimacy. However, if the mutual exchange of a glance can lay claim to and reveal a shared humanity, the denial of reciprocity—the refusal of mutuality—has the effect of transforming the other from person to object.

In what way do works of prose fiction and fictional films encourage non-reciprocal relations with readers or viewers? The claim may appear odd, but it is far from new. As Plato's Socrates pointed out to Phaedrus:

Yes, because there's something odd about writing, Phaedrus, which makes it exactly like painting. The offspring of painting stand there as if alive, but if you ask them a question they maintain an aloof silence. It's the same with written words: you might think they were speaking as if they had some intelligence, but if you want an explanation of any of the things they're saying and you ask them about it, they just go on and on forever giving the same single piece of information. Once any account has been written down, you find it all over the place, hobnobbing with completely inappropriate people no less than with those who understand it, and completely failing to know who it should and shouldn't talk to. And faced with rudeness and unfair abuse it always needs its father to come to its assistance, since it is incapable of defending or helping itself. (Plato 2002, 70)

The experience of reading a written text may mimic that of a conversation with another person, may provide us with a sense that we are interacting with (rather than merely responding to) the text, its narrator, its characters, or author, but this is not so. In the case of that particular set of fixed texts that we call fictional narratives—whether they are printed works of prose fiction, or films—we respond to the text but the text does not respond to us. The narrators of works of prose fiction and films may address us, but they do not interact with us; as readers and viewers we have a relationship with them that is a fundamentally non-reciprocal one. Observing the characters in such works may change us, but they can never return our gaze or answer our questions, and their lives as depicted are eternally unaffected by our interest in them. They may pose questions for us, but they do not listen to our answers; they are somewhere else, as Plato's Socrates has it, off "hobnobbing with completely inappropriate people," giving new readers the same false sense of intimacy and interaction they gave us. When we return to a novel a second time, our reading experience may be different, but that is not because the text is different but because *we* are (and we are different partly because of what the text did to us on first reading).

In her book *Having a Good Cry: Effeminate Feelings and Pop-Culture Forms,* Robyn R. Warhol (2003) includes the testimony of a woman in her late twenties reflecting on her reactions to reading a Dickens novel: "'I had a distinct physical response—kind of a sigh or a change in my breathing. I looked up from the page even though there was no one in the room to share the experience with; I think I smiled, too'" (x). Jonathan Cole (1998) reports that "[c]hildren smile not when they open a present but when they turn to their parents; adults' joy at a strike at ten-pin bowling is shown not when they are pointing downlane at the pins, but when they turn to their friends" (59). The smile we make while reading a novel comes from that overwhelming sense we have that we are in the presence of another person or people capable of witnessing our facial movements, whether this person is the author, the narrator, or a character in the fiction. Rationally, if we consider the matter, we know this is not the case, but the power of fiction trumps our reason.[1] We may be amused watching those speaking on cell phones who gesture animatedly while talking to someone who cannot see their arm movements, but at least there is a genuinely reciprocal exchange going on in such situations to evoke such automatic—albeit redundant—behavior.

Certain postmodernist exceptions apart, the characters we encounter in novels and films, like the people portrayed in paintings mentioned by Plato, remain in blissful ignorance that we are observing them. In their most intimate moments, we are there, in their private spaces and even inside their heads. Our surveillance of their lives goes far beyond that which is possible in our relationships with our fellow human beings: in the case of fictional characters even their thoughts may be displayed for us to follow, including those thoughts of which they themselves may not be fully conscious. The fictions within which they live are like prequels to Peter Weir's 1998 film *The Truman Show*—with the telling difference that unlike Truman Burbank they never discover that they are being observed. Reading a novel, watching a film—there is a case for calling these activities the ultimate voyeuristic experiences. As readers we smile as if we can be seen by others, and yet at the same time, and paradoxically, we observe characters in their most private moments as if we cannot be seen by them (and indeed we cannot). All this may seem obvious when considered, yet novels and films typically manage to anaesthetize readers and viewers against an awareness of the voyeuristic aspects of their activity. It may be that the emergence of genuinely reciprocal forms of fiction using the Internet as host have set this characteristic of more traditional fictional forms in a historically novel relief in the last decade or so. But even before the development of interactive electronic fiction, some forms of representation called more attention than did others to the non-reciprocal relationship that they offered.

---

1. For further discussion of smiling behavior prompted by a sense of pseudo intimacy, see the discussion of certain scenes in Hitchcock's *Rear Window* in chapter 5, p. 175.

Roland Barthes (1993) contrasts the effect that photographs, on the one hand, and films, on the other, have on the viewer. He advances the hypothesis that "by attesting that the object has been real, the photograph surreptitiously induces belief that it is alive, because of that delusion that makes us attribute to Reality an absolutely superior, somehow eternal value; but by shifting this reality to the past ('this-has-been'), the photograph suggests that it is already dead" (79). At the same time, however, the photograph also "has this power . . . of looking me *straight in the eye*" (111; emphasis in original). Thus the photograph evokes reciprocity only to draw our attention to its absence: it looks us in the eye, induces a belief that it is alive, but at the same time its lack of movement reminds us that it is (already) dead. It invites communicative exchange only to confront us with the reality that such exchange is not possible. In contrast, Barthes (1991) claims, in the cinema as against the photograph, "the *having-been-there* vanishes, giving way to a *being-there* of the thing" (34; emphases in original). Because the "thing" appears to be "there" for us, we do not have our attention drawn to the fact that we are not there for it, as we do in the case of the photograph. Barthes perhaps exaggerates this difference between photograph and film, but the contrast he draws between the two media is nonetheless thought-provoking. With both media the viewer responds and waits for some reciprocal response. In the case of film the change and movement fundamental to the medium go some way towards satisfying our desire for response, even if on a rational level the viewer must know that the change and movement are not prompted by his or her presence or reaction. But the tantalizing fixity of the photograph gives the viewer no basis for even pretending that a response has been given. Movies, then, do not evoke death for us in quite the same way that photographs do. Unlike photographs, they divert our attention from the fact that our relationship with the characters and events they present is not a reciprocal or interactive one.

Photographs, like some paintings, may suggest or evoke a sequence of events but, unlike movies, they are not themselves narratives. It seems likely that there is something about the narrative function that serves to conceal the fact of non-reciprocity from the reader or viewer. What Barthes (1991) says about the *being-there* experience of watching a movie can also be applied to our readings of literary fiction, which also typically provide us with a sense of "being-there," although this sense may involve a relationship to the teller as much as if not more than to the characters and events. Barthes notes that "by dint of gazing, one forgets one can be gazed at oneself" (238); one may add that reading a novel or watching a film, by dint of responding one frequently forgets that one cannot be responded to—unless the author or narrator draws our attention to this fact.

Dramatic performances on the theatrical stage are clearly different. The behavior of the audience does affect the performance and the delivery of the words, even if the words remain the same, and individual members of the audience may influence one another as they applaud, or laugh, or gasp with surprise. A dramatic performance is, in this sense, more of an interactive event than the silent, individual reading of a novel—although this is *not* to say that it is interactive in the manner of a person-to-person conversation. The response of an audience may affect what the actors do on the stage both during the performance in question and in subsequent performances, but unlike the performance of, say, a stand-up comedian, this response will not change the words that are spoken. An audience's behavior during a performance of *Hamlet* may change how the actors deliver their lines, but it cannot and will not change the words that the characters (as against the actors playing them) utter on stage. I have, accordingly, included no plays among my chosen texts. The dialectic between the audience's interaction with the characters, and the characters' interaction with one another, has a certain overlap with my chosen topic, but it is different enough to have persuaded me to exclude it from the present study.

Introducing his 1988 book *The Novel and the Police,* D. A. Miller explains that it has a dual perspective. On the one hand, he asks how "the police systematically function as a topic in the 'world' of the novel," a question that appears to require an answer that takes the form of a relatively traditional, "thematic" study. But to this he adds the additional question, "how does the novel—as a set of representational techniques—systematically participate in a general economy of policing power?" (2). This question focuses attention not just on what happens in the world of an individual novel—within, that is, its created fictional world or diegesis—but on the manner in which the novel as genre and institution functions in the non-fictional world in which it is written, read, and discussed.

In the present book I have set myself a comparable dual aim. On the one hand I focus on depictions of spying, surveillance, fantasizing, and voyeurism in a number of films and works of prose fiction. But on the other hand I attempt to explore how these varied works encourage the viewer or reader themselves to engage in forms of observation that simulate or initiate activities such as spying, surveillance, fantasizing, and voyeurism—and, on occasion, to be conscious of what they are doing. Miller suggests that "[w]henever the novel censures policing power, it has already reinvented it, in *the very practice of novelistic representation*" (20; emphasis in original). I argue that something similar is frequently true of representations of the activities of the spy or the voyeur in films and works of prose fiction: the reader is led to disapprove of the actions of the spy, while spying on these actions; the viewer looks down on the pathetic voyeur while either surreptitiously indulging a guilt-free voyeuristic tendency by proxy or surrogate—or alternatively experiencing disquiet at the similarity between what he or she is doing as a reader and what the pathetic voyeur is doing within the diegesis of the film. If, as I argue in chapter 4 on Henry James's "In the Cage," James's telegraphist fantasizes about her rich customers as if they were characters in a fictional work, she is in her turn a character in a work of fiction about whom James's readers are tempted (or invited) to fantasize.

Different texts relate the activities of surveillance of one form or another *in* the depicted fictional world to the various forms of surveillance *of* characters and events in that same fictional world by director, narrator, viewer or reader, in varied ways. In some texts (and not only those produced since the modernist revolution) these different moments are brought together, and the reader or viewer is invited to compare and contrast the activities of a character or characters within the depicted fictional world with his or her own observing of this world and its hidden or secret aspects. Mark Romanek's 2002 film *One Hour Photo*, for example, opens and closes with the character Seymour Parrish (played by Robin Williams) seated in a police interview room, being observed through the one-way glass. This places the character in precisely the situation of the family that he himself has been spying on in the narrative time prior to this—the object of a one-way gaze (although, unlike them, he presumably knows that he is being observed). But it also places us, the viewers, in what previously was his situation: that of the unobserved observer. Seymour "sees more" than he should, but in spite of the pseudo intimacy that his spying provides for him he is without real human contact with those on whom he spies. And we, too, as we watch with the detectives through the one-way glass, are confronted with our own lack of any human contact with him: his isolation is our isolation; his illicit looking has become ours as, like a spectral presence, we become a ghostly observer alongside the detectives, looking down on him for having done what we have been and are now ourselves doing.

In other texts the demarcation line between the fictional and the extra-fictional worlds is used to effect a rigid demarcation between the two, so that rather than witnessing our own voyeuristic activity mirrored in the text and thus being forced to recognize it, we are like the detective observing the suspect through one-way glass, able to scrutinize and judge without ourselves being scrutinized or judged. A third alternative—one that I will argue later on in this book can be found in Charles Dickens's *Oliver Twist*—involves a separation between "good spying" and "bad spying," with the reader allowed to locate his or her voyeurism in the first category. The possibility of making such a separation is, I argue, also raised in Alfred Hitchcock's *Rear Window,* although the film does not underwrite such a possibility in quite so uncritical a manner as does *Oliver Twist.*

To a certain extent my interests in this book overlap with those theoretical strands of thought that are often granted a collective identity under the title of "The Gaze." Within the humanities, and especially within literary or film studies, the term evokes a complex body of theory emanating from a number of sources. First among these is Michel Foucault's (1979) metaphorical extension of Jeremy Bentham's "panopticon," an extension used to describe that condition of internalized surveillance to be found (according to Foucault) at the heart of modern Western culture (195–201). A more diffuse tradition that develops Jacques Lacan's (1998) critique of Jean-Paul Sartre (1969) is represented in its most influential manifestation by Laura Mulvey's article "Visual Pleasure and Narrative Cinema," first published in 1975. Mulvey attempts to link looking behavior in the classic Hollywood film with forms of gendered audience identification and viewpoint—and further with the ideological position that these support—and I will have more to say about Mulvey's work in chapter 5 when discussing Alfred Hitchcock's *Rear Window.*

From these and other roots have grown a critical tradition that typically relates the forms of looking depicted within texts to aspects of the narrative positioning of readers or viewers, and further to techniques of ideological interpellation. Such a tradition is relevant to my interests in this book because it is sensitive to inequalities and imbalances in looking relationships, both those involving exchanged looks and those concerned with one-way looking. However, it is a tradition that is not without its critics. In her book *The Distinction of Fiction* (1999), for example, Dorrit Cohn has a concluding chapter entitled "Optics and Power in the Novel," in which she builds on Gérard Genette's (1988, 74) argument that the term "omniscience" is inappropriate to discussion of fictional narrative. Cohn argues that

> such terms as "surveillance," "discourse of power," or "panoptic vision" make sense only when they are applied to relationships that are potentially reversible: master/slave (cf. Hegel), police/criminal, prison-guard/prisoner, parent/child, teacher/pupil, man/woman, and many more. They make no sense at all—no Foucauldian sense, at any rate—when they are applied to an author's (or heterodiegetic narrator's) relationship to his fictional characters. (171)

Well, I am not sure that my relationship to the surveillance cameras that track my progress through a big city (or to those individuals who study the images that these cameras record) is "potentially reversible" in any meaningful way. Indeed, one can counter that it is precisely the lack of a potential reversibility that gives comparisons between, on the one hand, the relationship between the voyeur and his victim, and, on the other hand, an author's relationship to a character, their force. This apart, one of the things that Cohn's account leaves out is the *reader's* relationship to fictional characters. Her objection does, however, serve as a useful warning, and one that I will attempt to heed in the pages that follow. In comparing the relationship between literary characters with the relationship between a reader or viewer and a literary character, we have one foot in the realm of metaphor, and as the narrator of George Eliot's (1988) *Middlemarch* reminds us, "we all of us, grave or light, get our thoughts entangled in metaphors, and act fatally on the strength of them" (70). In what follows I will do my best to avoid such entanglements.

Readers, Viewers, Audiences

Readers . . . the reader . . . so far I have used these terms somewhat indiscriminately, as many literary critics do. Recently, while preparing an article for submission to a journal, I was struck by the fact that the journal's house style did not permit references to "the reader" but insisted that such references should be to the plural "readers." "The reader" is of course a convenient and potentially misleading generalization. As Peter Rabinowitz puts it in his book *Before Reading: Narrative Conventions and the Politics of Interpretation* (1998), "the term *reader* is slippery, not only because all individual readers read differently, but also because for almost all of them, there are several different ways of appropriating a text" (20). Both parts of this sentence are, I think, worth pondering on. It is certainly the case that in the course of the past three decades critics and theorists have come up with an impressive (or bewildering) array of terms to distinguish between different readers or reader-functions. The implied reader, the inscribed reader, the model reader, the intended reader, the average reader, the actual reader, the contemporary reader, the super-reader (Michael Riffaterre), the informed reader (Stanley Fish)— all of these (especially if they are critics as well as readers) have engaged in symptomatic reading, oppositional reading, radial reading (Jerome McGann), mediation reading, transparency reading, feminist reading, resisting reading (Judith Fetterley), and so on, and so on. The very abundance of terms is revealing: it is because reading does not involve a reciprocal exchange between two parties in the manner of a conversation that we can choose from a range of alternatives when deciding how we read a text. Some ways may appear to be palpably more rewarding or revealing than others, but the text cannot object to our manner of reading in quite the way that a human interlocutor can protest at our responses to his or her conversational contributions.

Rabinowitz makes his comment about the slipperiness of the term *reader* in an early section of his book entitled *Who Is Reading?* He goes on to focus on a more limited set of terms: actual audience, hypothetical, or authorial audience, and narrative audience. This shift from *readers* to *audience* deserves note because the connotations of *audience* differ somewhat from those evoked by *readers*. Rightly or wrongly we associate more passivity with an audience; an audience receives impressions from the activity of others, others who are in some way or another performers. In a performer–audience relationship there may be an element of interaction (actors talk about good and bad audiences), but what is transmitted from performer to audience is more important than what is transmitted from audience to performer. The term *readers,* in contrast, is one that describes a doing, an activity (the verb "to read" can be used both transitively and intransitively). The use of both terms to describe the processes whereby individuals appropriate literary works reflects, I would suggest, a recognition of the fact that almost any individual is active in his or her creative encounter with a text (dealing with a rich, complex work of fiction requires, among other things, that one think hard), but also passive to the extent that he or she must work with a text that is unchangeable and that, to a significant extent, dictates its own terms. Be this as it may, Rabinowitz's distinctions are helpful and, in the light of the terminological fecundity inspired by this topic, reassuringly limited.

The actual audience is, as Rabinowitz (1998) puts it, "the audience that booksellers are most concerned with—but it happens to be the audience over which an author has no guaranteed control" (20). Pretty obviously this term covers a group of flesh-and-blood people spread over time and place who may have in common little beyond the fact that they are readers of the same book (in Plato's designation, they may well be "inappropriate," although that is a term that raises as many problems as it resolves). Rabinowitz's "hypothetical or authorial audience" is the product of an author's guesswork: some (but by no means all) authors attempt to envisage who will read what they write, and compose with this construction in mind. Their texts may therefore bear the traces of these surmises. But a writer's guesses may vary wildly in their accuracy. A writer who regularly produces a particular sort of novel, who knows what his or her readers expect (because they communicate their responses and wishes to him or her) is different from a writer who (like Emily Dickinson) publishes little or nothing in their lifetime, or who has no idea who is likely to read what he or she may or may not hope to publish. The British novelist Sid Chaplin delivered a telling reply when asked in an interview if he was conscious of writing for any particular audience: "It's just the same as when I started. A message in a bottle," although he added the interesting qualification that when writing one particular novel that was set in a coalfield, he knew that it would be read by those who worked in the industry, and he was right. "One miner wrote to me and said that he'd worn seven copies out!" (quoted in Pickering and Robins 1984, 149). I was myself present at a talk given by the novelist Margaret Atwood and asked her if she had a sense of a particular reader while she was writing, and she replied that when first she started writing she had a sense of a man looking over her shoulder and reading what she had written, while more recently (this was in the late 1980s) she had started to think of this ghostly reader as female.

Such activity on the part of writers—trying to write for the readers they expect to get—is matched by readers' attempts to read in the way they believe authors want them to (or, as is the case with the "resisting reader," to oppose the author's wishes). Moreover, this belief is partly the product of the author's rhetorical choices, choices that, as in the military, turn a group of diverse raw reader-recruits into, if not a highly disciplined army, at least a body of individuals who have more in common as readers than they do as ordinary individuals.

Why are such issues relevant to my topic in this book? Well, James Phelan, in a foreword to Rabinowitz's (1998) book written on the occasion of its reissue, writes that

> Rabinowitz's model of interpretation assumes the possibility of—and places considerable value upon—reciprocity between authors and their audiences. However, because the conventions are social constructs and because readers' decisions about which conventions a text is employing are affected by their starting points, readers' inferences and an author's implications may very well diverge. Furthermore, in some of these cases, the divergence may never be discovered because the interpretation the reader constructs will adequately account for the text. (xiv)

Phelan, it will be seen, confesses to a certain skepticism about Rabinowitz's belief, or hope, that the relationship between author and audiences may involve an element of reciprocity. The hope and the skepticism can both be understood. As I have suggested, a real-life ("actual") reader may well have built up a sense of what to expect in the work of a familiar author, or with regard to a particular genre within the constraints of which an author writes. An actual author too may well have learned by trial and error, and on the basis of sales and feedback, what his or her readers want and expect (although they may well want something that is not quite what they expect). Furthermore, it is worth noting that the special circumstances of serial publication do allow reader responses to influence the process of composition of a single text. A set of shared expectations, constructed and modified over time from book to book or installment to installment, may warrant use of the term "reciprocity." At the same time, the "divergence" to which Phelan refers will, when it occurs, justify a view of the author–audience relationship as a non-reciprocal one.

In his foreword, Phelan suggests a further sophistication of Rabinowitz's classifications: "the narratee is the narrator's addressee, while the narrative audience is the observer role we enter within the world of the fiction" (Rabinowitz 1998, xxii n5). In his earlier *Narrative as Rhetoric: Technique, Audiences, Ethics, Ideology* (1996), Phelan associates the concept of the narratee with the tradition of structuralist narratology and that of the narrative audience with rhetorical narratology. He concedes that the boundaries between the two terms are often shifting and other than clear, but he makes a strong case that the two terms serve complementary functions and are both needed (135). The terms clearly cover what are often overlapping identities or rôles, and what are perhaps on occasion indistinguishable ones. When I read a novel in which the narrator addresses a personified narratee, my own activity as reader is altered. In Phelan's terms, an address to a narratee will change the behavior (and self-conscious identity) of the narrative audience.

In the chapters that follow, accordingly, I will attempt to write in the light of such distinctions and, where appropriate, to distinguish between the narratee's relationship with the narrator, the narrative audience's relationship with the characters and events in the world of the fiction, and the actual reader's double rôle as real-world person relating to the work of another real-world person (author or director) and as real-world person consciously adopting an observer rôle within the fictional world of novel or film. These alternative rôles, in my experience, are not mutually exclusive in the way that Wittgenstein's image is either duck or rabbit but never both. Rabinowitz's theory of audience makes it clear that when we read a novel or watch a film we adopt the observer rôle without altogether abandoning our sense of our extra-fictional actuality (and indeed, not to do so would be to abandon an important part of the fun that fiction provides).

The sliding, chameleon nature of the identities we adopt while reading has persuaded me to abandon an earlier attempt to indicate these identities by means of a special notation. I had thought that using reader[A] to indicate the actual, flesh-and-blood reader, and reader[B] to indicate the reader as member of narrative audience, might make things clearer. But after trying out such a scheme I became convinced that our reading behavior is a lot messier than such a neat distinction would suggest: as readers we are like the "transformers" in children's cartoons, drifting in and out of identities, moving nearer to and further from our day-to-day personalities and realities. To keep things simple, however, I have chosen to use the term "actual reader" to refer to readers in their ordinary, flesh-and-blood lives, and the simple "reader" in the sense suggested by Rabinowitz and Phelan: "the reader as member of the narrative audience," or "the observer role we enter within the world of the fiction." This said, I want again to stress that even during the reading of a single text the dividing line between an actual reader and the reader as member of the narrative audience is not a hard-and-fast one but rather a boundary that roughly delineates overlapping identities. Sometimes, to adapt my abandoned notation, we become reader[A/B].

"Audience" evokes both the cinema and the theater. In the dramatic arts there is a reassuringly sharp distinction between human beings in the street and human beings sitting in rows of seats facing a screen or a stage. However, not all the time that an individual is sitting in the movie theater facing a screen is spent watching the film, even though common usage suggests that that individual is part of the audience even when munching popcorn and waiting for the lights to dim. When writing about film, then, I will generally use the term "viewer" as filmic equivalent of what in discussion of literary fiction I call the reader (in Phelan's term, the reader as member of the narrative audience). In brief, "reader" and "viewer" are what individuals become while they are experiencing, respectively, literary and film narratives. This unfortunately means that the word "audience" has a different force when I am writing about film from what it has when I am writing about literary fiction. I will do my best to avoid ambiguity in my use of this and other terms in the chapters that follow.

I would, in passing, draw attention to the fact that Phelan's term "observer role" is a revealing one: like audiences, observers typically watch but do not significantly interact; the function is by definition at least partly non-reciprocal and carries with it the same association with passivity that attaches to the term "audience." In some ways this sense of a "partly non-reciprocal" relationship between a reader or viewer on the one hand, and the characters of a literary or filmic fiction on the other, matches my sense that the rôle adopted or assumed by the reader or viewer is neither wholly inside nor utterly separate from the world of the fiction. Indeed, the word "rôle" draws attention to such doubleness: the actor may try to lose his or her own self in playing a part, but even for the most extreme of method actors the loss is never total. In like manner, we never lose complete contact with our quotidian self when we enter the world of a fiction that we are reading. I will say more about this blurring of identities and world-boundaries in my discussion of ontological issues below.

My academic journal's insistence that contributors refer to "readers" rather than "the reader" has special force when it comes to actual readers. Several decades of feminist and post-colonialist theory and criticism have made us aware of the fact that gender, race, history, and culture impinge on our reading in very significant ways. Judith Fetterley's (1978) concept of the resisting reader, for example, is a valuable one, not least in terms of the way it forces us to be aware of the fact that with regard to a given text, one group of readers (for example, women) may be more likely to resist the reading identity that the text appears to crave or to try to impose than will another. Divisions associated with gender, class, race, culture, and history do not all fade away when we enter the world of the fiction. In the chapters that follow I will pay special attention to the ways in which the identities we assume within the diegesis are affected, even conditioned, by who we are in our day-to-day lives, albeit not in any mechanical or predictable manner. The engagement of a film such as *Peeping Tom* with gender rôles inevitably has a different impact on male and female viewers, and the same can be said of *Typee* with regard to the inequalities of colonialism and imperialism, and of "In the Cage" with regard to the divisions of both gender and class. However, any consideration of the relationship—or contrast—between who we are in our ordinary lives and who we are when we enter imaginatively the world of a fiction inevitably propels us into the realm of ontology.

Worlds Apart: Reciprocity and Ontology

An actual reader is a flesh-and-blood individual living in time and space and subject to those laws that affect all of the living. "The observer role we enter within the world of the fiction," in contrast, takes us through that airlock that insulates living human beings from their fictional counterparts, and allows us to observe them as if we were within the diegesis. But we can only observe. As members of the narrative audience we experience what it is like to live within the world of the fiction, while at the same time finding ourselves subject to a strict "no fraternization" injunction. The point has important implications for the issue of reciprocity. As a human being I can, potentially, have a reciprocal relationship with any other living human being with whom I am able to communicate. Within the world of a fiction, characters can have either reciprocal or non-reciprocal relationships with one another, just as is possible between flesh-and-blood beings. But it is not possible for a living human being (for example Rabinowitz's "actual reader") to have an interactive or reciprocal relationship with a fictional being. Elizabeth Bennet can meet, quarrel with, become reconciled to, fall in love with, and marry Mr. Darcy. None of these possibilities are open to her so far as I am concerned, or indeed to me so far as she is concerned.

But—and this is a "but" that is central to my argument in this book—that fictional or quasi-fictional self that I become when I join what Phelan and Rabinowitz dub the narrative audience is *also* barred from a reciprocal relationship with the characters of the fiction, even though our ontological status is now much more like a shared one. Phelan's term "observer role" makes this clear, for although, as he says, the assumption of this rôle gives us entry to "the world of the fiction," we become honorary rather than full members, allowed to watch, sympathize with, or disapprove of the antics of those with full membership, but forever barred from direct contact with them, and indeed permanently invisible to them notwithstanding the occasional gesture contained in an address by the narrator to a narratee characterized as the "dear reader" that may be taken by the member of the narrative audience to apply to him or her too.

Per Krogh Hansen (2012) has considered some of these issues in a recent essay on literary character. Basing his discussion on insights taken from a number of works by the Swedish narrative theorist Lars-Åke Skalin, he is critical of views that deny the extent to which readers experience literary characters as in some way or another like "actual" human beings. These views range from those expressed in L. C. Knights's 1933 essay "How Many Children Had Lady Macbeth?" to those delivered by more recent narrative theorists who either have found the concept of character to be irrelevant to the concerns of narratology, or who have reduced character to "rôles in a plot structure," "narrative agents or actants," or "subject positions in the narrative syntax" (Hansen 100). Hansen agrees with Skalin that "interpretive realism is grounded on a theory of interpretation based on an 'as-if' strategy where literary characters are approached as if they were real people, not aesthetic structures—that is as 'de re,' not 'de dicto'" (103). The "as if" strategy requires that the actual reader assume a changed ontological identity to become a member of the narrative audience. "This understanding of character as a non-existing individual implies that we as readers place ourselves at the same ontological level as the fictional character: We are approaching the characters of the fiction as if we ourselves were characters in their world" (103). The "as if" formulation is important and lies at the heart of the non-reciprocal relationship readers have with literary characters. We behave as if we were in the fictional world, but we are not in it in the way we are in our everyday world as flesh-and-blood individuals. However, when we are not reading a novel but, for example, talking about it and its characters, this shared ontological identity no longer holds. Again following Lars-Åke Skalin, Hansen puts it as follows:

> Skalin rightly asks whether we actually approach literary characters as we approach real persons. He argues that we hardly ever talk about

them as real persons we can have a personal opinion about. Rather we always judge them in accordance with the perspective the text establishes on the character, and furthermore on the basis of the aesthetic totality the character is part of. . . . To remove a character from a work of fiction is therefore not as easy a task as, say, moving a Swede to Denmark. (103)

To this I would add that even if "we as readers place ourselves at the same ontological level as the fictional character" while actually reading a work of fiction, this act of ontological repositioning still does not allow us to interact with the characters in the text. We inhabit a sort of ontological halfway house: treating the characters as if they were real people in a world we have entered, but unable to interact with them as they interact with one another, and unable to have our existence recognized as they recognize one another's existence. This may become clearer if we contrast the experience of, say, reading about Jane Eyre's life in Charlotte Brontë's text, and dreaming that we are in Jane Eyre's presence. In a dream, we lack that sense—however fleeting or suppressed—that Jane is not a real person. In the dream world she has the same ontological status as Justin Bieber or a member of our family. Reading Brontë's text, in contrast, can never make Jane seem real in the way that Mr. Bieber does.

I should perhaps insert a couple of qualifications at this point. First, that a central element in the reading of fiction does seem to be the production of fantasy experiences within which we do imagine interaction with literary characters while not actually reading. There is an episode of the British comedy science fiction TV series *Red Dwarf* in which characters project themselves into "Pride and Prejudice land" (a sub-division of "Jane Austen world") and interact with characters. Although played for laughs (the episode involves one character driving a modern army tank towards the garden tea-party at which other characters from the series are conversing with the Bennet sisters), the scene evokes an odd sense of familiarity: in an absurd manner it does represent what we do with our fictional reading or viewing experiences. In such fantasies an element of reciprocity can exist, and they do seem to be an integral part of the experience of fiction, but in my experience they typically occur not during a reading of the text but in the interstices in and aftermath of reading: direct encounter with the text in the actual process of reading dissipates them. Fantasies of this sort usually begin when we put the book down, and end when we pick it up again. Internet fan-fiction seems to provide a textualization of such fantasy activities.

My second qualification picks up a comment I made on page 4 that includes the proviso "certain postmodernist exceptions apart." Timothy Findley's 1993 novel *Headhunter,* for example, opens in the following arresting manner.

> On a winter's day, while a blizzard raged through the streets of Toronto, Lilah Kemp inadvertently set Kurtz free from page 92 of *Heart of Darkness*. Horror-stricken, she tried to force him back between the covers. The escape took place at the Metropolitan Toronto Reference Library, where Lilah Kemp sat reading beside the rock pool. She had not even said *come forth*, but there Kurtz stood before her, framed by the woven jungle of cotton trees and vines that passed for botanic atmosphere.
>
> "Get in," Lilah pleaded—whispering and holding out the book. But Kurtz ignored her and stepped away. (3; emphasis in original)

Headhunter is a wonderful novel, profound, amusing, and intellectually challenging. And like many recent works of fiction that may be categorized as "postmodernist," it constantly plays with the idea that fictional characters may escape from the world of the diegesis into the world that the author shares with the reader—or, alternatively, with the idea that the reader may enter the world of the diegesis and interact with fictional characters. At a much later stage in *Headhunter* the character Kurtz, who is a psychologist and who may or may not be the escaped Kurtz of Conrad's novella, is on the receiving end of a comparable experience. Reading an account written by a patient named Fabiana Holbach, he has "the unnerving impression that Fabiana Holbach had looked up off the pages and had seen him" (240). But even here there are qualifications to be made. Psychiatrist Kurtz is himself descending into mental illness, and Lilah Kemp is a schizophrenic and a psychiatric patient, and although her symptoms grant her access to truths to which her sane fellow-characters (and there are not so many of these!) are denied access, they may also present themselves in the form of experiences that the reader is allowed to ascribe to her medical condition. Moreover, even in her case she is ignored by the Kurtz who is set free from the first page of *Heart of Darkness*: there is no interaction between them. Finally, we may note that while we can choose to believe that Kurtz leaves *Heart of Darkness* to enter Lilah's world, neither of them leave *Headhunter* to enter the world of its readers, other than in a metaphorical sense. In the world of Conrad's Kurtz and Findley's Lilah, the member of the narrative audience is like a visitor allowed into a high-security building wearing a little "Guest" badge; he or she is in but not of the community among whose members they are free to move, although unlike such visitors, in the world of the fiction they are invisible, to all intents and purposes, ghosts.

Access Denied: The Reader as Ghost

One of Jean Rhys's finest stories is also her shortest. "I Used to Live Here Once" (1979) is only a page and a half long, and starts *in medias res* with a woman back in the place of her childhood, observing both that which is familiar and that which has changed:

> The road was much wider than it used to be but the work had been done carelessly. The felled trees had not been cleared away and the bushes looked trampled. Yet it was the same road and she walked along feeling extraordinarily happy. (175)

She comes to her childhood home and again notices changes. She sees two children, a boy and a girl, waves and calls to them, "but they didn't answer her or turn their heads" (176). She speaks to them twice more, telling them that she used to live in the house. At this point the boy turns towards her and the story ends as follows.

> His grey eyes looked straight into hers. His expression didn't change. He said: "Hasn't it gone cold all of a sudden. D'you notice? Let's go in."
> "Yes let's," said the girl.
> Her arms fell to her sides as she watched them running across the grass to the house. That was the first time she knew. (176)

The woman and the reader as member of the narrative audience discover simultaneously in this shock ending that the woman has indeed returned to her childhood home, but as a ghost. She can see the children but they cannot see or hear her, and the only evidence of her presence for them is a sense of chill—comparable to the chill of understanding that hits the reader at this point. (When first I read this story I felt this shock almost physically, as if the knowledge froze my chest and affected my breathing.)

It is tempting to relate the woman's experience to that of Rhys's own experience of being a ghostly presence while still living; like Ralph Ellison's invisible man, the invisibility of the typical Rhys heroine is also related to social and cultural exclusions. Such exclusions have to do with race in Ellison's case; in Rhys's case, while race may also on occasion be a factor, more often the exclusions have to do with gender, age, and economic situation. But beyond this, the fictional woman's ghostly presence has an added shock value for the reader because the reader, too, is a ghost in the world of the fiction. As we read we too feel that we see the house and we encounter the children; as readers we imagine ourselves *there* (indeed, as members of the narrative audience we *are* there, so much so that for us it is *here* not *there*), but like the woman we are ghosts in this observed world, lacking even the ability to spread a chill. There is safety in invisibility, but at the same time there is impoverishment. The story's closing lines compel us to share the woman's sudden sense of exclusion: we are, like her, denied the warmth of human interaction. We can look but we cannot touch or be touched; we can see but we cannot be seen. Furthermore, Rhys's use of a third-person, non-character narrator in the story also serves to cut the woman off from any human contact. Had she told her own story, she would have had to have had some sense of a reader or interlocutor to whom the account could be addressed; as it is, the story ends with her sense of utter isolation. We are told about her by a narrator with whom she cannot communicate: she herself has no one to whom she can talk.

Now, one could object to my identification of the character in the story here with the reader of the story on two grounds. First, one might insist that reader and character occupy distinct ontological realms. And second, one could argue that whereas the woman in the story has no one with whom she can communicate, in the process of reading the story the reader makes contact with someone who does exist in his or her own ontological realm: the author. These objections are not without force, but I am not wholly convinced by them. First, I have already argued that in reading a work of fiction, the flesh-and-blood individual holding the book assumes a rôle within the diegesis when he or she becomes part of the narrative audience. And second, because (as many accounts of the reading process have argued) in reading we think of the author only in a very intermittent and partial way. My own experience is that as I read "I Used to Live Here Once" my sense of Jean Rhys has been pushed very far to the back of my mind, leaving only a vague sense that the story is perhaps set in Dominica, where Rhys grew up, and that the heroine may in some way be like Rhys herself.

However, once I have finished the story, and am stepping back from and observing my own experiences during the reading process, I may well go back through that airlock that separates the fictional and real worlds and think of the flesh-and-blood author. But whether we talk of the relationship between narrative audience on the one hand, and characters and narrator on the other, or of me as flesh-and-blood individual relating to flesh-and-blood Jean Rhys, makes little difference so far as the absence of reciprocity is concerned. With a living author the situation might be somewhat dissimilar, although two comments from a respected source give me leave to doubt that it makes much difference so far as this particular argument is concerned whether the author is alive or dead: "if authors are as good after they are dead as when they were living, while living they might as well be dead"; and "If the real author is made of so little account by the modern critic, he is scarcely more an object of regard to the modern reader." Both comments are to be found in essays written not in the late twentieth century by Roland Barthes or Michel Foucault, but by William Hazlitt (n.d.) in the early nineteenth century, in, respectively, "On Thought and Action" and "On Criticism" (107, 214). The comments give me some confidence that my almost complete loss of any awareness of the author Jean Rhys while reading her story is not the product of too much reading of poststructuralist theory.

The ontological divide between readers and fictional characters is then an important factor to take into account in discussing the extent to which the reader or viewer of a fictional text is involved in a reciprocal exchange, but it is one that requires a nuanced perspective. As I have argued, in our rôle as member of the narrative audience we are in an in-between state, half in the world of the diegesis and half retaining an albeit dim sense of our own flesh-and-blood selfhood. I believe, incidentally, that this ability to assume such an ontologically hybrid state is one of the reasons why fiction offers us something unique and valuable.

Varieties of the Non-Reciprocal Gaze

At this stage, however, I should provide some provisional definitions of a set of key terms that are used to specify a range of different non-reciprocal ways by means of which we access the hidden activities, thoughts, and feelings of our fellows, ranging from the operation of what is termed "social intelligence" to such activities as spying, voyeurism, and surveillance.

1. Social Intelligence

It may seem odd to associate "social intelligence" with spying and voyeurism, but in ordinary social interaction we observe our fellows for clues to what is going on in their heads. Some do it more, or better, than others, which allows us to attribute more social intelligence to them. "Social intelligence" sounds like a positive quality, and indeed it is generally seen as such, but it does involve the conscious or unconscious gathering of information about other people by means of the interpretation of clues that often have not been offered willingly (or in some cases, knowingly) by those so studied. Sometimes this information-gathering may involve reciprocity; we often hope that our fellows will notice that we are sad, or angry, or tired, without having to tell them this. But sometimes it involves doing what the spy or the voyeur does: retrieving information that someone is trying to keep secret.

To illustrate what I have in mind I would like now to turn to a short passage in which a character does not exactly attempt to spy on another, but does attempt to penetrate into the thoughts and feelings that another character is attempting to keep to himself. The passage is from Jane Austen's *Sense and Sensibility,* and it traces Elinor's reaction to Mrs. Jennings's suggestion that Colonel Brandon is romantically interested in Elinor.

> [Colonel Brandon's] behaviour to her in this, as well as in every other particular, his open pleasure in meeting her after an absence of only ten days, his readiness to converse with her, and his deference for her opinion, might very well justify Mrs. Jennings's persuasion of his attachment, and would have been enough, perhaps, had not Elinor still, as from the first, believed Marianne his real favourite, to make her suspect it herself. But as it was, such a notion had scarcely ever entered her head, except by Mrs. Jennings's suggestion; and she could not help believing herself the nicest observer of the two;—she watched his eyes, while Mrs. Jennings thought only of his behaviour;—and while his looks of anxious solicitude on Marianne's feeling in her head and throat, the beginning of an heavy cold, because unexpressed by words, entirely escaped the latter lady's observation;—*she* could discover in them the quick feelings, and needless alarm of a lover. (Austen 1995, 258–59; emphasis in original)

This passage, from chapter 42 of the novel, surely exemplifies qualities and characteristics that lie right at the heart of why we read Jane Austen. It details the subtle and acute powers of observation that are typically possessed by her heroines, and it allows us to associate ourselves vicariously with the pleasure and satisfaction of reading other, normally less perceptive characters—and *their* less accurate readings. Those advanced skills of interpersonal interpretation possessed by the character or characters who perform a focalizing rôle in the novels seem, as we read, to be ours too. Elinor, who is not in thrall to romantic notions and who is more governed by her reason than is her younger sister Marianne, is, her rationality notwithstanding, a more sensitively perceptive observer and analyst of her fellow human beings than Mrs. Jennings. Her scrutiny of Colonel Brandon's eyes gives her access to his feelings; she *sees* into the colonel's inner world, into his emotions and sensibilities, and uncovers things there that remain hidden to Mrs. Jennings—who observes Colonel Brandon's behavior, but not his eyes, and who hears his words but does not follow his looks.

In one sense Elinor's reading of Captain Brandon is non-reciprocal: he does not deliberately share knowledge about his "attachment" to Marianne with her, and the clues that she interprets are involuntary and, we presume, unsuspected tokens of his attachment, rather than information that is intentionally imparted. But there is little or nothing here that merits the description "illicit": in company we know that others may read off information from our face, our gestures, and our words. We naturally attempt to manage such sources of knowledge by controlling our expression, our movements, and our utterances—more in some situations than others. We cannot hold another person morally responsible for having detected something by means of a careful reading of, say, our facial expression—although we may get irritated with those who spend all their time searching for such information while trying assiduously to reveal nothing about themselves.

The passage, then, serves to remind us that not all inquiry into the secrets of others is, or is considered to be, morally wrong. Confronted with the bald question "do we like people who try to find out the secrets of others or to invade their privacy?" most would answer "no" without significant hesitation. But Jane Austen knew better; being able to discover some things about our fellows that they might rather keep secret is not only a necessary skill to ease normal social intercourse, it is also on occasion a moral duty. In practice, those people who are lacking in such skills are adjudged "insensitive," a term that, among other things, carries with it more than a hint of moral inadequacy. The more fully we can understand our fellows, the better we can take their interests into account.

The quoted passage serves well to exemplify what Lisa Zunshine (2008) has termed "embodied transparency": that is, those moments when people are put "into such trying emotional situations that they can't control their behavior and so their feelings are written all over their bodies" (66). Using the findings of cognitive evolutionary psychology, Zunshine argues that human beings read inner states from outer appearance in their fellows, and also expect that others will do the same to them—with such processes being so much a part of our daily lives that our perceptual systems do not necessarily make all the information so gleaned available to us for our conscious scrutiny (67). Such skills, as her article makes clear, are of great interest to those attempting to represent the intricacies of interpersonal communication, and she notes the existence of a

> representational tradition, which manifests itself differently in different genres and individual works, of putting protagonists in situations in which their bodies spontaneously reveal their true feelings, sometimes against their wills. Such moments are carefully foregrounded within the rest of the narrative. In each case an author builds up a context in which brief access to a character's mental state via her body language stands out sharply against the relative opacity of other characters or of the same character a moment ago. (72)

What is of special interest in the present context is what Zunshine says of the reader's experience of such moments, for as she notes, if characters may notice or may miss such moments of embodied transparency,

> we readers are always made to notice them. We may perceive such moments as perceived by characters in the story or as *not* perceived by them, but, either way, they offer us a dazzling possibility of an escape from our double perspective of the body as a highly privileged and yet unreliable source of information about the mind. (74; emphasis in original)

And indeed, reading this passage and watching Elinor observe Colonel Brandon, we do experience that unique sort of exhilaration that stems from the ethically questionable pleasure we gain from an accurate penetration into another individual's privacy while secure in the knowledge that they are in no position to return the favor. The skill that Elinor practices we feel that we too are practicing by proxy as the narrator displays Elinor's judicious perceptiveness to us. And just as Elinor sees things to which Mrs. Jennings is blind, and can feel superior to "the needless alarm" of Colonel Brandon, so too are we made privy to a notion that "had scarcely ever entered" Elinor's head. If Elinor outstrips both Mrs. Jennings and Colonel Brandon in the acuteness of her interpersonal perceptions and the soundness of her interpretations of the behavior and situation of other characters, and if our knowledge not only encompasses but exceeds Elinor's, then our reading is likely to underwrite our sense of the superiority of our own skills of perception and interpretation. But only for a while: as it turns out, Colonel Brandon is correct to be worried about Marianne's illness, and Elinor is wrong to dismiss his concerns as "needless alarm." One of the lessons that Austen's fiction consistently teaches is that confidence in the superiority of one's own judgments is typically the prelude to error. Reading this passage, we sense that as Elinor learns something about the limitations of her judgments, so too do we, and this sense of accompanying Elinor in her interpretive activities and moral assessments legitimizes our own reading behavior. What Zunshine refers to as the "dazzling possibility" of escaping from the unreliability of the body's information about the mind turns out (like many dazzling possibilities, alas) to open up for embarrassing errors. If Colonel Brandon's romantic preference is clearly signaled to Elinor through the embodied transparency of his eyes, Marianne's illness is not embodied transparently enough for Elinor to read it.

But this element of vulnerability has its positive side, for as we read *Sense and Sensibility* we are led to feel that we are exercising and extending skills that are useful both for us as real-world individuals and for society at large: the pitfalls into which we stagger have their educational function. Our own inadequacies lead us to be more sympathetic to the shortcomings of others, so that although we witness the suffering caused to herself and to others by a character who is fundamentally good but who lacks these skills—Marianne—we realize that we share with her a need constantly to learn from our misreadings—whether of texts or of people.

In the quoted passage, the fact that Elinor's observation of Colonel Brandon is accompanied by candid interaction with him makes her uncovering of the secret of his preferences seem less culpable: after all, he could, if he wished, attempt to read her in the way that she is reading him. Such at least potential reciprocity makes the narrator's and our observation of all of these characters, including Elinor, appear less morally problematic.

If in Austen's fiction it is a social, perhaps moral, responsibility to develop those skills of interpersonal sensitivity that allow us to find out things not deliberately displayed by other people, we should remember that especially for her female characters it is also a duty to keep certain things secret. The main polemical thrust of *Sense and Sensibility* is to present Elinor's keeping her emotional suffering to herself in a positive light, and Marianne's ostentatious display of her own lovesickness to others in a way that is demeaning for her and burdensome for them, in a negative light. Characters in Austen are typically engaged in a struggle to learn more about their fellows, while revealing about themselves only that which they choose to reveal. Such a struggle contains ethical tensions that Austen, moralist though she be, does not dwell on. Her novels do not, accordingly, generally lead the reader to wonder all that often whether his or her desire to know as much about her characters as is possible has itself an ethically questionable aspect.

2. The Spy and the Voyeur

The third chapter of the seventh book of Frances Burney's monumental novel *Cecilia, or Memoirs of an Heiress* is entitled "An Incident." At this point in the novel the heroine, Cecilia, is despairing of ever being able to marry the man she loves, Mortimer Delvile. The terms of her inheritance require that whoever marry her must adopt her name if she is to come into wealth. At the time the novel is set, such a provision might be expected to inspire hesitation in the mind of even the most besotted of suitors, but with Mr. Delvile there is the additional problem that his father is one of the most proud and prejudiced of individuals (Jane Austen almost certainly obtained the title of her most popular novel from the repeated—and capitalized—juxtaposition of the words "Pride and Prejudice" at the end of Burney's novel), and he is inordinately proud of the family name.

Cecilia, we learn, "considered her separation from Delvile to be now, in all probability, for life" (Burney 2008, 545–56). Believing herself to be quite alone except for Mr. Delvile's spaniel Fidel (she is in "a summerhouse in the garden"), she addresses the dog out loud.

> Her tenderness and her sorrow found here a romantic consolation, in complaining to him of the absence of his master, his voluntary exile, and her fears for his health: calling upon him to participate in her sorrow, and lamenting that even this little relief would soon be denied her; and that in losing Fidel no vestige of Mortimer, but in her own breast, would remain; "Go, then, dear Fidel," she cried, "carry back to your master all that nourishes his remembrance! Bid him not love you the less for having some time belonged to Cecilia; but never may his proud heart be fed with the vain glory of knowing how fondly for his sake she has cherished you!

Go, dear Fidel, guard him by night, and follow him by day; serve him with zeal, and love him with fidelity;—oh that his health were invincible as his pride!—there, alone, is he vulnerable—"

Here Fidel, with a loud barking, suddenly sprang away from her, and, as she turned her eyes towards the door to see what had thus startled him, she beheld standing there, as if immoveable, young Delvile himself! (546)

Her initial shock turns quickly to other emotions, and realizing that she has betrayed her love for him to Delvile, she is "overpowered by consciousness and shame" (547). Delvile, in contrast, is "penetrated with gratitude," and "filled with wonder and delight" which were "too potent for controul, and he poured forth at her feet the most passionate acknowledgments" (547). These do little to alter Cecilia's feelings, and she remains "in an agony of mortification and shame" (548).

From the perspective of the history of the novel we may suspect that the somewhat clumsy device of having Cecilia address the dog out loud may be associated with that process whereby novelists discovered progressively more satisfactory ways of granting the reader access to the inner lives of characters without the artificialities of this sort of semi-soliloquy. But Cecilia's public expression of her private thoughts here has the great advantage of allowing Burney to explore how her character responds to the knowledge that this announcement of her most intimate feelings has been overheard by the object of her affections. In the culture from within which and about which Burney is writing, the one "power" that a young gentlewoman possessed was that of retaining the secret of her preferences, thereby requiring that any man interested in obtaining her hand declare himself before being sure that he was the object of her affections. Cecilia's "agony of mortification and shame" is directly associated with the loss of this power: she has effectively declared herself to Delvile before he has declared himself to her. So affected is Delvile by Cecilia's reaction, however, that he promises her that "the words just now graven on my heart, shall remain there to eternity unseen" (549).

In 1933 the Russian writer Ilya Ehrenburg, long resident in Paris, published a book of photographs entitled *My Paris*. To take these photographs he made use of an early Leica camera with a lateral viewfinder—which meant that he appeared to be taking photographs of what was in front of him, but was actually snapping those at his side. Introducing the book, Ehrenburg (2005) related this duplicity to his profession as a writer:

A writer knows that to see people, he must remain unseen. The world changes when you stare straight at it: cowards become heroes, and heroes become puppets. This second world can be studied in the shop window of any provincial photographer: the frozen pupils, the feelings combed back like hair, and that undemanding game which none can resist. But the writer knows the arts of both cunning and pretence. He enters life under another's name. When he's looking at cars or at daisies, Comrade Pavlov or snub-nosed Valentina don't realize that he's looking at them. (2)

And he concludes: "I can talk about this without blushing: a writer has his own notions of honesty. Our entire life is spent peeping into windows and listening at the keyhole—that's our craft" (2).

"Peeping into windows and listening at the keyhole"—the classic, even clichéd—defining activities of the voyeur and the spy. And if the writer does this to produce his or her books, then what of the reader? If Delvile's promise to keep Cecilia's words "to eternity unseen" is kept within the world of the novel, within the world in which the novel is read it is not. As members of the narrative audience we have already been made privy to Cecilia's most intimate secrets and to her most private thoughts and feelings, just as we are taken into the private consciousness of Austen's Elinor, and into her penetration of the privacies of others. This after all is an essential part of what the common reader looks for in novels: the ability to play the voyeur without fear of discovery or of recrimination, and without experiencing even the remotest pangs of guilt. Fictional characters at the time that Burney and Austen are writing are never going to discover that their most intimate secrets are being studied by male and female readers of all ages and classes, or to challenge these readers. The privilege that Ehrenburg associates with the rôle of the writer—that of being able to admit to being a window-peeper and keyhole-listener *without blushing*—is one that the reader too enjoys. If someone approaches us while we are reading *Cecilia* or *Sense and Sensibility*, we do not normally attempt to hide the book or admit what we are doing shamefacedly. And yet an absolutely crucial pleasure that readers of novels look forward to is precisely what my quotation from Austen provides: the pleasure of gaining access to the private thoughts, feelings, and beliefs of the characters about whom we read—an activity for which we would feel extensive shame if caught doing it in the real world by reading a private letter or a diary, or eavesdropping on a private conversation. Delvile at least has the excuse that his knowledge of Cecilia's secret, and thus his trespassing into her private life, is accidental: he is neither spy nor voyeur. But what of the reader?

The spy and the voyeur may make use of similar techniques of observation, but in theory at least they are two different animals: the spy is a paid employee or ideologically committed operative gathering information in which he or she has no immediate personal interest, while the voyeur observes for (normally) his own personal satisfaction. While the spy attempts to obtain something that can be commodified—information that can be priced and exchanged like any other commodity—the voyeur is out after an experience that is valued in itself, either "as it happens" or as recalled or replayed in memory. The subtle distinctions between "secret" and "private" are relevant here. The spy is interested in obtaining secrets, although to do this he or she often has to invade privacies. The voyeur is interested in observing privacies so as to create a sense of pseudo intimacy, although to do this he or she must often uncover secrets.

Marx's distinction between exchange-value and use-value seems relevant here: information gathered by the spy has use-value for his or her employer but none for the spy. What it does have for the spy is exchange-value: it can be sold, used to justify the payment of a salary or retainer by an employer, or valued as a contribution to a political cause of one sort or another which the spy supports. From such a perspective the reader is more like a voyeur than a spy (although the academic literary critic, whose information may have exchange- as well as use-value, engages in activities that perhaps also have something in common with those of the spy).

Nonetheless, the neatness of such divisions between realms or between value-systems frequently crumbles in the encounter with the untidiness of any individual life. Many of the texts on which I will focus in this book confirm that keeping the private realm well insulated from the public often presents insuperable problems: the two value-systems inevitably leak into the wrong realm on occasion, when human considerations—conscience, for example—intrude into business, or when aspects of personal life start to be assessed in commercial terms. Moreover, the person who spies as a result of ideological commitment rather than merely for financial gain does have some personal interest in the information he or she is after, while the voyeur may seek to commodify the results of his snooping in the form of memories or fixed images which may be sold to others for their use. The spy may have to mimic a human interest in the people he or she is observing, people in whom his or her interest is actually financial or ideological rather than human, and the problem with mimicking human relationships is that mimicry can create that which it models. Pretend to have a human relationship with someone and it is hard not to stumble into the reality that is being feigned. I write this in February 2011, shortly after the exposure of a police infiltrator in radical ecological movements in Britain. The police agent, a Mark Kennedy, offered to give evidence for the defense in the trial of a number of activists, after allegedly "going native" (a revealing formulation, used in a number of media reports) and becoming emotionally involved with those whose organization he had infiltrated. If we think of von Donnersmarck's 2006 film *The Lives of Others* (*Das Leben der Anderen*), we can consider Mark Kennedy's behavior as a case of life imitating art.[2]

3. FROM FANTASY TO STALKING

The verb "to stalk" and its associated noun are dated back to the sixteenth century by the *OED*, but it is only in the last few decades that their primary meaning has involved the stealthy pursuit of a human being rather than an animal. Stalking can still be used in a military or a hunting context (think of the deerstalker hat, not inappropriately associated with Sherlock Holmes, although apparently without any textual justification), but it is increasingly associated with the physical or electronic pursuit of one individual by another, particularly a pursuit that has an obsessive and, especially, a sexual character. As such it is closely linked to voyeurism, except for its exclusive focus on one particular individual. It may be associated with delusions of reciprocity, and in many countries there are specific laws that render it illegal.

The act of stalking a woman by a man is clearly not a historically recent development, but the increased use of this particular term can be explained both by a greater openness concerning the existence of sexual deviation and violence to woman, and by the extended possibilities offered by new technologies. At what point a fascination with another person turns into stalking is a matter for discussion, and the sexual element in stalking would suggest that it represents a perversion of a normal aspect of sexual interest and attraction. I find it a useful category to bear in mind when discussing our relation to fictional characters, with whom we can also have a partly obsessive and certainly non-reciprocal relation-

---

2. A full account of the activities of undercover spies such as Mark Kennedy can be found in Paul Lewis and Rob Evans, *Undercover: The True Story of Britain's Secret Police* (2013).

ship that may engender personal fantasies. Indeed, it is important to hold on to an understanding that forms of fantasy or imaginative speculation are part of any rich subjective life and are thus as "normal" as talking to another person. Imagining "what I should have said to her," or "what life would be like married to him," or, more darkly, "what it must have been like to have been condemned to death" are not activities that are perverted: they are the mental and moral equivalents of healthy physical exercise. At what point such personal imagining becomes escapist fantasy or diseased voyeurism is a matter for discussion, but generally speaking it is once the imagining has been insulated and shut off from all or any reciprocal forms of human contact that a crucial dividing line has been passed. What I want to make clear at this point is that a healthy mental life can and should involve forms of imagining that are non-reciprocal, but a mental life dominated by non-reciprocal forms of human contact is likely to be an unhealthy one.

Generally speaking, the term "stalking" is applied to a form of aggressive and threatening behavior in which the target (a revealing term) of the stalker is made aware that she is being stalked (whereas the voyeur hopes that the person observed will not know they are observed). But forms of what is called cyberstalking may be covert, so that the stalker, like the traditional Peeping Tom or voyeur, attempts to keep his activities secret from the target figure. Such covert stalking offers a much richer form of comparison to the activity of the reader of fiction or the member of the cinema audience, as the reader or viewer's inability to interact with fictional characters matches the cyberstalker's hoped-for invisibility to the target.

4. SURVEILLANCE

According to David Lyon (2007), "surveillance refers to processes in which special note is taken of certain human behaviours that go well beyond idle curiosity" (13); "it is the focussed, systematic and routine attention to personal details for purposes of influence, management, protection or direction" (14). Lyon notes that surveillance is "always hinged to some specific purpose" (15), while the study of surveillance is "about power (among other things), and . . . about personhood as well" (23). Lyon relates particular sorts of surveillance to specific historical periods, distinguishing between pre-modern (direct, face-to-face), modern (rationalized using accounting methods and file-based coordination), and so-called post-modern methods "(digitally mediated and involving an electronic interface(s) between subject and surveillance system)" (75). Lyon locates his book within the academic disciplines of politics and sociology, but he makes the interesting comment that novels "are an important source of metaphor and simile, then, and help to alert us to significant dimensions of surveillance as well as helping the reader imaginatively to get inside characters who are either the surveillors or, more probably, the surveilled" (145). As he notes: "our understanding of surveillance is in part shaped by . . . popular media, from being sensitized by literary metaphors to vicariously sharing the vision of those who peep, snoop, observe and gaze" (155).

Although Lyon refers to "surveillors," there is in normal English usage no common term for the individual who engages in surveillance; unlike "spy" and "voyeur," "surveillor" sounds odd and in speech is likely to be misunderstood as "surveyor," so unusual is the formulation. The lack of such a word in common usage is revealing: surveillance is generally understood as spying industrialized, based not on the activities of a single and isolated operative, but on a corporate system of information-gathering that is collectively installed, maintained, and financed. If Jeremy Bentham's "panopticon" is often cited as the founding idea of modern electronic surveillance, it is so only imperfectly. In Bentham's model the prison was to be constructed in such a way that inmates would never know whether they were being observed or not, would thus at all times assume that they might be being observed, and would accordingly in time internalize the never-ceasing possibility of observation. Modern surveillance systems replace the possibility of observation with certainty. Walking down London's Oxford Street I know that I am leaving my trace on a succession of CCTV systems; there is no "perhaps" about it. (The United Kingdom reportedly has more CCTV cameras per person than any other country in the world.)

Surveillance systems can be operated both within the legal framework of a society and outside of it. They may be installed to gratify the needs of either spy or voyeur, but they are frequently there to act as a deterrent: you see the camera, it is transmitting and/or recording what you are doing, if you do anything wrong that too will be transmitted and/or recorded. The driver is often given advanced warning of a speed camera designed to trap those going too fast: rather than the surveillance being covert and unexpected, the whole point is that it is known of in advance, intended to deter much like a policeman standing outside a jewelry store.

The Case Studies

As my earlier quotation from Plato's *Phaedrus* makes clear, the absence of that reciprocity found in person-to-person conversation in the reading of written texts is not something that is associated only with modernity. Spying and voyeurism are probably as old as the human race: they certainly took place centuries if not millennia before the present day, as the account of David, Bathsheba, and Uriah in the second book of Samuel confirms. A. C. Spearing's study *The Medieval Poet as Voyeur* (1993) makes it clear that even in the pre-industrial world a shared sense of the distinction between the public and the private opened up for transgressive penetration into the latter by the spy or the voyeur. As Spearing notes, "the private sphere"

> includes not just outward events transacted in the private space of the chamber or the orchard; it also includes all that we mean by the inner life—the thoughts and feelings, perhaps betrayed only fleetingly and ambiguously by glances or lowered eyes, blushing or turning pale, that are otherwise the most secret realm of all—"the chambir of my thought" as a late-medieval poet puts it. There must be some connection, though its precise nature is hard to specify, between these two kinds of privacy— the existence of objectively private space and the cultivation of a subjective realm of individual being. (23)

Many centuries after the period about which Spearing is writing, Virginia Woolf was to remind her readers that not everyone—and certainly not every woman—had access to a "chambir" or a room of one's own. Privacy is often a privilege enjoyed by the wealthy or those singled out by social status or gender. But such social-class inequalities in the enjoyment of privacy are complicated by historical variations in the nature of privacy and in the possibilities for violating it.

Of these variations, urbanization must be accounted the most important. Before the growth of large towns it was just not possible for most people most of the time to live among other human beings about whom they knew next to nothing, with whom they hardly communicated, and among whom they were themselves as anonymous and unknown as these people were to them. In a sense towns can be said to have bestowed on the poor a privilege that prior to this only the rich had been able to enjoy— that of being, if they wished, anonymous in the midst of those who lived around them. Anyone who has lived in a village knows that in a small community the ability to keep aspects of one's life secret is significantly diminished in contrast to the opportunity for a private life offered by a large town. At the same time, and paradoxically, this same lack of privacy makes undetected spying more difficult in a village than it is in a city.

The other crucial historical variation in the possibility of enjoying privacy resides in the development of various technologies. The first of these variations is arguably that of writing itself. As Plato points out, the written document can engage in promiscuous intercourse with all and sundry, while its author remains anonymous, or unaware of who is reading what they have written. But the development of the spyglass, the telegraph, the telephoto lens, the electronic bug, GPS tracing, and the Internet all have a double potentiality so far as secrecy and privacy are concerned. Most obviously, all open up new possibilities for penetrating private spaces. But at the same time they also offer the spy or the voyeur greater possibilities for keeping their illicit activities undetected.

Bring together urbanization and new technologies, and the realms of the public and the private are redefined along with the opportunities for crossing the boundaries between these realms. In this respect the telegraphist in Henry James's "In the Cage" and Jeff in Alfred Hitchcock's *Rear Window* are representative figures. They are both able to observe the private lives of people they do not know, people who may be unaware that they are being observed and who, if they did discover that they were being spied on, would not know the person who was observing them. It is worth reminding ourselves that this ability is not one that has been universally available in human history. In a small, pre-modern community, gaining access to the private lives of those who know nothing of your existence is just not possible, because in such a community everybody knows everybody. In the title of this book and in many of its chapters I refer to the mythic figure of the "Peeping Tom." In chapter 5, for example, while discussing *Rear Window*, I note that one of the characters alludes to "Peeping Tom," a mention that has the effect of linking Jeff's activity to a mythic figure associated with a pre-modern era, although actually dating from a much later period (see the discussion in chapter 1, p. 49). But the mythic Peeping Tom did not enjoy Jeff's anonymity, and, moreover, he was far more vulnerable than Jeff, who gets caught only when he is involved with an active intervention into the life of the person on whom he is spying—when he, or rather his agent, moves from voyeurism to action.

I have selected texts based on two criteria. First, I have picked texts that not only represent and thematize non-reciprocal human relations of various sorts, but that also allow or encourage the reader or viewer to consider analogies between these relations and the activities of reading literary fictions or watching fictional films. These are texts that I suggest may be assigned to a subgenre that could be called "fictions of non-reciprocity." Second, I have generally focused on texts that explore the new possibilities for non-reciprocity enabled by two key aspects of modernity: urbanization and the development of various technological extensions of the power to penetrate privacies. The two exceptions are Nathaniel Hawthorne's *The Scarlet Letter* and Herman Melville's *Typee*, both of which are set in communities that in technological terms can be described as pre-modern. I start with *The Scarlet Letter* because I know of no better text to exemplify some of the paradoxical processes associated with secrecy and surveillance, including those associated with readers' penetration of the secrecies of fictional characters. So far as *Typee* is concerned, Melville's text allows me to link the operation of what E. Ann Kaplan (1997) has termed "the imperial gaze" both to the character Tommo's experiences of looking and being looked at, and to the American or European male reader's non-reciprocal engagement with the Typee. Apart from these two texts, the novels, stories, and films that I have chosen all depict the activities of the spy or the voyeur in urban settings and involve the use of new technologies of surveillance. But every one of the texts I consider also allows or even encourages the reader or viewer to associate his or her reading/viewing activity with the activities of spying or voyeurism depicted in the fictional world created by the text. This has, inevitably, resulted in a group of texts that would otherwise be unlikely to be gathered together in a single study. I crave the reader's indulgence on this issue.

One anonymous response to an earlier version of this study noted that all my chosen authors and film directors were male, and commented on the "creepiness" of the project. There are female spies and female voyeurs, but these activities (and especially the latter) are very much associated with men rather than with women, both in life and in fiction. "In the Cage," although written by the male Henry James, does focus on the voyeuristic activities of a woman, but my other texts are by men and about the spying and voyeuristic activities of men. The interest in the penetration of privacies exemplified by my examples from Austen and Burney in this introduction are clearly of a different (and arguably less disturbing) sort from those investigated in the chapters that follow. As for the creepiness: what interests me is how activities that certainly are creepy in the real world become, when we engage in them in the pages of a novel or the darkness of a film theater, by common consent quite other than creepy. But perhaps this book may change that.

There are doubtless historical reasons for my interest in the topics I consider in this book. In particular, the varieties of new fictional forms associated with the Internet, many of which are commonly referred to as "interactive," have had the effect of making me conscious of the lack of interaction between reader or viewer and author or text in more traditional forms. I could have extended my concern to such recent developments, but they are so varied and so fast-changing that I became convinced that any study of the forms of interaction they offer would require a book of its own. The scope of the book could also have been extended backwards to encompass literary texts from before the nineteenth century. My chosen starting point is an arbitrary one: I have chosen texts with which I am familiar that fit my purposes. Both my familiarity with texts and my purposes could have been extended, but they are what they are.

In my first chapter, on *The Scarlet Letter,* I have chosen to explore analogies between readings of people *in* the text and readings *of* the text in what I suppose could be described as a New Critical manner—focusing on the text itself and paying less attention to the social, historical, or cultural determinants of the writing or reading processes. From then on I have attempted to redress this balance in a number of ways. Writing about *Oliver Twist,* I have devoted particular attention to the socio-historical context in and about which the novel was written, especially with regard to the importance of urbanization. As I have noted above, my discussion of Herman Melville's *Typee* in chapter 3 includes a consideration of "the imperial gaze"—the ways in which inequalities between peoples and nations condition and control contact and communication between individuals. Chapter 4, on "In the Cage," permits exploration of the parallels and interaction between, on the one hand, the indirect forms of communication that are mediated through a new technology such as the telegraph, and, on the other hand, the ways in which economic and class differences interfere with or prevent full reciprocity in human intercourse in the society about which James is writing and in which he resides. Technology is important too with regard to *Rear Window, Peeping Tom,* and *The Conversation,* in all of which investigative or recording tools (the telephoto lens, the hidden movie camera, the electronic bug) facilitate a non-reciprocal surveillance of human targets. These films, and especially *Rear Window* and *The Conversation,* also investigate the ways in which new technologies emerge from, and in part constitute, new socio-political states and developments.

The potential for reciprocity in human interaction arguably exists most fully in direct person-to-person conversation. In such a situation communication takes place simultaneously on a number of levels or, to speak metaphorically, through a number of channels. While I am speaking to you I am also observing you—your expression, your bodily stance and movements, your seeking or avoiding eye contact. I am listening to your interjected grunts or words and perhaps even feeling you lay your hand on my shoulder. You, while all this is going on, are registering all these things in my behavior as they accompany and qualify my speech and the way this speech is delivered. When I stop speaking and you start, our positions are reversed. Of course there are inequalities even (perhaps especially) in such simple forms of interpersonal communication, and these have been documented by a succession of researchers. In communication between a person of power and a subordinate there are significant differences in the use of eye contact or avoidance, and these reflect, signal, or perhaps challenge such inequalities. Reciprocity, as I have already noted, does not entail equality.

Such direct, immediate, person-to-person contact is still crucial to human experience. In the day of the Internet, the cell phone, Skype, and Google, most of us still spend a substantial amount of most days facing another person and talking to them. But it is clear that the history of the human race is one that involves progressively more time devoted to more varieties of indirect and mediated communication. For most of this history the biggest technological leap allowing for such new and less intimate forms of communication was that of writing. Having access to the words of the dead or the far distant, or being able to send one's own words to those never to be met in person—this possibility was one for which our biological inheritance prepared us only inadequately. Where biology runs out, culture has to take over, and a crucial element in our cultural armory is provided by means of fictional narratives: stories, novels, and films.

I have, however, deliberately started with two texts that, at the thematic level, focus on acts of human communication that are not conducted through distances of time and place. From then on, things become more complicated.

Nathaniel Hawthorne's *The Scarlet Letter* and the Paradoxes of Privacy

MUCH OF the more recent critical response to Nathaniel Hawthorne's *The Scarlet Letter* (1983) has had an overtly historicist thrust and has attempted to relate the novel's concerns to the Puritan and New England contexts of its setting and its composition. It is certainly the case that Hawthorne's concern with issues of sin, guilt, secrecy (and the uncovering of secrets) cannot fully be explained independently of his own family history and cultural heritage. On a personal level, Hawthorne was clearly fascinated by attempts to penetrate into the privacies of others, and by attempts to prevent such penetration. His use of the motif of the veil in works such as *The Blithedale Romance* and "The Minister's Black Veil" confirms that this fascination is by no means limited to *The Scarlet Letter.* So far as the characters of *The Scarlet Letter* are concerned, they must negotiate the particular norms and beliefs of the society in which they live, especially those norms and beliefs that concern sexuality, sin, confession, and the individual conscience. However, for all that biographical and historicist-cultural criticism has much of importance to tell us about *The Scarlet Letter,* this is a novel that has a very sharp eye for a set of culture-independent paradoxes relating to such matters as private conscience and social conformity, and especially to those relating to the opposing claims of secrecy and openness.

At the core of the novel are two principles that, if not opposed, certainly make demands on the individual that are not always easy to reconcile. First, that it is bad (for both individual and community) "to hide a guilty heart through life" (Hawthorne 1983, 93), and second, that it is also bad to attempt to violate "the sanctity of a human heart" (212). Ironically, both of these phrases are quoted from utterances delivered at different times in the novel by the same character: the Reverend Arthur Dimmesdale—whose life and fate do indeed confirm how utterly destructive it is to hide a guilty heart through life. But in spite of his awareness that hiding a guilty heart through life is a form of self-destruction, Dimmesdale continues to do just this. Moreover, the reader is led to believe that even though at an abstract level Dimmesdale understands that it would be better for his psychic, moral, and spiritual welfare to make public his guilt, the minister eventually also perceives that the man who has attempted to penetrate his heart and uncover his guilt—Chillingworth—has destroyed himself and has done something morally wrong by attempting to violate the sanctity of another's heart in order to bring a guilty secret to light. Hiding a guilty secret from the world is wrong, but attempting to uncover a guilty secret in the heart of another is also wrong, even if the person possessed of the guilty secret would be better off were the secret made public.

In the course of this book I will consider cases in which the overt or implied justification for doing something morally wrong (spying on others to discover their secrets, for example) is that the results are good—an individual is relieved of a guilty secret, a crime is discovered (or a crime may be prevented: the by-now standard justification for spying and surveillance in our contemporary world). Hawthorne's novel is uncompromising in its stance: apparently "good" results of this sort do not justify the "bad" action, and indeed they engender bad as well as good results. Most strikingly, Chillingworth's attempt to prize Dimmesdale's secret out of him has the (again paradoxical) effect that it transforms Chillingworth himself into a man who has his own guilty and self-destructive secret. Looking at Chillingworth late in the narrative, his unacknowledged wife Hester is

> shocked, as well as wonder-smitten, to discern what a change had been wrought upon him within the past seven years. It was not so much that he had grown older; for though the traces of advancing life were visible, he bore his age well, and seemed to retain a wiry vigor and alertness. But the former aspect of an intellectual and studious man, calm and quiet, which was what she best remembered in him, had altogether vanished, and been succeeded by an eager, searching, almost fierce, yet carefully

guarded look. It seemed to be his wish and purpose to mask this expression with a smile; but the latter played him false, and flickered over his visage so derisively, that the spectator could see his blackness all the better for it. (187)

The result of "eager searching"—attempting to penetrate the secrets of another—is to produce secrets in oneself, secrets that have to be guarded by means of "carefully guarded" looks and masked expressions. But—and here the paradoxes engender paradoxes—this attempt to hide his expression is an abject failure, and the truth of his changed self is displayed for all to see on his face. This moral—that the more we spy on others, the more we produce and even display in ourselves that which we wish but are often unable to conceal—we will see repeated again and again in the different texts considered in the pages that follow. Essential to the activities of both spy and voyeur is an ability to conceal what one is up to: accordingly, so soon as we venture to gain access to the privacies of others do we add something to that private area of our own lives that we must shield from the gaze of our fellows.

In the case of Chillingworth, however, there is another corrupting element. Chillingworth wishes to uncover Dimmesdale's guilty secret not in order that Dimmesdale will be relieved of its burden and made able to atone for his sin, and not in order that the community will benefit, but in order that he may *possess* Dimmesdale. Told by Hester that he will never discover who the father of Pearl is, Chillingworth replies:

"Never know him! Believe me, Hester, there are few things,—whether in the outward world, or, to a certain depth, in the invisible sphere of thought,—few things hidden from the man, who devotes himself earnestly and unreservedly to the solution of a mystery. Thou mayest cover up thy secret from the prying multitude. Thou mayest conceal it, too, from the ministers and magistrates, even as thou didst this day, when they sought to wrench the name out of thy heart, and give thee a partner on thy pedestal. But, as for me, I come to the inquest with other senses than they possess. I shall seek this man, as I have sought truth in books; as I have sought gold in alchemy. There is a sympathy that will make me conscious of him. I shall see him tremble. I shall feel myself shudder, suddenly and unawares. Sooner or later, he must needs be mine." (100–101)

He repeats his confident prediction. "'Thou wilt not reveal his name? Not the less he is mine,' resumed he, with a look of confidence, as if destiny were at one with him. 'He bears no letter of infamy wrought into his garment, as thou dost; but I shall read it on his heart. . . .'" (101). Chilling-worth's search is corrupted at source because it is a search not for truth but for power: he wants the man with whom Hester has sinned to belong to him, to be in his power, to be "mine." There is thus a world of dif-ference between Elinor's exercise of her social intelligence in penetrating into the secrets of Colonel Brandon's heart and Chillingworth's attempt to read on Dimmesdale's heart the secret of Pearl's paternity. At the same time, it is somewhat worrying for the reader of Hawthorne's novel to find Chillingworth's corrupt and self-destructive search associated with the search for "truth in books" and with the skill of reading, even though it is a heart and not a book that is being read.

The passage reminds us that knowledge is power, and that the spy searches to uncover secrets in order to provide his or her employer with power over the possessor of these secrets. But the passage is also of inter-est because it reveals that in certain circumstances this search for power through illicitly obtained knowledge is necessarily ill-fated. Chillingworth does not obtain power over Dimmesdale; instead he himself is increas-ingly imprisoned by his obsession. Hawthorne's allusion to the search for gold in alchemy is surely deliberate: just as the alchemists never suc-ceeded in producing gold from base metal, so too will Chillingworth fail to find what he is looking for, even though he does eventually succeed in uncovering Dimmesdale's secret. This desire for possession produces a further paradoxical result: the man searching to uncover the truth becomes unwilling that the secret he seeks be broadcast to the world, as it is possession of this secret that grants him at least the illusion of power. Chillingworth insists to Hester that she keep secret the fact that he is her legal husband, and when Dimmesdale finally announces his guilt to the community, Chillingworth perceives this action as Dimmesdale's escape from his power: "'Hadst thou sought the whole earth over,' said he look-ing darkly at the clergyman, 'there was no one place so secret,—no high place nor lowly place, where thou couldst have escaped me,—save on this very scaffold!'" (266). To escape from Chillingworth's clutches, Dimmes-dale must declare his sin in public. Just as legalizing narcotics destroys the power of the drug dealer, so too making public declaration of one's sin destroys the power of the spy: who will buy what is freely available?

○

Throughout *The Scarlet Letter* Hawthorne gestures towards an ideal that his text repeatedly concedes is unattainable: that of a community in which there are no secrets. By so doing it puts pressure on the reader to consider more rigorously the ethics of secrecy. What is the relationship between secrecy and privacy? Are there good secrets and bad secrets? At the end of the novel, the narrator attempts to draw out the most important moral from the story that has been told:

> Among many morals which press upon us from the poor minister's miserable experience, we put only this into a sentence:—"Be true! Be true! Be true! Show freely to the world, if not your worst, yet some trait whereby the worst may be inferred!" (271)

Even in these two short sentences there is a tension: "show freely," but perhaps only "some trait" that will allow the observer to infer what it indicates. Hawthorne knew that guilty secrets destroyed their possessors, but he knew, too, that the dream of a community in which there were no secrets—guilty or otherwise—was just that: a dream. Even Hester Prynne, whose secret is displayed to the world first by her pregnancy and then by the scarlet letter on her breast, has her secrets. Not only is she coerced by Chillingworth to conceal the fact of their marriage relationship, but her isolation from normal social intercourse allows her mind to wander outside the limits set by her community. While she feels of her shame that "all nature knew of it" (110), she is also possessed of secrets of which she herself is at best only partly aware.

> It might be, too—doubtless it was so, although she hid the secret from herself, and grew pale whenever it struggled out of her heart, like a serpent from its hole,—it might be that another feeling kept her within the scene and pathway that had been so fatal. There dwelt, there trode the feet of one with whom she deemed herself connected in a union, that, unrecognized on earth, would bring them together before the bar of final judgment, and make that their marriage-altar, for a joint futurity of endless retribution. Over and over again, the tempter of souls had thrust this idea upon Hester's contemplation, and laughed at the passionate and desperate joy with which she seized, and then strove to cast it from her. She barely looked the idea in the face, and hastened to bar it in its dungeon. What she compelled herself to believe,—what, finally, she reasoned upon, as her motive for continuing a resident of New England,—was half a truth, and half a self-delusion. (105)

If "it was the clergyman's peculiarity that he seldom, now-a-days, looked straightforth at any subject" (151), Hester cannot look the idea of union

with Dimmesdale "in the face." That universal measure of honesty—
meeting the eyes of another in a frank exchange—becomes in its absence
the mark of a corruption of the integrity of the individual self. The passage gives us a classic example of self-deception, that process whereby
knowledge that we wish we did not have is pushed to the back of the
mind where we do not have to confront its implications.

Writing about our contemporary world, Thomas Docherty (2012)
has argued persuasively that the "culture of transparency means the end
of our right to a private life" (136). For him "confessional discourse,
far from endorsing the idea of a strong identity or selfhood, is precisely
responsible for a weakening of individual liberal autonomy and freedom
in the face of the pressure to 'reveal'" (xiii). There is much in *The Scarlet
Letter* to underwrite such a view with regard to the very different society about which Hawthorne is writing, but the novelist pushes further to
investigate the paradox that while selfhood dissolves if there is no realm
of the private and if there are no secrets, selfhood is also threatened by an
excess of secrecy. At different points in the novel the effect on the individual of an abandonment of frank and open exchange with others is seen
to lead to either a loss or a fragmentation of self. Such a loss of self is
described directly by the authorial narrator:

> It is the unspeakable misery of a life so false as his, that it steals the pith
> and substance out of whatever realities there are around us, and which
> were meant by Heaven to be the spirit's joy and nutriment. To the untrue
> man, the whole universe is false,—it is impalpable,—it shrinks to noth-
> ing within his grasp. And he himself, in so far as he shows himself in a
> false light, becomes a shadow, or, indeed, ceases to exist. The only truth,
> that continued to give Mr. Dimmesdale a real existence on this earth, was
> the anguish in his inmost soul, and the undissembled expression of it in
> his aspect. Had he once found power to smile, and wear a face of gayety,
> there would have been no such man! (166)

If we do not show who we are, we lose life-giving contact with the world
around us and, in a real sense, abandon more and more of our unique
identity. In opposition to the view that what is most fundamentally the
essence of an individual is a hidden core of private selfhood, the narrative
asserts that our real self is not that which we keep to ourselves, but that
which we develop in interchange with others. The character-narrator of
Joseph Conrad's novel *Under Western Eyes* (2003), talking of the unwilling secret agent Razumov, notes that "A man's real life is that accorded

to him in the thoughts of other men by reason of respect or natural love" (11). If the thoughts of others are directed towards a self that is a constructed façade rather than a genuine expression of personhood, then there is a sense in which the individual has no such "real life."

With regard to the fragmentation of self, Hawthorne's narrator comments with reference to Dimmesdale's dishonesty that "No man, for any considerable period, can wear one face to himself, and another to the multitude, without finally getting bewildered as to which may be the true" (231). Dimmesdale—like Conrad's Razumov—attempts to circumvent some of these problematic issues by telling the truth about himself in utterances that he knows will be misunderstood by those who hear them:

> More than once—nay, more than a hundred times—he had actually spoken! Spoken! But how? He had told his hearers that he was altogether vile, a viler companion of the vilest, the worst of sinners, an abomination, a thing of unimaginable iniquity; and that the only wonder was, that they did not see his wretched body shrivelled up before their eyes, by the burning wrath of the Almighty! Could there be plainer speech than this? Would not the people start up in their seats, by a simultaneous impulse, and tear him down out of the pulpit which he defiled? Not so, indeed! They heard it all, and did but reverence him the more. They little guessed what deadly purport lurked in those self-condemning words. (164)

A form of words that is technically true but that the utterer knows will be misunderstood by those who read or hear it is not an honest statement, but an exercise in hypocrisy.

> The minister well knew—subtle, but remorseful hypocrite that he was!—the light in which his vague confession would be viewed. He had striven to put a cheat upon himself by making the avowal of a guilty conscience, but had gained only one other sin, and a self-acknowledged shame, without the momentary relief of being self-deceived. He had spoken the very truth, and transformed it into the veriest falsehood. And yet, by the constitution of his nature, he loved the truth, and loathed the lie, as few men ever did. Therefore, above all things else, he loathed his miserable self! (164–65)

I noted, above, the way in which Chillingworth's attempt to violate the sanctity of Dimmesdale's heart and expose his secret is compared to the striving of the alchemist to produce gold from base matter. This comparison of the doctor to a prospector for gold is repeated later in the text:

> Old Roger Chillingworth, throughout life, had been calm in temperament, kindly, though not of warm affections, but ever, and in all his relations with the world, a pure and upright man. He had begun an investigation, as he imagined, with the severe and equal integrity of a judge, desirous only of truth, even as if the question involved no more than the air-drawn lines and figures of a geometrical problem, instead of human passions, and wrongs inflicted on himself. But, as he proceeded, a terrible fascination, a kind of fierce, though still calm, necessity, seized the old man within its gripe, and never set him free again, until he had done all its bidding. He now dug into the poor clergyman's heart, like a miner searching for gold; or, rather, like a sexton delving into a grave, possibly in quest of a jewel that had been buried on the dead man's bosom, but likely to find nothing save mortality and corruption. Alas, for his own soul, if these were what he sought! (150)

Let us step back from the world of the novel at this point and consider what is going on from a somewhat greater distance. What is the narrator doing at this point—and what in their turn are readers of the novel being encouraged to do? A slight digression may be needed prior to suggesting an answer to such questions; given my discussion of readers in the introduction, who exactly do I have in mind when I ask about "readers"?

This is a complex issue, and its complexity should be admitted. On the one hand, I mean readers as members of the narrative audience, defined by Peter Rabinowitz and James Phelan as "the observer role we enter within the world of the fiction" (Rabinowitz 1998, xxii n5), although I resist some of the connotations of passivity that for me at least cling to the word "observer." Because that rôle is situated within the world of the fiction, our desire to discover Chillingworth's secret mimics the desire that one real-world individual has to discover the secrets of another real-world individual. But at the same time, that unwillingness to cease from turning the pages of the novel is something that the reader as member of what Rabinowitz dubs the "actual audience" experiences. It is not the reader who belongs to the world of the fiction who finds it hard to put the book down, it is the reader as flesh-and-blood individual. As flesh-and-blood individual I find it hard to put the book down because my alter ego within the diegesis is so fascinated by what is unfolding in front of him that he cannot bear to stop watching. Thus our reading, as I argued in the course of my earlier discussion of Jean Rhys's "I Used to Live Here Once," involves distinct yet overlapping selves that exist on different ontological levels. Most important, I would argue, is that these different levels are not hermetically sealed from one other; our narrative-audience desire to penetrate into Dimmesdale's heart seeps into our actual-audience experience, seducing our ordinary-world self to desire to continue enjoying the experience of such a transgression.

As for the narrator, as he narrates the quoted passage, is not he digging into Chillingworth's heart in the way that Chillingworth is digging into Dimmesdale's? And is not the ontologically double reader also being encouraged by the narrator to read on to satisfy his or her own terrible fascination with the story that promises to reveal the inner secrets of Dimmesdale, Chillingworth, and Hester? How is it, then, that Chillingworth's quest is one that we are told threatens his own soul, while narrator and reader (and implicitly, too, author) are exempted from the prohibition against violating the sanctity of the human heart? If Dimmesdale is charged with the sin of hypocrisy, are not we too equally guilty of this failing, a failing that the novel encourages us to indulge? How—and why—does the novel anaesthetize us against this attribution of guilt; how does it lead us away from identifying ourselves with Chillingworth?[1]

○

The most obvious technique used by the narrator is that of laying claim to an ignorance of the inner lives of the characters, an ignorance that is belied by what he tells us of these lives. Take the following sentence, from a passage that I have already quoted: "It might be, too—doubtless it was so, although she hid the secret from herself, and grew pale whenever it struggled out of her heart, like a serpent from its hole,—it might be that another feeling kept her within the scene and pathway that had been so fatal" (105). From this point on, as can be confirmed by looking at the quoted passage in its entirety, the narrator treats the hypothetical reason as an actual one, informing us that "Over and over again, the tempter of souls had thrust this idea upon Hester's contemplation, and laughed at the passionate and desperate joy with which she seized, and then strove to cast it from her" (105). By these means the narrator has his cake and eats it too: he is at one and the same time an outside observer

---

1. I have explored some of these questions in different ways in an article that considers a range of different textual examples. See Hawthorn (2013).

merely hypothesizing about what is going on in Hester's heart (and in real life there is little or no ethical prohibition against doing that—rather the reverse) and an all-seeing narrator capable of penetrating her soul and revealing the secrets of her heart.

This sort of narrative duplicity—for that, surely, is what it is—runs through the whole novel. Words and phrases such as "it might be," "perhaps," and "seems" continually disavow the insight into characters that the narrator then goes on to confirm that he must possess. In the passage cited above that outlines Chillingworth's corruption by the investigation he has initiated, the insight comes first and the avowal of ignorance follows. At the start of the passage the narrator can inform us of Chillingworth's character and temperament "throughout life," but the word "possibly" in the penultimate sentence leads into a disavowal of knowledge in the final quoted sentence about what Chillingworth actually was seeking. The narrator starts with an authoritative declaration about Chillingworth: "He had begun an investigation, as he imagined, with the severe and equal integrity of a judge, desirous only of truth," only for the reader to find a few lines further on that the information is not of something known but of something partly hypothesized. "He now dug into the poor clergyman's heart, like a miner searching for gold; or, rather, like a sexton delving into a grave, possibly in quest of a jewel that had been buried on the dead man's bosom, but likely to find nothing save mortality and corruption. Alas, for his own soul, if these were what he sought!" It is dangerous to generalize about the effect on the reader of such inconsistency. For some readers, the avowals of ignorance may serve merely to grant reassurance that no unethical invasion of privacy or voyeuristic pleasure in uncovering a character's secrets is taking place. Other readers may pick up on the inconsistency and relate it to an uncertainty at the heart of the novel with regard to the ethics of finding out things about people that they wish to keep private.

Beyond such issues, we can note that terms such as "sexton," "mortality," "corruption," and "soul" all have ecclesiastical associations, but they are linked to activities that are of this world rather than the next: digging for gold, looking for a jewel. Although the comparisons are those of the narrator and are not chosen by Chillingworth himself, they suggest a propensity on Chillingworth's part to ascribe religious motives to earthly and unworthy desires. It is significant, too, that the passage ends with a declaration of sympathy for Chillingworth and hope on the part of the narrator that he is mistaken about Chillingworth's aims. This declaration situates the narrator as a human being looking at and expressing concern for another human being, rather than as a god-like and omniscient observer who is apprised of Chillingworth's behavior "throughout life." The effect is to dull the reader's sense of a cold and distanced view of Chillingworth that takes in both his outer behavior and his inner qualities, by shifting over to a warmer, human, concern for a fellow human being whose inner qualities can be guessed at but not known for sure. To put it another way: the narrator of *The Scarlet Letter* actually knows as much as the narrator of *Sense and Sensibility,* but often pretends that he knows only as much as Elinor knows of Colonel Brandon, or Colonel Brandon knows of Marianne. It may be that Hawthorne wishes the reader to see what the narrator is up to, and thus to extend an ethical criticism of Chillingworth to the narrator, but I find it hard to be sure about this.

Second, even if this shift to a pretended ignorance were not to have taken place, it is doubtful whether the opening part of this passage would have led the reader to worry that he or she was engaged in precisely the activity for which Chillingworth was being condemned: violating the sanctity of a human heart. Omniscience does not seem like an invasion of privacy: where all is seen and known, there is no privacy to violate. God presumably cannot choose to not know anything, and a god-like narrator does not *invade* privacies—these privacies are *displayed* to him or her in a manner that is indistinguishable from the lives that, within the fictional world, are public to those living in that world. God does not spy on mankind; He just sees everything. In like manner, a narrator who sees and knows everything can hardly be understood to invade the private lives and histories of his or her characters. Following what we are told by an omniscient narrator, then, does not make us feel guilty that we are invading the privacy of another person: through the narrator's involuntary perceptions we are merely witnessing what is openly displayed. The conventions of omniscient narrative were, even in Hawthorne's day, sufficiently fixed and familiar for most readers not to have felt that a narrative that abided by them was in any way ethically problematic. However, the more human characteristics a narrator displays the more he or she becomes subject to ethical judgments, and it is at precisely these points when the narrator claims ignorance of his characters' inner lives that he becomes most human.

Of course, the *author's* display of these perceptions is not involuntary but rather deliberate and considered. However, my earlier argument that as we are reading we are not generally conscious of the real-life author is relevant here. If it is the case, as I argued, that we think of the author mostly during gaps in our reading, or following our reading, then "think-ing about the author" and "witnessing the inner lives of a character," are not usually experienced at the same time or during the same process. In general terms this argument seems to have force, but the specifics of vari-ous works of fiction need to be taken into account here. In *The Art of Fiction* Henry James (1984) presents the classic case against the author making an appearance *in propria persona* within a work of fiction, noting Anthony Trollope's "want of discretion in this particular. In a digression, a parenthesis or an aside, he concedes to the reader that he and this trust-ing friend are only 'making believe.' He admits that the events he narrates have not really happened, and that he can give his narrative any turn the reader may like best. Such a betrayal of a sacred office seems to me, I con-fess, a terrible crime" (46). In a personal communication James Phelan has suggested to me that what James seems most to object to in Trollope's practice is the way in which the reader of fiction's tacit awareness of an authorial constructor is forced to become an explicit awareness of an actual human author. This I find convincing, although I do retain a sense that even in those post-modernist moments at which an author announces his or her presence within the diegesis, there are often ontological trans-formations to be seen. Alfred Hitchcock's famous "cameos"—those very brief scenes in which he appears in his own films as a character, but recog-nizable as himself—offer an interesting case in point.

The third method which helps to insulate the reader from any bad conscience about discovering the secrets of characters involves our dis-placing our guilt onto a character in the text. Writing about the history of the Lady Godiva legend, Daniel Donoghue (2003) notes that with "guilt assigned to Peeping Tom and Godiva's shame aesthetically transformed, the reader assumes a voyeuristic perspective with impunity," adding that even so, "the eroticism still provides the legend with its energy" (5). The figure of Peeping Tom was first added centuries after the initial account of Lady Godiva's ride (Donoghue 69) but rapidly became an integral com-ponent of the legend. As Donoghue suggests, the scapegoat in the text allows the reader or viewer to have their cake and eat it too. In *The Scar-let Letter* the reader is spared any guilt about his or her curiosity concern-ing Dimmesdale's secret by being able to displace any such guilt onto the character who is most concerned with penetrating to this secret—Chill-ingworth. Having a spy or voyeur in a work of fiction gives the reader or viewer the best of both worlds: we can maintain our disapproval of such activities, while profiting from them. Once one becomes aware of this scapegoating technique it is striking how often it can be witnessed in works of fiction, and there are good examples in the texts that I consider in the pages that follow. Thus while the narrator expresses sympathy for Dimmesdale and abhorrence of Chillingworth's satanic quest in search of Dimmesdale's secret, the reader's potential guilt concerning his or her own desire to learn Dimmesdale's secret, and concerning his or her spying on Chillingworth, is sidetracked. It is also the case that Dimmesdale's hypocrisy allows the reader to feel that the minister deserves to have his inner self violated, as he is misusing his right to privacy. (If you are—say—a practicing homosexual then this is none of my business; but if you argue in public that practicing homosexuals should all be imprisoned, then arguably you have forfeited the right to keep this part of your personal history private.)

Fourth, if we can hide our own guilt behind our righteous indignation at Chillingworth's heartlessly obsessive pursuit of Dimmesdale's secret, we are also able to shelter behind our sympathy and pity for Dimmesdale—emotions that alternate with our feeling of outrage in response to his hypocrisy. Generally speaking it is only towards the end of the novel that criticism of Dimmesdale's character goes beyond a sense of him as a man who has been betrayed into sin by a powerful passion. Thus so late as chapter 17 we are told of him that in contrast to Hester Prynne, he "had never gone through an experience calculated to lead him beyond the scope of generally received laws; although, in a single instance, he had so fearfully transgressed one of the most sacred of them. But this had been a sin of passion, not of principle, nor even purpose" (217). By chapter 20, however, a more negative side to Dimmesdale's character is suddenly revealed in his response to the knowledge that the date fixed for his flight with Hester will not prevent him from preaching the Election Sermon.

> "At least, they shall say of me," thought this exemplary man, "that I leave no public duty unperformed nor ill performed!" Sad, indeed, that an introspection so profound and acute as this poor minister's should be so miserably deceived! We have had, and may still have, worse things to tell of him; but none, we apprehend, so pitiably weak; no evidence, at once so slight and irrefragable, of a subtle disease, that had long since begun to eat into the real substance of his character. No man, for any considerable period, can wear one face to himself, and another to the multitude, without finally getting bewildered as to which may be the true. (231)

The heavy irony in the narrator's use of the word "exemplary" in this passage strikes a new note for the reader. But even at this point, however, the narrator situates himself in a position of sympathy vis-à-vis Dimmesdale, expressing sadness at his corruption and explaining it in a way that comes close to suggesting that to understand is to forgive. Moreover, the use of disease imagery here half characterizes Dimmesdale's guilt not as something for which he is himself responsible, but as something that can be attributed to an outside infection that is not part of what he actually is, something external that "had long since begun to eat into the *real substance* of his character" (my emphasis).

Fifth, the reader's invasion of Dimmesdale's private self can be justified because we have been led to believe that it is in Dimmesdale's interest that his secret be revealed. Indeed, Dimmesdale's public address to Hester in the third chapter of the work sums up why his secret should be divulged.

> "Be not silent from any mistaken pity and tenderness for him; for, believe me, Hester, though he were to step down from a high place, and stand there beside thee, on thy pedestal of shame, yet better were it so, than to hide a guilty heart through life. What can thy silence do for him, except it tempt him—yea, compel him, as it were—to add hypocrisy to sin? Heaven hath granted thee an open ignominy, that thereby thou mayest work out an open triumph over the evil within thee, and the sorrow without. Take heed how thou deniest to him—who, perchance, hath not the courage to grasp it for himself—the bitter, but wholesome, cup that is now presented to thy lips!" (93–94)

What Hester dare not do, or will not do for reasons of unacknowledged self-interest, the reader can associate him- or herself with doing. The reader can shelter behind the moral duty to help Dimmesdale by linking him- or herself with the narrative's crusade to expose his guilt and thus prevent him from adding hypocrisy to sin.

I suspect, however, that it is my sixth reason for our lack of guilt that is the most telling. Unlike the characters in the novel, we know that we cannot get caught. (We can of course be caught *reading a novel,* but we cannot be caught *vicariously enjoying violating the privacy of the characters in that novel* because in the world of the novel we are invisible to characters.) Chillingworth has to proceed very carefully to avoid alerting Dimmesdale to what his real motives are.

> He groped along as stealthily, with as cautious a tread, and as wary an outlook, as a thief entering a chamber where a man lies only half asleep,—or, it may be, broad awake,—with purpose to steal the very treasure which this man guards as the apple of his eye. In spite of his

premeditated carefulness, the floor would now and then creak; his garments would rustle; the shadow of his presence, in a forbidden proximity, would be thrown across his victim. In other words, Mr. Dimmesdale,
whose sensibility of nerve often produced the effect of spiritual intuition,
would become vaguely aware that something inimical to his peace had
thrust itself into relation with him. But Old Roger Chillingworth, too,
had perceptions that were almost intuitive; and when the minister threw
his startled eyes towards him, there the physician sat; his kind, watchful,
sympathizing, but never intrusive friend. (151)

The floor never creaks when we pick up the book and start reading, and
our interest in Dimmesdale cannot be communicated to him. The guilt
associated with being a spy or a voyeur is intimately associated with the
fear that we might be caught; the shame associated with these activities is
the result of having been caught.

Film can simulate the experience of being observed by a character,
as I will discuss in chapter 5 with reference to Alfred Hitchcock's *Rear
Window*. When a character in a film looks at the camera they look, or
appear to look, at the viewer (at me, rather than us). Moreover, both cinema and theater involve collective audiences rather than private, individual readers. In the cinema, for example, we witness certain responses
of other audience members (laughter, fear, embarrassment) and they are
able to detect the same in us. We can, accordingly, be embarrassed in the
cinema in a way that we are rarely if ever embarrassed while reading a
novel, although in the chapters following I will look at some of the ways
in which works of literary fiction can give their readers the sense that they
are being observed and interrogated.

In this context it is revealing that Hawthorne's essay "The Custom-
House," which provides a discursive account of how *The Scarlet Letter* came to be written and was included in the first edition of the novel,
contains a comment on the writer–reader relationship that talks directly
about veiling the inner self and refraining from violating the rights of
the other. Talking of his writing, Hawthorne imagines a single, sympathetic reader and comments that "it may be pardonable to imagine that
a friend, a kind and apprehensive, though not the closest friend, is listening to our talk; and then, a native reserve being thawed by this genial
consciousness, we may prate of the circumstances that lie around us, and
even of ourself but still keep the inmost Me behind its veil. To this extent,
and within these limits, an author, methinks, may be autobiographical,
without violating either the reader's rights or his own" (35–36). Even

before they start reading *The Scarlet Letter,* then, the actual reader has been reassured that no one will violate his or her rights or peep behind the veil hiding their "inmost Me"—while they, once they become members of the narrative audience, are given *carte blanche* to peep into the inmost Me of the characters in the novel. In stark contrast to this, as I shall argue, is the scene towards the end of Alfred Hitchcock's *Rear Window* in which the spied-on murderer stares back at his observer and apparently too at each of us viewing the film.

There is one additional reason why observing the private self of a literary character may not trigger the reader's guilt. In ordinary life we can only experience our own thoughts, and so experiencing the thoughts of a literary character is half like being that character. Only "half," because we do not so much have a sense that we *are* them, but more a sense of having a sort of magical, unforced access to their inner selves. And just as we cannot invade our own privacy, cannot feel guilty about spying on ourself, so too we feel no guilt experiencing "being another person" from the inside. "Intimacy," after all, is what we feel in relation to another person, not in relation to ourself, it is that flash of utterly reliable exchange of inner thoughts and feelings that occurs between two individuals who respect each other's separate identity. When we catch someone's eye in a group and exchange a smile, such a moment of intimacy occurs: we are not forcing our way into another person's private self but rather being given access to that person's inner self at the same time as they are granted a comparable access to our own private domain. Fictional narratives that allow access to the inner worlds of characters can mimic the experience of such moments, using words rather than smiles. In such cases, even though we are not opening ourselves to scrutiny by the characters whose thoughts we follow, the reading experience evokes a sense of intimacy rather than of invasion.

○

In her introduction to an edition of the novel, Nina Baym argues that Hawthorne "was writing about what goes on inside people, 'the truth of the human heart,' rather than what goes on outside and around them" (10). Actually, Hawthorne was surely writing about both, about the relationship between what goes on inside people and what goes on outside and around them—with one striking exception. The one character into whose interiority the narrative never really penetrates, although it is clear that she is possessed of a rich inner self, is Pearl, the child born of the adulterous relationship between Hester and Dimmesdale. In a passage that presents Pearl to the reader through her mother's perceptions of her, the child's unfathomability is linked to her lack of social contact.

> This outward mutability indicated, and did not more than fairly express, the various properties of her inner life. Her nature appeared to possess depth, too, as well as variety; but—or else Hester's fears deceived her—it lacked reference and adaptation to the world into which she was born. The child could not be made amenable to rules. (114)

It is as if in order to be read by others, an individual must learn to display his or her inner life through contact with others, as if an individual must have grown up as an integrated part of a functioning community if others are to be capable of making contact with his or her private self. But "Pearl was a born outcast of the infantile world" (117). We have here the narrator's word that Pearl's outward mutability does "not more than fairly express" the various properties of her inner life, but the reader is never granted access to this inner life, and in the sentence following the narrator records only that her nature "appeared" to possess depth.

Why does Hawthorne include a character in his novel whose inner life is hidden from the gaze not just of other characters, but from the otherwise all-seeing eye of the narrator? And a perhaps even more puzzling question follows. Many actual readers may, I suspect, find it strange that the character who throughout the novel has been portrayed in a manner that suggests oddity if not some sort of supernatural possession (in the novel's closing pages the narrator refers to Pearl as "elf child" and "demon offspring" even!) appears by the end of the novel to have achieved a conventional existence denied to all the other characters—although this normality is not witnessed at first hand but is reported from, revealingly, a land far away.

> In fine, the gossips of that day believed,—and Mr. Surveyor Pue, who made investigations a century later, believed,—and one of his recent successors in office, moreover, faithfully believes,—that Pearl was not only alive, but married, and happy, and mindful of her mother; and that she would most joyfully have entertained that sad and lonely mother at her fireside. (274)

How is it that the strangest character in *The Scarlet Letter* apparently ends up enjoying what it seems fair to term some sort of normal life, a normal life denied to all the others in the narrative? There are, I suggest, two overlapping answers to such questions that can be proposed. The first of these is that, as a number of commentators have recognized, Hawthorne's portrayal of Pearl seems to have owed much to his and his wife's view of their first child, Una. In a passage from his notebooks dated July 30, [1849], he writes:

> But, to return to Una, there is something that almost frightens me about the child—I know not whether elfish or angelic, but, at all events, super-natural. She steps so boldly into the midst of everything, shrinks from nothing, has such a comprehension of everything, seems at times to have but little delicacy, and anon shows that she possesses the finest essence of it; now so hard, now so tender; now so perfectly unreasonable, soon again so wise. In short, I now and then catch an aspect of her, in which I cannot believe her to be my own human child, but a spirit strangely min-gled with good and evil, haunting the house where I dwell. The little boy is always the same child, and never varies in his relation to me. (Hawthorne 1972, 430–31)

In spite of this disturbing view of his daughter, Hawthorne knew that Una was human, and clearly hoped for a fulfilling life for her. This hope may go some way to explaining Pearl's later conventional happiness, which can be read as what Hawthorne hoped for for his Pearl-resembling daughter.

But linked to this is the possibility that Pearl's impenetrability is pre-cisely what allows her to escape the abnormalities of a culture in which everyone is engaged in peering into the hearts of their fellows. From this perspective the narrative's preservation of the sanctity of Pearl's inner self is directly related to her final escape into normality. Biographical specula-tion apart, the text of *The Scarlet Letter* does appear to link the achieve-ment of normality with the preservation of the privacy of one's own inner self, with "the sanctity of the human heart." In Alfred Hitchcock's *Rear Window,* it is the apartment of the seemingly normal family to which the viewer gains no access. To enjoy a normal life, it might appear, an indi-vidual must be possessed of a private self to which only he or she has access.

Seeing Is Believing

Power and the Gaze in Charles Dickens's
The Adventures of Oliver Twist

TO MOVE from *The Scarlet Letter* to Charles Dickens's *The Adventures of Oliver Twist*[1] (henceforth *Oliver Twist*) is in terms of publication dates to move back in time, albeit only two years. But in a crucial sense this movement represents a leap forward, from the sort of community that had hitherto characterized most of the existence of the human race, to a historically new way of living: that of the gigantic city. Such a leap forward had and has fundamental implications for the possibility of spying on one's fellows—or of being spied on by them. In a big city most of the people encountered in the street or in public meeting-places are strangers. In a village you notice if someone keeps walking past your home; in a big city you quite probably do not. In the city you can easily be spied upon by a stranger without realizing it, something that is much less likely to happen (at least in the days before electronic surveillance) in a village. At the same time, the typical city dweller knows far less about even his or her neighbors than the inhabitant of a village knows about more or less everyone in the local community. It is more difficult to find oneself

---

1. The novel was first published in *Bentley's Miscellany* 1837–39 under the title *Oliver Twist; or, The Parish Boy's Progress*, by Boz, and, before the concluding installment was issued, in a three-volume edition under the same title in 1838. The second edition was published in 1839 as *Oliver Twist*, by Charles Dickens. The 1846 edition was published as *The Adventures of Oliver Twist*, with the 1838 subtitle. Later editions retained this title but dropped the subtitle.

lonely in a small community, and people are more willing to give assistance because those in need are known. And in a village if you do want to find out things about your neighbors often you do not have to spy on them; you just need to keep your eyes open.

Another way of putting this is that in a small community nearly all non-written communication between individuals has a reciprocal aspect to it. In order to spy on Dimmesdale, Chillingworth has to enter into a relationship with him. But in a big city—even in the pre-electronic age—the spy's target may not ever register the presence of the person tracking him or her. However, if this situation was historically new for those living in London from the middle of the eighteenth century, in a weird sense some people had had a foretaste of this aspect of what it was like to live in a big city before actually doing so: they had read novels. As readers they had had the experience of observing the lives of others in intimate detail, others who did not know them, who would remain eternally unaware that they were being observed, and who could not return the compliment and observe the life of the person doing the observing. And if it is not quite the case that the urban spy can never be caught, such an occurrence is much less likely to occur in the city than in a small village.

In *Oliver Twist,* then, there are links between (i) looking relations *in* the novel (between characters, and between the narrator and characters), (ii) the ways in which readers as members of the narrative audience are situated by the narrative in relation to characters through various technical choices, and (iii) an ideological agenda that while ostensibly arguing that reciprocal, person-to-person contact is still adequate to the task of establishing the truth in these new circumstances, actually seeks to underwrite new methods of social knowledge and control in the England of the 1830s, methods that have in part been called into being by the growth of London and other vast towns. In the London of *Oliver Twist* a spy or a voyeur may operate with limited fear of detection—just like readers of Dickens's novel. But *Oliver Twist* is not set exclusively in London, and the geographical movements in the novel from town to country—which are in a sense movements from present to past—allow Dickens to highlight the contrast between a way of life in which human communication is a necessarily reciprocal affair and a way of life in which some relationships may be reciprocal in nature but some may not.

This natural desire for reciprocity in human communication is highlighted relatively early in the novel when Oliver, rescued from Fagin and taken home with Mr. Brownlow, confronts a painting of his mother—

although he is unaware that the portrait is of her. Mrs. Bedwin, observing his interest in the portrait, asks him if he is afraid of it.

> "Oh no, no," returned Oliver quickly; "but the eyes look so sorrowful; and where I sit, they seem fixed upon me. It makes my heart beat," added Oliver in a low voice, "as if it was alive, and wanted to speak to me, but couldn't." (Dickens 1985, 80)

Like Plato's Socrates, Oliver is frustrated by the way in which the portrait appears to invite an interactive relationship with the viewer that it cannot in fact offer. The reader is of course in exactly the same relation to Oliver as is Oliver to the lady in the picture: able to empathize, but unable to communicate reciprocally, with him. However, as readers watch and engage emotionally with Oliver, they escape his frustration: they guess who the lady is, they feel superior to his ignorance, and this shields them from their own inability to interact with Oliver.

Oliver's special concern with the eyes of the depicted lady is representative: a concern with these organs of sense runs through the whole novel. References to looking and to the eyes in *Oliver Twist* have small chance of functioning as dead metaphors; the novel is crammed with acts of literal looking and seeing, and with descriptions of material eyes and physical faces. An electronic search of the text of *Oliver Twist* gives 289 hits for the word "eye" and its cognates in the novel, a count that is high even for Dickens, whose novels consistently make repeated reference to eyes and seeing. (*Hard Times*, a slightly longer novel, has 150 hits, while *Bleak House*, which is twice as long as *Oliver Twist*, has only 115 hits.) A search for the word "look" and its cognates yields nearly 500 hits in *Oliver Twist*.

If this is a novel crammed with acts of spying and non-reciprocal communication, it is also one in which the reciprocal nature of ordinary, direct person-to-person communication is repeatedly stressed. In this novel characters exchange glances and they avert their eyes, they spy upon one another and they read one another's expressions, they attempt to deceive but reveal the truth through their looks and their countenances. When we are told of Mr. Bumble's relation to the paupers, subsequent to his marriage to Mrs. Corney, that he "was degraded in their eyes" (328) the phrase has a literal force: we witness Bumble actually being looked at and mocked by the paupers. Shortly after this humbling, Monks, "looking keenly into Mr Bumble's eyes," challenges him: "You have the same eye to your own interest, that you always had, I doubt not?" (330). Mr. Bumble's eyes are indeed literally devoted to the pursuit of his own interest. The very many idioms involving sight and the eyes ("strike me blind," "before my very eyes," "damn your eyes") that the novel contains have a force on the literal plane of meaning as well as on their more familiar metaphorical one. Take for example the following comment: "I promise you that in that case, if the truth is forced from him, there the matter will rest; there must be circumstances in Oliver's little history which it would be painful to drag before the public eye" (412). The final courtroom scene involving Fagin's trial demonstrates that in the world of *Oliver Twist* being "before the public eye" is not a dead metaphor: it involves having the eyes of members of the public focused upon one.

Given that metaphors involving looking and the eye are so relentlessly exposed to the pressure of the literal in this novel, it might be expected that *Oliver Twist* would keep the reader close to the truth of the physical world, to those "facts" the worship of which Dickens was later to treat with such suspicion and disdain in *Hard Times* (1854). But literalism is not the same as truth, nor are the literal-minded immune from fanciful beliefs or ideological confusions. Indeed, as *Hard Times* demonstrates, those committed to the primacy of hard facts are likely to be more rather than less subject to social misperceptions and human blindnesses. And at the heart of *Oliver Twist* lies a fundamentally ideological (and, I would argue, nostalgic) belief in the power of the eye to both perceive and display the truth. It is ideological because it is based upon what Dickens would like to be the case rather than upon what he has observed is the case, and it is nostalgic because it yearns back to an England that existed before or apart from the growth of London and other giant cities, in which literal face-to-face encounters could expose falsity and establish the truth. Time and time again in the novel characters perceive truths by literally seeing something, especially in the faces of those they encounter; time and time again characters reciprocate by revealing and displaying the truth of their own character, personality, history, and morality through their eyes and in their faces. In a world full of secrecies and immensely complex chains of mediation (in space as well as in time), we are assured that the truth is nonetheless visible and can always be *seen*. Words—whether spoken or written—may mislead, but the face of an interlocutor cannot but reveal or betray the truth.

If *Oliver Twist* engages with and reflects a society moving from the basic unit of the small, rural community to a domination by the sprawling urban conglomeration, at its ideological heart lies the implicit claim that what we can term the "moral technology" of this new order is identical to that of the old: in both orders, direct interpersonal contact between two individuals mediated by the eye is what makes it possible to distinguish good from evil, and truth from falsehood. But this claim is advanced half-heartedly; alongside this optimistic view is a rather different, only half-admitted recognition that the opportunities for secrecy, concealment, and deception in the big city are so extensive that a network of spies and surveillance is needed to monitor those whose faces cannot be seen. In *Oliver Twist* we move backwards and forwards between scenes in which the truth is perceived instantly in the face of another person, and scenes in which it can be uncovered only by complex undercover surveillance operations.

If words can mislead, what then of those assemblages of words we call novels? For the reader to be able to rely on what he or she learns, that ontological transformation from flesh-and-blood individual holding a book to simulated consciousness within the diegesis must take place. If the actual reader is—obviously—reading about characters and unfolding events, the reader as member of the narrative audience must be given the sense that he or she is actually seeing flesh-and-blood individuals and witnessing their reality.

This might seem to run counter to those repeated points in this novel—and, indeed, in Dickens's fiction in general—at which the narrator addresses the reader directly from what appears to be an extradiegetic standpoint. Take the following passage from chapter 17:

> As sudden shiftings of the scene, and rapid changes of time and place, are not only sanctioned in books by long usage, but are by many considered as the great art of authorship: an author's skill in his craft being, by such critics, chiefly estimated with relation to the dilemmas in which he leaves his characters at the end of every chapter: this brief introduction to the present one may perhaps be deemed unnecessary. If so, let it be considered a delicate intimation on the part of the historian that he is going back to the town in which Oliver Twist was born; the reader taking it for granted that there are good and substantial reasons for making the journey, or he would not be invited to proceed upon such an expedition. (169)

It would be foolish to ignore the humorous aspect of this passage, in which Dickens (and there is a strong case for saying that it is Dickens, who has here merged his identity with that of his narrator) jokes with the

reader about the conventions and clichés of the novel. But jokes notwithstanding, the mention of "books," the "art of authorship," "characters,"
and "chapter" clearly indicates and initiates a move outside the diegesis. Such a passage must surely have the effect of pulling the reader out
of the world within which the characters are encountered by the narrative audience as real people, and into the world of flesh-and-blood author
and actual reader in which the characters are fictional beings constructed
through the art of an author. However, even here the final conceit that
the text is the work not of an author but a historian, and that a shift
of scene is a physical journey, reinserts the reader into the diegesis after
having offered him or her the pseudo intimacy of a pretended reciprocal
exchange with the author-narrator.

Such minuscule movements between ontological levels mirror those
larger ones that would regularly have been experienced by those early
readers who consumed the novel in installments. Serial publication not
only imposes decisions on the reader about when he or she will abandon membership of the narrative audience and exit from the world of
the fiction, but also allows for a particular sort of reciprocity between
author and readers. Dickens monitored reactions to his novels as they
were published in installments, and adapted the process of composition
in response to such reactions. Furthermore, for readers of the installments
as they appeared, the reality-illusion was greater to the extent that in the
world of the fiction, as in the real world, the last page had not yet been
written.

○

The only words that are given to Oliver's mother prior to her death in the
opening pages of the novel are "Let me see the child, and die" (46). Her
request is granted, and her seeing initiates a chain of looks that we both
observe and share, a relay race in which the exchanged glances function as
a baton that, by the end of the novel, allows evil to be exposed and right
to triumph. But if the humanist ideology which underpins *Oliver Twist*
rests on a belief that the ills of the big city and of a new urban society
can be solved by those interpersonal skills developed in a now obsoles-
cent pre-industrial society, it nevertheless has to offer some explanation
as to how these traditional skills and their moral accoutrements can be
adapted to the England of the 1830s. The substantially increased potential
for secrecy to be found in the big city must be simultaneously challenged
and exploited by a vastly increased force of looking and surveillance, one

that is outwardly paternalistic and benevolent but that in the last resort is a despotic system of panoptical knowledge attained through spying. Paradoxically, then, in arguing for the old, Dickens's novel is forced to underwrite some rather new forms of surveillance and control.

A Window on the Soul

In chapter 14 of the novel Mr. Brownlow notices that Oliver surveys the shelves of books in his house (which reach "from the floor to the ceiling") with curiosity, and he makes Oliver a promise: "'You shall read them, if you behave well,' said the old gentleman kindly; 'and you will like that, better than looking at the outsides,—that is, in some cases; because there *are* books of which the backs and covers are by far the best parts'" (145). If the literal truth of the saying that one cannot tell a book from its cover appears here to be asserted, its more usual metaphorical implication is not: so far as the characters of the novel are concerned, truths about their moral and existential selves *can* generally be read from their physical appearances, and, especially, from their faces and their eyes. Accordingly the tales told by faces and eyes are implicitly believed. At the workhouse, when after three months of starvation a tall boy hints to his companions that "unless he had another basin of gruel per diem, he was afraid he might some night happen to eat the boy who slept next him, who happened to be a weakly youth of tender age," the response of his companions is revealing. "He had a wild, hungry eye; and they implicitly believed him" (56).

Much more seriously, in one of the best-known scenes in the novel, it is what can be read from Oliver's face by the "old gentleman" magistrate rather than anything that Oliver says that saves him from being signed over to the horrifying Mr. Gamfield.

> "And this man that's to be his master—you, sir—you'll treat him well, and feed him, and do all that sort of thing, will you?" said the old gentleman.
>
> "When I says I will, I means I will," replied Mr Gamfield doggedly.
>
> "You're a rough speaker, my friend, but you look an honest, open-hearted man," said the old gentleman: turning his spectacles in the direction of the candidate for Oliver's premium, whose villainous countenance was a regular stamped receipt for cruelty. But the magistrate was half blind and half childish, so he couldn't reasonably be expected to discern what other people did.

"I hope I am, sir," said Mr Gamfield, with an ugly leer.

"I have no doubt you are, my friend," replied the old gentleman, fixing his spectacles more firmly on his nose, and looking about him for the inkstand.

It was the critical moment of Oliver's fate. If the inkstand had been where the old gentleman thought it was, he would have dipped his pen into it, and signed the indentures, and Oliver would have been straightway hurried off. But, as it chanced to be immediately under his nose, it followed, as a matter of course, that he looked all over his desk for it, without finding it; and happening in the course of his search to look straight before him, his gaze encountered the pale and terrified face of Oliver Twist: who, despite all the admonitory looks and pinches of Bumble, was regarding the repulsive countenance of his future master with a mingled expression of horror and fear, too palpable to be mistaken, even by a half-blind magistrate. (65)

Even such an inadequate observer as the old gentleman—whose need for glasses and his literal short-sightedness ("half-blind") are clearly equated with a lack of human perceptiveness—is forced to read the truth written on Oliver's face, just as Oliver has read the message so clearly displayed in Gamfield's visage. Not so very long after this scene takes place, even the morally corrupt beadle is similarly affected by Oliver's face and the undeniable truth of that which it displays: "Mr Bumble regarded Oliver's piteous and helpless look with some astonishment for a few seconds; hemmed three or four times in a husky manner; and, after muttering something about 'that troublesome cough,' bade Oliver dry his eyes and be a good boy" (73).

Not only does Oliver's look reveal an incontrovertible truth: it is also possessed of existential moral force, a force which imposes a human and moral burden upon whoever observes it—even if that someone is Mr. Bumble. We are not surprised to learn, shortly after this exchange, of Mr. Sowerberry's view that Oliver "would make a delightful mute" (79). A child with such an expressive face hardly needs the power of speech.

Oliver Twist offers several instances of what was to become a recognizable topos in Dickens's fiction: the face (actual or represented) which presents a message at first only partially decoded by a puzzled observer. Oliver's response to the portrait of his mother is of this sort, as is the later response of Mr. Brownlow to Oliver's face.

"There is something in that boy's face," said the old gentleman to himself as he walked slowly away, tapping his chin with the cover of the book, in a thoughtful manner; "something that touches and interests me. *Can* he be innocent? He looked like.—By the bye," exclaimed the old gentleman, halting very abruptly, and staring up into the sky, "God bless my soul! Where have I seen something like that look before?"

After musing for some minutes, the old gentleman walked, with the same meditative face, into a back ante-room opening from the yard; and there, retiring into a corner, called up before his mind's eye a vast amphitheatre of faces over which a dusky curtain had hung for many years. "No," said the old gentleman, shaking his head; "it must be imagination."

He wandered over them again. He had called them into view, and it was not easy to replace the shroud that had so long concealed them. There were the faces of friends, and foes, and of many that had been almost strangers peering intrusively from the crowd; there were the faces of young and blooming girls that were now old women; there were others that the grave had changed to ghastly trophies of death, but which the mind, superior to its power, still dressed in their old freshness and beauty, calling back the lustre of the eyes, the brightness of the smile, the beaming of the soul through its mask of clay, and whispering of beauty beyond the tomb, changed but to be heightened, and taken from earth only to be set up as a light, to shed a soft and gentle glow upon the path to Heaven. (119; emphasis in original)

"[T]he beaming of the soul through its mask of clay" is, on a literal level, the recalling of a person's soul after their death by means of a picturing of their face, but given the conventional association of "clay" with "flesh" the phrase also suggests that the face is indeed a window through which the truth of the soul can shine.

Even the distortions and corruptions of the face have their own story to tell. In "The Three Cripples" Inn, we are told, it

was curious to observe some faces which stood out prominently from among the group. There was the chairman himself, (the landlord of the house,) a coarse, rough, heavy built fellow, who, while the songs were proceeding, rolled his eyes hither and thither, and, seeming to give himself up to joviality, had an eye for everything that was done, and an ear for everything that was said—and sharp ones, too. Near him were the singers: receiving, with professional indifference, the compliments of the company, and applying themselves, in turn, to a dozen proffered glasses of spirits and water, tendered by their more boisterous admirers; whose countenances, expressive of almost every vice in almost every grade, irresistibly attracted the attention, by their very repulsiveness. Cunning, ferocity, and drunkenness in all its stages, were there, in their strongest aspects; and women: some with the last lingering tinge of their early freshness almost fading as you looked: others with every mark and stamp of their sex utterly beaten out, and presenting but one loathsome blank of profligacy and crime; some mere girls, others but young women, and none past the prime of life; formed the darkest and saddest portion of this dreary picture. (237)

The truth is there to be read upon these and other faces, but such reading requires the sharp eye of the landlord—or of the narrator.

Accurate reading of the testimony written on the face or in the expression requires sharpness and attention (unless it is so glaringly obvious that even a half-blind magistrate can decipher it), but it also requires moral rectitude and disinterest. Oliver is lucky to meet with all of these, and of him it can be said that, literally, his face is his fortune.

"Queer name!" said the old gentleman. "What made you tell the magistrate your name was White?"

"I never told him so, sir," returned Oliver in amazement.

This sounded so like a falsehood, that the old gentleman looked somewhat sternly in Oliver's face. It was impossible to doubt him; there was truth in every one of its thin and sharpened lineaments. (130)

Doubt is *impossible,* and what is read in Oliver's face are not facts, but *truth.* (Later on in the novel, Oliver's "earnest face" convinces Harry Maylie and Mr. Losberne that he really has seen Fagin [313].)

This is not the only point in the novel where we are told that characters' lives and experiences are written on their faces. As in *The Scarlet Letter,* the virtues and sins of an individual are inscribed on his or her face.

Alas! How few of Nature's faces are left alone to gladden us with their beauty! The cares, and sorrows, and hungerings of the world, change them as they change hearts; and it is only when those passions sleep, and have lost their hold for ever, that the troubled clouds pass off, and leave Heaven's surface clear. It is a common thing for the countenances of the dead, even in that fixed and rigid state, to subside into the long-forgotten expression of sleeping infancy, and settle into the very look of early life; so calm, so peaceful, do they grow again, that those who knew them in their happy childhood, kneel by the coffin's side in awe, and see the Angel even upon earth. (223)

Behind such a claim can be located a clearly ideological argument: the concealments and corruptions of a modern society, in which people are forced to deal with those they do not know, can be resolved through the use of those skills of reciprocal interpersonal perception that serve to distinguish truth from falsity in a small community. A corrupt individual such as Monks can hide *in* the city, but he cannot conceal his corruption *from* his face. In the course of Monks's first meeting with both Mr. and Mrs. Bumble—when the revealing topic of conversation is that of the ability of women to keep secrets—Monks suddenly removed his hands from his face, and "showed, to the unspeakable discomposure of Mr Bumble, that it was much distorted, and discoloured" (337). In the world of *Oliver Twist,* if you are shrewd and upright then you *can* tell a book by its cover. In the final courtroom scene of the novel, Fagin is condemned not so much by proffered evidence as by the collective gaze of those observing him.

Misreading is still possible, but only if those doing the looking project their own shortcomings on to what they see.

> Men who look on nature, and their fellow-men, and cry that all is dark and gloomy, are in the right; but the sombre colours are reflections from their own jaundiced eyes and hearts. The real hues are delicate, and need a clearer vision. (307)

Thus when the doctor tells Rose that although he believes Oliver's story, he does not think that "it is exactly the tale for a practised police-officer," she asks him why. "'Because, my pretty cross-examiner,' replied the doctor: 'because, viewed with their eyes, there are many ugly points about it; he can only prove the parts that look ill, and none of those that look well,'" and after detailing the suspicious circumstances surrounding Oliver's account he asks Rose: "Don't you see all this?"

> "I see it, of course," replied Rose, smiling at the doctor's impetuosity; "but still I do not see anything in it, to criminate the poor child."
>
> "No," replied the doctor; "of course not! Bless the bright eyes of your sex! They never see, whether for good or bad, more than one side of any question; and that is, always, the one which first presents itself to them." (276–77)

The exchange works in two directions. On the one hand it repeats a conventional view of the lack of logic possessed by women, but on the other hand, of course, the reader knows that Rose is correct in what she "sees" and that the police officers are not. Deciding to attempt to deceive the police, Mr. Losberne declares, "All I know is . . . that we must try and carry it off with a bold face" (277). In a world of bold faces, one might assume that truths are not unproblematically to be read by the observer, but so far as Oliver is concerned it seems that Dickens believes that innocence has the power to distinguish itself from the "bold face" of an assumed appearance.

Reciprocity and the Look

> The girl [Nancy] drew closer to the table, and glancing at Monks with an air of careless levity, withdrew her eyes; but as he turned his towards Fagin, she stole another look, so keen and searching, and full of purpose, that if there had been any bystander to observe the change, he could hardly have believed the two looks to have proceeded from the same person. (354)

Human interpersonal looking is naturally reciprocal. We *exchange* looks. Even when we avert our eyes, we thereby reveal something to an alert interlocutor or observer. In person-to-person communication we *inter*act. We both receive and transmit information non-verbally in a cumulative process of reciprocal exchange. Human beings often want to gather information without paying the reciprocal price of providing information about themselves to others—including the information that they want to gather information. The numerous acts of looking that take place in *Oliver Twist* fall naturally into two categories: the reciprocal and the one-way. There are those that are genuinely interactive and there are those that—like the look of the voyeur or the spy—resist and evade reciprocity. As we will see, reciprocity is associated with the honest, the natural, and the true, while the one-way is at least initially associated with the unnatural, the perverted, and the false. But this picture is far from being absolutely consistent, and as the novel proceeds, the right to engage in one-way looking is progressively transferred from the bad to the good.

Reciprocity in looking may be natural but it is not necessarily pleasant, as the early example of Mr. and Mrs. Sowerberry illustrates.

Mr and Mrs Sowerberry—the shop being shut up—were taking their supper in the little back-parlour, when Mr Sowerberry, after several deferential glances at his wife, said,

"My dear—" He was going to say more; but, Mrs Sowerberry looking up, with a peculiarly unpropitious aspect, he stopped short.

"Well," said Mrs Sowerberry, sharply.

"Nothing, my dear, nothing," said Mr Sowerberry.

"Ugh, you brute!" said Mrs Sowerberry. (78)

The unsophisticated pun by which their marital name is constituted tells the whole story: the fruits of this marriage are indeed far from sweet. Sweetness is not to be found, either, in the relationship between Fagin and Sikes, but there is a reciprocity of evil in their looks nevertheless.

"Hear me speak a word," rejoined Fagin, laying his hand upon the lock. "You won't be—"

"Well," replied the other.

"You won't be—too—violent, Bill?"

The day was breaking, and there was light enough for the men to see each other's faces. They exchanged one brief glance; there was a fire in the eyes of both, which could not be mistaken.

"I mean," said Fagin, showing that he felt all disguise was now useless, "not too violent for safety. Be crafty, Bill, and not too bold." (421)

In both of these cases, looks speak more fully and eloquently than do words, and it is for this reason that, on a number of occasions in the novel, eyes are averted. But such averting of the eyes is also communicative. In interaction with another, it is impossible to convey nothing: as Watzlawick, Beavin, and Jackson (1968) put it, because "one cannot *not* behave . . . no matter how one may try, one cannot *not* communicate" (48; emphases in original).

"Yes. I have come from Bill," replied the girl. "You are to go with me."

"What for?" asked Oliver, recoiling.

"What for?" echoed the girl, raising her eyes, and averting them again, the moment they encountered the boy's face. "Oh! for no harm."

"I don't believe it," said Oliver; who had watched her closely.

"Have it your own way," rejoined the girl, affecting to laugh. "For no good, then." (198)

Once again, Nancy's eyes speak more truthfully than do her words. There
is indeed a sort of moral double-take in this passage: although Nancy lies
to the boy, the fact that she has to avert her gaze bears witness to the
fact that she cannot lie with her eyes, and this inability betokens an inner
honesty beneath her corrupt exterior (of which her words at this stage of
the narrative form a part). Oliver, we may note, is no longer a complete
innocent abroad at this point: he watches Nancy closely, and he knows
what her avoidance of eye contact betokens. His skills are shared by Mr.
Brownlow, and seem generally to serve as a badge of moral goodness.
Confronting Monks, Mr. Brownlow reminds him of his father's situation
when, estranged from Monks's mother and with "his prospects blighted,"
he fell among new friends:

> "*This* circumstance, at least, you know already."
>
> "Not I," said Monks, turning away his eyes and beating his foot upon
> the ground, as a man who is determined to deny everything. "Not I."
>
> "Your manner, no less than your actions, assures me that you have
> never forgotten it, or ceased to think of it with bitterness," returned Mr
> Brownlow. (436; emphasis in original)

Even the underworld characters display gradations of moral corruption
in their ability or inability to maintain eye contact; after the murder of
Nancy, when Sikes visits Fagin's den, "[i]f an eye were furtively raised and
met his, it was instantly averted" (447). Finally even Sikes, facing Charley's horror-struck gaze, is stared down: "[t]he man stopped half-way, and
they looked at each other; but Sikes's eyes sunk gradually to the ground"
(448).

At the same time, one of the advantages of communicating by means
of looks rather than by words is that looks can be used to exclude as well
as to inform:

> Bill Sikes merely pointed to the empty measure. The Jew, perfectly under-
> standing the hint, retired to fill it, previously exchanging a remarkable
> look with Fagin, who raised his eyes for an instant, as if in expectation
> of it, and shook his head in reply; so slightly that the action would have
> been almost imperceptible to an observant third person. It was lost upon
> Sikes, who was stooping at the moment to tie the boot-lace which the
> dog had torn. Possibly, if he had observed the brief interchange of sig-
> nals, he might have thought that it boded no good to him.

"Is anybody here, Barney?" inquired Fagin; speaking, now that Sikes was looking on, without raising his eyes from the ground.

. . .

Now, whether a peculiar contraction of the Jew's red eyebrows, and a half-closing of his deeply-set eyes, warned Miss Nancy that she was disposed to be too communicative, is not a matter of much importance. The fact is all we need care for here; and the fact is, that she suddenly checked herself, and with several gracious smiles upon Mr Sikes, turned the conversation to other matters. In about ten minutes' time, Mr Fagin was seized with a fit of coughing; upon which Nancy pulled her shawl over her shoulders, and declared it was time to go. (155–56)

Fagin's ability to target his looks and to shield any telltale elements in his eyes from those he wants to exclude from a circle of knowledge bears testimony to his skill in restricting communicative reciprocity. But it is a skill that in the dog-eat-dog underworld of the novel can also be used against him.

Given the natural reciprocity of eye contact, a look can both offer and canvass emotional succor and recognition of a shared humanity. The doomed child Dick tells Oliver that he dreams "so much of Heaven, and Angels, and kind faces that I never see when I am awake" (96–97). It is because of her wish to escape or be spared the mute appeal posed by Oliver that Nancy wishes him away from her.

"The child," said the girl, suddenly looking up, "is better where he is, than among us; and if no harm comes to Bill from it, I hope he lies dead in the ditch, and that his young bones may rot there."

"What!" cried the Jew, in amazement.

"Ay, I do," returned the girl, meeting his gaze. "I shall be glad to have him away from my eyes, and to know that the worst is over. I can't bear to have him about me. The sight of him turns me against myself, and all of you." (239–40)

Nancy can meet Fagin's gaze, but she wishes Oliver away from her eyes. She is able morally to confront the eyes of Fagin, but not those of the innocent and abused child.

However, it is Nancy's own eyes that pose the most powerful moral challenge in the novel. Sikes has to deny himself the sight of his own act of murder: Dickens's narrative presents us with a "ghastly figure": "[t]he murderer staggering backward to the wall, and shutting out the sight with his hand, seized a heavy club and struck her down" (423). But that which he wishes to shield himself from pursues him: after her death, in one of Dickens's most powerful extended sequences, he cannot escape from Nancy's accusing eyes, just as, after the murder, even Sikes's dog can read his own threatened fate in Sikes's eyes. The last words uttered by Sikes are "The eyes again!" (453). There is no clearer demonstration of Dickens's reliance upon the look as active guarantor of knowledge and of justice.

Even the look of defiance or aggression enters into reciprocal exchange.

> "Mrs Bumble, ma'am."
>
> "Well," cried the lady.
>
> "Have the goodness to look at me," said Mr Bumble, fixing his eyes upon her. ("If she stands such a eye as that," said Mr Bumble to himself, "she can stand anything. It is a eye I never knew to fail with paupers, and if it fails with her my power is gone.")
>
> Whether an exceedingly small expansion of eye be sufficient to quell paupers, who, being lightly fed, are in no very high condition; or whether the late Mrs Corney was particularly proof against eagle glances; are matters of opinion. The matter of fact is, that the matron was in no way overpowered by Mr Bumble's scowl, but, on the contrary, treated it with great disdain, and even raised a laugh thereat, which sounded as though it were genuine.
>
> On hearing this most unexpected sound, Mr Bumble looked, first incredulous, and afterwards amazed. He then relapsed into his former state; nor did he rouse himself until his attention was again awakened by the voice of his partner. (323)

The genuine if grim reciprocity of this exchange is in marked contrast to the assumed reciprocity of the contrived *oeillades* involved in Mr. and Mrs. Bumble's earlier courtship maneuverings.

Who Owns the Look of Power?

Acts of one-way looking within the story of *Oliver Twist* fall into two dominant categories: the look of lust or of voyeurism, and the look of the spy or of surveillance. Both of these forms of looking are more interested in possession and power than in interaction, both treat the person or persons surveyed as object for use rather than as human being to be respected. But, as the novel progresses, ownership of the one-way look of power is progressively transferred from the morally corrupt and the criminal to characters who are either "good" or associated with official power—with the police or the judiciary. This process ensures that while at the start of the novel the bad characters have power over the good, by the end of the novel the good have power over the bad.

The clearest example of the gaze of lust or voyeurism is that directed by Fagin at young Oliver. The rather obvious suggestiveness of Dickens's insistence on calling (only) Charley Bates "Master" is one of a number of hints associating Fagin's relationship with the boys with tabooed forms of sexuality. After his recapture by Fagin's gang, Oliver is given a warning by "that gentleman" that he will be given up to be hanged unless he cooperates. Oliver is particularly struck at this point by Fagin's scrutiny of him.

> As he glanced timidly up, and met the Jew's searching look, he felt that his pale face and trembling limbs were neither unnoticed nor unrelished by that wary old gentleman.
> The Jew, smiling hideously, patted Oliver on the head, and said, that if he kept himself quiet, and applied himself to business, he saw they would be very good friends yet. (178)

The statement that Fagin "relishes" Oliver's "trembling limbs" has an inescapably sexual set of connotations. When Noah Claypole is fed oysters by Charlotte, he takes them with "intense relish," and this scene plays heavily on both the aphrodisiacal properties of oysters as well as on the popular association between the oyster and the female genitals. (Charlotte even offers Claypole an oyster "with such a beautiful, delicate beard!" [251].) As with Fagin's lustful gaze at Oliver, this earlier scene also associates sexuality with looking: Charlotte tells Noah that "I like to see you eat 'em, Noah dear, better than eating 'em myself," something Noah finds "queer" (251). At any rate, Fagin's "relishing" of Oliver's pale face and trembling limbs, and his promise that Oliver and he will, if Oliver behaves, become "very good friends," attach a clearly voyeuristic and lustful character to his scrutiny of Oliver. Later on in the novel, Bill Sikes poses a pertinent question:

> "And wot," said Sikes, scowling fiercely on his agreeable friend, "wot makes you take so much pains about one chalk-faced kid, when you

know there are fifty boys snoozing about Common Garden every night, as you might pick and choose from?"

"Because they're of no use to me, my dear," replied the Jew, with some confusion, "not worth the taking. Their looks convict 'em when they get into trouble, and I lose 'em all." (192)

The answer is not wholly implausible, but the fact that Fagin's answer is delivered "with some confusion," along with his familiar use of the term "my dear" to a man, provides a clear indication that there is more to the matter than he admits.

In itself this characterization of the look of lust as objectifying, demeaning, and non-reciprocal is unremarkable. But the two characters primarily responsible for such forms of looking—Fagin and Noah Claypole—are also the two characters most associated with spying: the most important form of non-reciprocal looking in the novel. *Oliver Twist* is a work riddled with the activities of spying and surveillance at the story level; it even includes a story about an "active officer" named Jem Spyers. Fagin, moreover, represents a classic example of Foucault's power-knowledge with its attendant machinery of clandestine information-gathering. (The potentiality for a punning double-meaning in the repeated references to his "pupils" smolders throughout the novel, as the boys do indeed serve as his eyes.) The Cripples public house provides a striking example in miniature of a Benthamite panopticon—except that we can presume that the subjects of the controlling gaze are generally unaware that they are being watched. When "Morris Bolter" (Noah Claypole as was) and his "wife" (Charlotte) enter the public house they are shown into a back room:

Now, this back-room was immediately behind the bar, and some steps lower, so that any person connected with the house, undrawing a small curtain which concealed a single pane of glass fixed in the wall of the last-named apartment, about five feet from its flooring, could not only look down upon any guests in the back-room without any great hazard of being observed (the glass being in a dark angle of the wall, between which and a large upright beam the observer had to thrust himself), but could, by applying his ear to the partition, ascertain with tolerable distinctness, their subject of conversation. The landlord of the house had not withdrawn his eye from this place of espial for five minutes, and Barney had only just returned from making the communication above

related, when Fagin, in the course of his evening's business, came into
the bar to inquire after some of his young pupils. (380)

There is a loving quality to the manner in which Dickens provides such
a detailed description of this secret observation-point, one that solicits
the reader's own excitement at being made a party to the observations
that it renders possible. This drawing of the reader into the act of surveillance constitutes a significant move in the progressive legitimation of
surveillance, even though at this point the reader shares his or her secret
view with corrupt characters such as the landlord and Fagin. Although
this identification of the reader with the characters who are engaged in
spying and surveillance is not made explicit, the fact is that the reader is
given access to the information that these activities generate. That process of safe, one-way scrutiny that the reader as member of the narrative audience enjoys during the reading process is thus merged with the
safe, one-one scrutiny of characters by Fagin and the landlord. As readers we are thereby thrust into the role of privileged but corrupt viewers,
being shown the machinery of secret surveillance along with the information thus obtained—and in this instance the ontological status of "we"
is decidedly mixed: half in the real world and half in the world of the
diegesis.

There is a comparable, again very detailed, description of the vantage
point from which Claypole's spying is conducted, one which is almost as
lovingly detailed as is the "place of espial" in the public house:

> These stairs are a part of the bridge; they consist of three flights. Just
> below the end of the second, going down, the stone wall on the left ter-
> minates in an ornamental pilaster facing towards the Thames. At this
> point the lower steps widen: so that a person turning that angle of the
> wall, is necessarily unseen by any others on the stairs who chance to be
> above him, if only a step. The countryman looked hastily round, when he
> reached this point; and as there seemed no better place of concealment,
> and, the tide being out, there was plenty of room, he slipped aside, with
> his back to the pilaster, and there waited: pretty certain that they would
> come no lower, and that even if he could not hear what was said, he
> could follow them again, with safety. (408)

The text prior to and following this paragraph is in the traditional historical past tense of fictional narrative: the steps "were those," the man

"hastened unawares," "he heard the sound of footsteps." The effect of (and reason behind) the switch to the present tense in this paragraph is complex, and may vary from reader to reader. But my own response suggests that it has the (intended) effect of jolting the reader out of the diegesis and into the real world: these stairs *are* part of the bridge and they *consist* of three flights—not just in the imaginative world of the novel but in the world of Dickens's contemporary readers. I would go even further, and propose that the use of the present tense at the start of this passage marks a further move in the involvement of the reader in surveillance activities. What we observe taking place within the diegesis (spying from the vantage point of the place of concealment on the stairs of the bridge) is available for the same purpose outside the diegesis to Dickens's contemporary readers and, by implication, to any reader of the novel then and now, whether or not that particular bridge has survived. Even the present-day reader assumes, on his or her encounter with this passage, that there really was a London bridge that really did have these characteristics. (The description of the secret vantage point in the public house, in contrast, is given in the standard past tense of fictional narrative.) If ontological parity between readers and characters is generally achieved in this and other novels by having the flesh-and-blood reader move into the world of the fiction and become a member of the narrative audience, in this passage the fictional location is moved out into the world of the flesh-and-blood reader. This movement is necessary for the underlying thrust of Dickens's argument to work: as readers we need to associate ourselves with the operation of spying in our world for the ideological interpellation to function as it should.

We are being moved, in other words, in the direction of participating in and hence legitimizing spying in the extra-fictional world in this passage, just as Noah Claypole is being moved slowly and surely in the direction of incorporation into the legal machine. By the end of the novel he has become an "Informer," reporting publicans whom he has lured into dispensing brandy during church time. As Mr. Brownlow's private surveillance of Monks reaches a natural conclusion, the formal machinery of law and order appropriates Noah Claypole to its own uses. Surveillance, which for most of the novel has appeared to be the prerogative of the criminal classes, is ultimately incorporated into the shady outer suburbs of authority—and we the readers have in turn been incorporated into these same acts of surveillance. We are thus positioned to accept the surveillance of the state as something in which we participate.

The Panoptical Narrative

The penultimate chapter in the novel, entitled "Fagin's Last Night Alive," clearly evokes the genre of the sensational prison account or confession. Here Fagin the watcher becomes Fagin the watched, the objectifier objectified. From the opening paragraph of the chapter the members of the public attending the trial are reduced to faces and eyes:

> The court was paved, from floor to roof, with human faces. Inquisitive and eager eyes peered from every inch of space. From the rail before the dock, away into the sharpest angle of the smallest corner in the galleries, all looks were fixed upon one man—the Jew. Before him and behind: above, below, on the right and on the left: he seemed to stand surrounded by a firmament, all bright with gleaming eyes. (466)

These words invite the reader to surrender to the lure of the sadistic gaze, and to indulge in that spirit of the lynch mob that is condemned when Oliver is chased by the crowd after Mr. Brownlow's pocket is picked.

The prospect of interpersonal visual interaction with Fagin in the condemned cell is too terrible for a single warder: "[Fagin] grew so terrible, at last, in all the tortures of his evil conscience, that one man could not bear to sit there, eyeing him alone; and so the two kept watch together" (470). But the sight of the conscience-racked Fagin is certainly not deemed too terrible for the reader to contemplate; indeed, there is a palpably voyeuristic and sadistic indulgence in Dickens's prolonged description of Fagin's suffering that calls to mind Fagin's earlier sadistic relishing of Oliver's trembling limbs. Too terrible for a warder to contemplate, Fagin's exposure to the objectifying gaze of the crowd—and the narrative audience—is stretched out over eight pages. Sikes has been pursued by imagined eyes—and has succeeded in hanging himself and sparing the judicial system the effort. Fagin is surrounded by actual eyes: he is reduced to an object of vision, unable in any real way to interact with those who look at him or to reciprocate their gaze.[2] And these eyes are all looking at—at what the narrative audience, too, is observing. It is at this

---

2. It is well known that Dickens used accounts of Jonathan Wild's career in constructing the character of Fagin. Lucy Moore (1997) quotes interestingly from *Mist's Weekly Journal* of May 29, 1725, describing the vast crowds that turned out to witness Wild's execution: "In all that innumerable crowd, there was not one pitying eye to be seen, nor one compassionate word to be heard; but on the contrary, wherever he came, there was nothing but hollowing and huzzas, as if it had been on a triumph" (254).

point that the narrative completes its transfer of responsibility for surveillance from the criminal class to the forces of established authority.

I have suggested that at the heart of *Oliver Twist* there is a paradox. On the one hand, the novel asserts an ideologically directed belief in the power of the eye to both perceive and display the truth, a belief that skills of interpersonal perception and acuity are sufficient to pierce and subdue the concealed crimes and secrecies of a burgeoning industrial society and its urban conglomerations. But at the same time the novel progressively underwrites the judicial appropriation of techniques of surveillance that would not be necessary were it actually the case that all truth and villainy are displayed for the honest citizen to read off the faces of the good and the bad.

Furthermore, the novel's varied narrative techniques and perspectives contribute to this legitimation of judicial surveillance by inviting participation in forms of seeing which are non-reciprocal and which mimic the activities of the voyeur and the spy. Fagin has relished the powerlessness and fear of Oliver: we are invited to relish the powerlessness and fear of Fagin. Fagin uses spies: Mr. Brownlow has subjected Monks to comparable forms of surveillance, the results of which are offered to the reader to enjoy along with Monks's discomfiture. Fagin peers through a concealed window at those who are unaware that they are being watched and overheard—just as the reader sees and overhears Dickens's characters at their most private moments and when they are presented as believing themselves to be alone and unobserved.

> The house to which Oliver had been conveyed, was in the neighbourhood of Whitechapel. The Jew stopped for an instant at the corner of the street; and, glancing suspiciously round, crossed the road, and struck off in the direction of Spitalfields.
>
> The mud lay thick upon the stones, and a black mist hung over the streets; the rain fell sluggishly down, and everything felt cold and clammy to the touch. It seemed just the night when it befitted such a being as the Jew to be abroad. As he glided stealthily along, creeping beneath the shelter of the walls and doorways, the hideous old man seemed like some loathsome reptile, engendered in the slime and darkness through which he moved: crawling forth, by night, in search of some rich offal for a meal. (186)

Seemed to whom? The passage is a disturbing one for a number of reasons. For a modern reader it strikes immediate chords with anti-Semitic

Nazi films in which cuts between shots from Jewish ghettos and shots of swarming rats make a similar identification to that made between "the Jew" and "some loathsome reptile" in the quoted passage. The phrase "such a being as the Jew" has a generalizing effect and seems to grope towards "such a being as a Jew." Reading this passage myself I am very conscious of being positioned in a "looking-down" relation to Fagin; the objections of Gérard Genette and Dorrit Cohn notwithstanding (see p. 9), I find the concept of omniscience hard to avoid here. Moreover, the omniscience of the narrative focus appears to go along with a sense of physical elevation. I am not sure quite why this is—perhaps because we assume that reptiles are low on the ground, so that to picture Fagin as reptile is to suggest that we are looking down upon him from a height. While "glided stealthily" suggests the movement of a snake, "creeping" and "crawling" imply a limb-driven movement: it is almost as if while we read this passage Fagin metamorphoses from snake to lizard to old man.

At the same time, a phrase such as "everything felt cold and clammy to the touch" implies physical presence, for we do not, surely, assume that it is Fagin's sense of the cold and clammy that is being evoked: he is at one with his surroundings, whereas "we," as members of the narrative audience, have a reaction to the cold and clammy atmosphere and objects because we, along with the narrator, are *not* at one with them. The passage thus positions readers in a dry, clean, warm, superior position, looking down on, and reacting with horror to, that which is wet, clammy, cold, and loathsome. Susan R. Horton (1981) includes this passage among a number of others from a range of Dickens's works, in all of which words such as "seems" or "appears" are used to indicate an exact match between how the observer interprets something, and what is actually the case. Regarding the passage in question, Horton comments, "again what seems to be is what feels true to the spirit" (51). But again, the question is: seems *to whom?* As no other character is present, one might assume that it can only be to the narrator, who, as Dorrit Cohn reminds us, knows as much about Fagin as the author (who has created them both) decides. But the passage clearly also appeals to pre-existing prejudices in actual *readers:* men like Fagin (or, worse, Jews) are as bad as they look. How things seem to the narrator is how the reader is encouraged to assume they would seem to him or her—or even how they do so seem.

○

We are now in a position to outline an "economy of the gaze" in *Oliver Twist.*

1. Good and evil are displayed on the face and are impossible to conceal.

2. Good people can be divided into two categories:

   The innocent good, especially pure women and children, whose main function is to be seen rather than to see; although they can perceive wickedness and good, they can also be deceived.

   The wise good, normally men, or women like Nancy who have lost their innocence, whose active gaze searches out and punishes wickedness, who are hard to deceive, and who generally see rather than are seen.

3. The wicked do all in their power to avoid being observed, especially by the wise good. The eyes of others are recognized as a principal danger by all the evil characters, who seek to avoid them. As a result, the forces of good need a machinery of surveillance.

4. Moral rectitude is finally associated with being the subject rather than the object of the look, especially at the end of the novel when the spies are incorporated into the legal system and villains such as Sikes and Fagin become the focus of a moral-judicial avenging gaze. The plot and its resolution in the novel consist of a gradual transference of the active gaze from the wicked to the good, and a gradual passivization and visual objectification of the wicked. This process allows the reader to share the narrator's voyeurism and scopophilia with a clear conscience, and to feel part of—incorporated in—the machinery of judicial surveillance outlined in the novel. Whereas *The Scarlet Letter* closes by insisting upon the need to preserve the inviolability of the heart and by associating privacy with healthy normalcy, *Oliver Twist* ends with a strong assertion of the need to protect a vulnerable normalcy by means of a paternalistic surveillance operated by a benevolently stern authority that includes the narrative audience. By a sort of narrative sleight of hand, then, the novel allows the reader to reconcile a commitment to the primacy of the interpersonal reciprocal gaze (it is through the reading of faces and eyes that intimacy with characters is achieved) with an acceptance of the need for a paternalistic, non-reciprocal gaze that exposes the wicked and protects the weak.

If we think back to the way in which Jane Austen valorizes social intelligence in her fiction by associating skill in reading their fellows with those characters who best measure up to the implied moral standards of her narratives, there is a sharp contrast with what we meet with in *Oliver Twist*. Social intelligence, perceptual perspicacity, can and should be learned and improved by those who inhabit the world of Austen's fiction. Such a honing of the interpretive edge of our insight into others allows us to take their interests more fully and, if necessary, more diplomatically into account. In the world of *Oliver Twist*, in contrast, virtue and vice are displayed on the faces of the good and bad, ready to be read by the virtuous and the wicked alike. Where faces are not available to be seen in the burgeoning city, new social institutions such as the spy and the informer must be created to discover that which can no longer be observed as it once was in the community of the village. Where a need arises for the faces of the wicked to be read so that their actions can be challenged, Austen places a strong ethical responsibility at the door of the individual, while Dickens delegates such a responsibility to social institutions created by the state.

The Voyeur and the Imperial Gaze

Herman Melville's *Typee*

HERMAN MELVILLE's first book initially appeared under the title *Narrative of a Four Months' Residence among the Natives of a Valley of the Marquesas Islands; or a Peep at Polynesian Life*. The book, published in Britain by John Murray in the "Colonial and Home Library Series" in 1846, was subsequently issued in a somewhat censored American edition with the title *Typee: A Peep at Polynesian Life*. Given the work's first title, it must have seemed apparent to early readers that the individual who does the peeping is the first-person narrator, and as the account presents itself as a memoir rather than as a work of fiction a further natural assumption would have been that this narrator is also the author, or his alter ego "Tommo." But the book also offers the actual reader the chance to situate her- or (most likely) himself within the diegesis in the position of Peeping Tom(mo): the reading experience itself is the peep, the view, the spectacle that the narrative audience can enjoy just as the mythical Peeping Tom enjoyed the sight of the naked Lady Godiva. Even before getting very far into the pages of the book, then, early readers—and especially those male readers who had some previous knowledge of travelers' accounts of the Marquesas—must have had some well-formed ideas concerning what they would encounter in Melville's work. This is not quite the same as saying that Melville's work itself textually constructs an implied reader who is looking for salacious details; indeed, the reader ostensibly implied in the text appears to be a more innocent individual than the actual readers that Melville must surely have known would have had their attention caught by his title. And as a specific actual reader, I frequently find myself resisting the pressure to read in the manner that Melville, I think, invites me to do.

Given such well-focused readerly expectations, less specification is required of an author. As Henry James (1999) noted in the preface to the volume of his New York Edition containing "The Turn of the Screw"— "Only make the reader's general vision of evil intense enough . . . and his own experience, his own imagination, his own sympathy . . . and horror . . . will supply him quite sufficiently with all the particulars" (128). Melville appears to have expected the male reader of *Typee* to supply "particulars" of a rather different sort in much the same way; in any event, a number of early reviewers certainly perceived that this was the case. T. Walter Herbert Jr. (1980) quotes from an amusing but revealing comment in a contemporary review of *Typee*, in the *New-York Evangelist* (issue 17; April 9, 1846, p. 60):

> "We have long noted it as true in criticism," the Evangelist asserted, "that what makes a large class of books bad, immoral, and consequently injurious, is not so much what is plainly expressed, as what is left to be imagined by the reader." (183)

The comment can revealingly be set alongside another, perhaps yet more amusing, contemporary reaction quoted by Milton R. Stern (1982).

> A gentleman signing himself G. W. P. and writing in the *American Review* (1847, Vol. IV, pp. 36–46) was scandalised by Melville's habit of presenting "voluptuous pictures, and with cool deliberate art breaking off always at the right point, so as without offending decency, he may excite unchaste desire." After discovering in Melville's writing a boastful lechery, this gentleman undertakes to discountenance Melville on three scores: (1) only the impotent make amorous boasts; (2) Melville had none of Sir Epicure Mammon's wished-for elixir; (3) the beauty of Polynesian women is all myth. (66)

What these reviewers object to, it seems, is not what *Typee* reveals about the inhabitants of the South Seas but what it exposes in European or North American readers, especially male heterosexual readers. The reader-voyeur may hope to displace all his voyeuristic guilt onto peeping Tommo, but just as he observes Tommo peeping, so in their turn do the guardians of morality observe him peeping at the voluptuous pictures painted in words in the book. I argued earlier that in the world of a literary fiction the voyeuristic member of the narrative audience cannot be caught, but in the world outside that fiction the actual reader may discover that the very nature of the book being read may give some strong clues as to what his ontologically transformed self is getting up to within the diegesis. Thus while looking at the nakedness of the South Sea maidens, the reader within the fiction that Melville has created discovers that his peeping strips the reader clutching the book more naked than the ostensible object of his illicit look.

The mention of impotence is, however, interesting, and the comment is reinforced by the reference to Sir Epicure Mammon's wished-for elixir, which in Ben Jonson's *The Alchemist* was supposed to be able to make old men young and potent. As Melville was a young man when he wrote and published *Typee*, the comment suggests a fixation on the sexual possibilities hinted at in the work. More recent commentators have seen Tommo's injured leg (like Jeff's broken leg in Hitchcock's *Rear Window,* about which I will have more to say in chapter 5,) as symbolic of a form of castration or castration fear, and all of these reactions to the text assert what is a traditional link between the Peeping Tom and impotence. Given the parallels suggested in the work between cultural observation and sexual voyeurism, the innuendo that the Peeping Tom is impotent involves not just Tommo, but also the European or North American explorer (through voyages of discovery or the reading of books) of other cultures.

Peeping whether by voyeur or by reader is ostensibly a one-way activity: it is non-reciprocal looking, observing without being observed. Webster's 1828 dictionary defines the noun as follows: "PEEP, n. First appearance; as the peep of day. 1. A sly look, or a look through a crevice. 2. The cry of a chicken." The second definition of the verb is also of interest; it provides two unreferenced quotations, the second of which may pun on the two definitions given for the noun. "2. To look through a crevice; to look narrowly, closely or slyly. 'A fool will peep in at the door.' 'Thou are a maid and must not peep.'"

By virtue of its non-reciprocity the sly peep serves as appropriate token or symbol of the unequal relationship between American or European on the one hand, and "native" or "savage" on the other. In his now canonical study *Orientalism* (1979), Edward Said has drawn attention to the implicit exercise of power involved in a relationship in which one group has the authority to describe and define another, but is itself exempt from a reciprocated study or inquiry. Said acknowledges the influence of Michel Foucault's work on his own use of Jeremy Bentham's "panopticon"—a prison in which each and every prisoner is under surveillance by a central authority but cannot return this gaze of power or communicate with other prisoners. In the past three decades the idea of the panopticon has provided a much-cited model for the unequal looking relations involved in colonialism and imperialism. There is a double aspect to this coupling of the gaze with power. First, power confers the right to observe: those with power are generally allowed to look at anything they want, while the disempowered are expected to avert their eyes from authority. Second, looking serves both as token and as source of power: those who look garner more information than those who avert their eyes, and knowledge is then convertible to power. If those who own the gaze also have a monopoly on literacy and on powerful technologies of communication, the inequalities stretch out further and further in the world, and further and further inside the consciousnesses and self-understanding of both observers and observed.

E. Ann Kaplan, in her 1997 study *Looking for the Other: Feminism, Film, and the Imperial Gaze,* bases her concept of the "imperial gaze" on a distinction between look and gaze. For her, "look" connotes "a process, a relation," while the word "gaze" she reserves to indicate "a one-way subjective vision" (xvi). Moreover "[t]he gaze is active: the subject bearing the gaze is not interested in the object per se, but consumed with his (*sic*) own anxieties, which are inevitably intermixed with desire" (xviii; parenthetical insertion in original). Extending this definition to the colonial or imperialist situation, Kaplan explains that "[t]he imperial gaze reflects the assumption that the white western subject is central much as the male gaze assumes the centrality of the male subject. As noted before, anxiety prevents this gaze from actually seeing the people gazed at" (78). In Kaplan's usage, then, looking is a reciprocal activity while gazing is not:

> The gaze of the colonialist thus refuses to acknowledge its own power and privilege: it unconsciously represses knowledge of power hierarchies and its need to dominate, to control. Like the male gaze, it's an objectifying gaze, one that refuses mutual gazing, mutual subject-to-subject recognition. It refuses what I am calling a "looking relation." (79)

In an afterword to her book Kaplan briefly considers whether the gaze can be reversed, whether "racial intersubjective looking" (292) is possible. My argument in this chapter is that already in Melville's first published work we have documented a resistance to the objectifying force of the gaze of the colonialist, although in terms of *reversal* rather than *rejection*. A one-way gaze that is reversed is still a one-way gaze, and not—as Kaplan defines it—a "looking relation." It is not accidental that this reversal is, in Melville's work, inescapably linked to a struggle for power. It is only because the isolated Tommo and his companion are cut off from the firepower of their culture that they can be made subject to the reversed, or returned, gaze.

As I will argue below, it would go too far to claim that Melville's (or Tommo's) imperial gaze actually fails to see the people gazed at. It is, however, to suggest that Tommo's scrutiny of the people he encounters and, accordingly, his understanding of who and what these people actually are has to negotiate a prefabricated image of them that is indeed deeply imbricated in anxieties. These anxieties—self-doubts and insecurities—are not unique to Tommo, but are shared with Melville and, I contend, with male readers past and present.

The definitions from Webster's dictionary remind us that the word "peep" was not without its negative connotations even at the time that Melville wrote *Typee*. If Said's Orientalist enjoys a relatively unselfconscious authority, a confident assumption of the right to look and the right to remain unobserved and unscrutinized, the Peeping Tom is classically the social outcast: the guilty individual who is punished by blindness or (in some versions) by death. If the prison warder or governor at the heart of the panopticon enjoys power without a bad conscience, the Peeping Tom is forever looking over his own shoulder to make sure that he in his turn is not the object of someone else's gaze. Melville's *Typee* thus effects a self-critical and destabilizing turn not uncommon in the literature of the colonial gaze: while offering its readers an inviting "peep" into the forbidden it associates this activity with that of the sexual voyeur and thus undercuts their sense of moral superiority. Instead of the unreflecting superiority of the scholarly Orientalist, the responses to the work from which I have quoted suggest that the reader ends up with the self-conscious unease and guilty pleasure of the impotent voyeur. Michael Clark (1982) has argued that the word "peep" also had rich connotations for Melville, involving the discovery not just of the forbidden and unknown, but also of things physically and morally desirable (217). *Typee* is certainly a book crammed with acts of looking, and there are two aspects to these acts which are of special significance for the present discussion. First, that looking in *Typee* is never a matter of cold or clinical observation but is always informed and orchestrated by expectations, ideas, and desires. And second, that the invitation to indulge in unobserved, one-way looking that is offered by the book's title is not honored. Those who look (a group that includes both Tommo and the book's narrative audience) are made uncomfortably aware that they too are the object of often critical scrutiny: they are made the objects of a returned gaze. As a result, on repeated occasions Tommo's discomfiture is also the discomfiture of the white, male, reader.

○

Perhaps the most-quoted passage from *Typee* is the following one, taken from the third page of the work.

> "Hurra, my lads! It's a settled thing; next week we shape our course to the Marquesas!" The Marquesas! What strange visions of outlandish things does the very name spirit up! Naked houris—cannibal banquets— groves of cocoa-nut—coral reefs—tatooed chiefs—and bamboo temples; sunny valleys planted with bread-fruit-trees—carved canoes dancing on the flashing blue waters—savage woodlands guarded by horrible idols— *heathenish rites and human sacrifices.*
>
> Such were the strangely jumbled anticipations that haunted me during our passage from the cruising ground. I felt an irresistible curiosity to see those islands which the olden voyagers had so glowingly described. (Melville 1996, 13; emphasis in original)[1]

The most striking thing about this passage is that it contains in summary so much of the three hundred or so pages that follow. What is presented as an adventure or a set of discoveries thus to a significant extent turns out to be a confirmation of Tommo's pre-existing *visions* of outlandish things; what he feels "an irresistible curiosity to see" turns out to be what he actually *does* see—and what he presents to our reading eyes. The search for the new becomes the confirmation of the already known. Geoffrey Sanborn (1998) agrees that Tommo's "anticipations" are indeed "strangely jumbled," and he notes that the "naked bodies of the islanders first appear as feminized objects of lust, then instantly reappear as masculinized agents of lust" (78)—an indecisiveness concerning the appor-

---

1. *Typee* was first published in 1846; the edition cited reproduces the text edited by Harrison Hayford, Hershel Parker, and G. Thomas Tanselle, and published in 1968 by the Northwestern University Press and the Newberry Library.

tioning of subject and object that will increase as the work progresses. Sanborn also draws attention to the Saidean *textuality* of Tommo's visions.

> *Typee* presents itself to its readers as an "Orientalist" narrative, one that promises to explore what Edward Said describes as an "imaginative geography." The region it turns toward in this passage is purely textual, consisting of nothing but "that collection of dreams, images, and vocabularies available to anyone who has tried to talk about what lies east of the dividing line." (79)

Once reciprocity is denied, however, the objectification of the other quickly threatens an objectification of the self. Prepared to impose a preformed, stereotyped identity on those upon whom his imperial gaze falls, Tommo soon finds that he is in danger of being paid back in kind. In particular, he fears especially two forms of objectification, two ways in which he himself may have his personhood denied by being reduced to an object: cannibalism (he becomes an item for consumption), and tattooing (he becomes a human canvas for the display of the art of another culture).

Typee thus traces a battle in and for Tommo: a battle between what he expects, and what he experiences. This battle concerns not just the nature of the people he meets, but also the nature of himself. The returned gaze of the imperial subject redefines him just as his imperial gaze attempts to impose a predefined identity onto the people he sees. For the European or North American, "primitive peoples" are both mysterious and exotic *and* essentially already known, familiar. *Typee* is, accordingly, able to illustrate how an *idea* or "vision" of such "primitive peoples" actually conditions what is seen. But the conditioning is far from absolute; it is partial, volatile, and challenged. On occasions the white man's preconceptions may actually give him such a clear "vision" that this is imposed upon an unfamiliar and alien reality. But when the gap between the expected and the observed is too great to bridge, the result is a sighting that unsettles the observer's own native assumptions. Later readers encounter a similar failure to match the vision with the actuality in Joseph Conrad's *Lord Jim*. Daydreaming while a naval cadet, Jim is unable to cope with the shock of the real:

> On the lower deck in the babel of two hundred voices he would forget himself, and beforehand live in his mind the sea-life of light literature. He

saw himself saving people from sinking ships, cutting away masts in a hurricane, swimming through a surf with a line; or as a lonely castaway, barefooted and half naked, walking on uncovered reefs in search of shellfish to stave off starvation. He confronted savages on tropical shores, quelled mutinies on the high seas, and in a small boat upon the ocean kept up the hearts of despairing men—always an example of devotion to duty, and as unflinching as a hero in a book.

"Something's up. Come along."

He leaped to his feet. The boys were streaming up the ladders. Above could be heard a great scurrying about and shouting, and when he got through the hatchway he stood still—as if confounded. (Conrad 2012, 11)

Jim, like Tommo, sees before he witnesses, and his vision is so strong that it prevents him from acting in the world in which he finds himself.

Jim's visions come from books, but they have a Quixote-like effect on his behavior in the real world of trade, colonialism, and imperialism. Conrad too wrote of the effect on his youthful self of reading accounts of the great explorers, and of Stanley and Livingstone, and it is well known that the mismatch between the romantic visions inspired by such reading and the sordid reality encountered in Africa finds partial expression in *Heart of Darkness* (1899). In his essay "Geography and Some Explorers" (2010a), Conrad details his youthful fascination with the great explorers and then records how he exposed himself to "the derision of my school-boy chums" by "putting my finger on a blank spot in the very middle of the, then white, heart of Africa" and declaring "that some day I would go there" (14). Conrad's own account of a captain whose ship is approaching an exotic island (in this case the unnamed Mauritius) also stresses the element of expectation. At the start of his story "A Smile of Fortune" (2008), when the captain-narrator makes out land, he notes: "It was a well known Island; known for centuries. The more enthusiastic of its inhabitants delighted in calling it in picturesque and hackneyed phrase: The Pearl of the Indian Ocean. A very good name. Let us call it The Pearl" (15).[2] Conrad's story, like Melville's, also depicts an ultimately abandoned relationship between European character-narrator and "native," albeit white, woman.

---

2. I quote from the new Cambridge edition of *'Twixt Land and Sea*, which restores a deleted opening to "A Smile of Fortune." In all previously published versions the paragraph from which I quote opens the tale; here it occurs on the tale's third page.

Ironically enough, there is a thought-provoking account of the effect that the reading of *Typee* had on Jack London, one which calls to mind Conrad's account of the effect on him of his own youthful reading. Milton R. Stern (1982) quotes the following extract from London's *The Voyage of the Snark* (1911).

> "How often had we pored over the chart and centred always on that midmost bight and on the valley it opened—the Valley of Typee. 'Taipi' the chart spelled it, and spelled it correctly, but I prefer 'Typee.' When I was a little boy, I read a book spelled in that manner—Herman Melville's 'Typee'; and many long hours I dreamed over its pages. Nor was it all dreaming. I resolved there and then, mightily, come what would, that when I had gained strength and years, I too, would voyage to Typee. . . . The years passed, but Typee was not forgotten[."] (11)

There is a sort of economy of the colonial dream to be constructed from such accounts: the child who reads the fantasy-inspiring books which prompt his (it is nearly always his) voyage to a disappointing reality which in turn is used as the basis for a literary expression that will inspire a new set of male fantasies in a subsequent generation. As we will see in my next chapter, in the nineteenth century novel or short story the fantasies inspired in a woman by her reading are, according to Henry James, typically more domestic in scope.

What I want to argue, then, is that *Typee* is structured around a central opposition. On the one side there is what we can term the "Orientalist," or "conservative-voyeuristic," view of the Marquesas, one which involves an essentially one-way, confirmatory imposition on the realities encountered of certain dominant European and North American myths and fantasies about the South Seas. This aspect of the work tends to be dominant when Melville deals with the sexually suggestive relation between Tommo and Fayaway. But on the other side there is a more subversive, disturbing depiction of the returned gaze of the "primitive" or "savage" people, one which exposes and undercuts precisely those attitudes which fuel the "conservative-voyeuristic" view, and which offers a critique of North American cultural assumptions on the part of Tommo—and of his readers.

Tommo's experiences among the Typee are certainly informed and structured by the myths and models of his own cultural heritage: Lady Godiva and Peeping Tom, the Noble Savage ("the noble Mehevi" [100]), the Garden of Eden ("Fayaway—I must avow the fact—for the most part clung to the primitive and summer garb of Eden" [109]), an indeterminate fairyland ("like the enchanted gardens in the fairy tale" [66]), and Rasselas in his Happy Valley. Tommo reports that

> if ever disagreeable thoughts arose in my mind, I drove them away. When I looked around the verdant recess in which I was buried, and gazed up to the summits of the lofty eminence that hemmed me in, I was well disposed to think that I was in the "Happy Valley," and that beyond those heights there was nought but a world of care and anxiety. (151)

I have above cited E. Ann Kaplan's argument that anxiety prevents the imperial gaze from actually seeing the people gazed at, and here it is specifically "a world of care and anxiety" that causes Tommo to look up to the summits of the mountains that hem him in and see—a scene taken from Samuel Johnson's 1759 romance *Rasselas*!

Moreover, when Tommo's gaze falls upon "the grotesquely-tattooed form of Kory-Kory," and finally encounters "the pensive gaze of Fayaway, I thought I had been transported to some fairy region, so unreal did everything appear" (162). It is, we should note, both "unreal" and also capable of being allotted to a category provided by his own culture: "some fairy region." The reference to Johnson's *Rasselas* is particularly ironic. Johnson wrote this semi-philosophical narrative about an Abyssinian prince without ever having visited Abyssinia and lacking any firsthand knowledge of the East. The work belongs to that sub-genre that we can perhaps name "the exotic pastoral," in which real or invented lands are used as settings in which the transposed problems of Europe are displayed and dramatized. Unhappy in a real exotic setting, Tommo imagines himself not back in his native North America, but in another fantasy exotic setting, one imagined by an eighteenth-century English writer who only once traveled outside the British Isles—to France. Edward Said's argument that Orientalism is how the West manages the East needs to be expanded with the recognition that it is also how the West manages and defines itself against a part-imagined but part-resistant other.

Looking, then, is never a neutral or mechanical process in *Typee*. In the course of the work it is made clear that it is not only beauty that is in the eye of the beholder: much of what is "seen" is actually inflicted upon, rather than discovered in, an unfamiliar reality. Thus we find repeated descriptions of eyes and looking that suggest the *imposition* rather than the *neutral reception* of meaning: "his evil eye," "gazing wistfully," "so strange and steady a glance," "the strange gaze," "my unaccustomed sight," "gazing intently," "the pensive gaze," "eyeing us intently," "angry glances," "glanced their eyes suspiciously," "the nervous eloquence of their looks and gestures," "looking wistfully," "with the eye of faith," "opened my eyes to a new danger," "my melancholy eye," "gazing earnestly," "a fixed and serious eye," "I looked imploringly."

One of the contradictory aspects of Melville's first work—and I would argue that it is a function of the divided nature of *Typee*—is that it both enacts and exposes such semiotic imperialism. On the one hand, as I have suggested, *Typee* gives its actual readers what they were expecting when they bought the book—which is what Tommo describes himself as anticipating on the third page of the work. But because it reveals the mechanics of such processes of culturally determined perception, *Typee* also raises the possibility of mounting a critique of them, a possibility bolstered by other aspects of the work.

Chief among such other aspects is that second sort of looking that is described in *Typee:* "the returned gaze." While Tommo looks forward to "looking at," he finds to his dismay that all too frequently he is "looked at." This "returned gaze" of the "native" is an important element in a number of works that critique colonialism or imperialism. Homi K. Bhabha (1985), for example, has noted that part of the subversive force of mimicry is that "[i]t unsettles the mimetic or narcissistic demands of colonial power but reimplicates its identifications in strategies of subversion that turn the gaze of the discriminated back upon the eye of power" (35). The returned gaze has a crucial symbolic role in resisting and denying the "object status" of the "native," and in insisting upon his or her identity as a self-determining individual, capable of and entitled to interrogate the colonial interrogator. As Jean-Paul Sartre (1969) has put it, "[t]o be looked at is to apprehend oneself as the unknown object of unknowable appraisals—in particular, of value judgments" (267), and "[i]n the phenomenon of the look, the Other is on principle that which can not be an object" (268). Martin Jay (1993) quotes from an English translation of Sartre's 1948 preface to an anthology of African texts edited by Leopold Senghor, in which Sartre told his French readers:

> I want you to feel, as I, the sensation of being seen. For the white man has enjoyed for three thousand years the privilege of seeing without being seen. It was a seeing pure and uncomplicated; the light of his eyes drew all things from their primeval darkness. The whiteness of his skin was a further aspect of vision, a light condensed. The white man, white because

he was a man, white like the day, white as truth is white, white like virtue, lighted like a torch all creation; he unfolded the essence, secret and
white, of existence. Today, these black men have fixed their gaze upon us
and our gaze is thrown back into our eyes. . . . By this steady and corro-
sive gaze, we are picked to the bone. (Jay, 294–95)

Here non-reciprocal looking is the product and support of colonial and
imperial power, and conversely the challenge to non-reciprocal looking
posed by the returned gaze is also a challenge to colonialism and imperialism—it is the empire looking back. Throughout *Typee* the "sensation of
being seen" is one that resists the cultural colonialism of Tommo's attempt
to paint the Typee with the brush of his own culture. Milton R. Stern
(1982) quotes a contemporary review of *Typee* from the London *Times* of
April 6, 1846, which puzzles over Herman/Tommo's desire to escape from
Typee Valley and advances a number of explanations, of which the concluding one is perhaps most interesting:

> Nothing but pure physical delight; sunny days, bright skies, absence of
> care, presence of lovely woman. Fayaway—who gave her that name?—is
> in herself sufficient to enchain a human heart to a dungeon for life, yet
> she failed to wed the soul of Herman to this happy valley. Like Rasselas,
> his pleasures palled. He wished to be beyond the mountains, to be freed
> from luscious imprisonment; for it has to be told that Herman is close
> prisoner in the valley, is well cared for, fed, and housed (not clothed),
> but, for some mysterious reason, *watched* during every hour of the day
> and night. (30; emphasis in original)

Even though he is watched, as Robert E. Abrams argues in his essay
"*Typee* and *Omoo*: Herman Melville and the Ungraspable Phantom of
Identity," to the Typee "Tom is largely an invisible man," one who in
large measure "the savages simply *do not see*" (Stern 1982, 204; emphasis
in original). But this apparent paradox—continually watched but never
seen—is not hard to explain. What is watched, as in Bentham's panopticon, is external conformity or otherwise to a set of rules; what is not
seen are the processes taking place within the individual. The dehuman-
izing process of being considered only in terms of one's external appearance and behavior, a process typical of the European or North American
treatment of the "savage," is here turned back upon the observed white
man. Edward Said (1979) has argued that Orientalism "is premised upon
exteriority," meaning that it is the European or "Western" scholar who

"makes the Orient speak" (20). In *Typee* Tommo is made to experience what such treatment is like. Like the narrator of Jean Rhys's "I Used to Live Here Once," he is frequently forced to experience what it is like to see without being seen. And, I would argue, the experience of reading *Typee,* like the experience of reading Rhys's story, displays for the narrative audience the alienating effect of seeing other people in terms of our own created image of them. The male reader of *Typee* in a sense gets what he wants—his own animated fantasies—but is unlikely to want what he gets—the self-aware isolation of the Peeping Tom coupled with the experience of being not the owner of the gaze, but (through the proxy white male Tommo) its object.

Right at the start of the work, it is as if the animal kingdom itself is prophesying that henceforth Tommo must expect to be the object of an unsympathetic gaze:

> Far off, the lofty jet of the whale might be seen, and nearer at hand the prowling shark, that villainous footpad of the seas, would come skulking along, and, at a wary distance, regard us with his evil eye. . . . That piratical-looking fellow, appropriately named the man-of-war's hawk, with his blood-red bill and raven plumage, would come sweeping round us in gradually diminishing circles, till you could distinctly mark the strange flashings of his eye; and then, as if satisfied with his observation, would sail up into the air and disappear from the view. (19)

But this warning that the white man will be the object of not necessarily conciliatory or respectful gazes is not the first in the work.

> An intrepid missionary, undaunted by the ill-success that had attended all previous endeavours to conciliate the savages, and believing much in the efficacy of female influence, introduced among them his young and beautiful wife, the first white woman who had ever visited their shores. The islanders at first gazed in mute admiration at so unusual a prodigy, and seemed inclined to regard is [it] as some new divinity. But after a short time, becoming familiar with its charming aspect, and jealous of the folds which encircled its form, they sought to pierce the sacred veil of calico in which it was enshrined, and in the gratification of their curiosity so far overstepped the limits of good breeding, as deeply to offend the lady's sense of decorum. Her sex once ascertained, their idolatry was changed into contempt; and there was no end to the contumely showered upon her by the savages, who were exasperated at the deception which

they conceived had been practised upon them. To the horror of her affectionate spouse, she was stripped of her garments, and given to understand that she could no longer carry on her deceits with impunity. The gentle dame was not sufficiently evangelised to endure this, and, fearful of further improprieties, she forced her husband to relinquish his undertaking, and together they returned to Tahiti. (15)

If the difference between the white man or woman and the "savage" is signaled by the clothing of the former and the nakedness of the latter, such a response indicates that it is a difference that will not be respected by the "savage" and is one that may be hard to sustain in his or her presence.

It is apparent from the start of the work that looking is fundamental to the imposition of the power and authority of the white man. As soon as the shout "Land ho!" is heard on Tommo's ship, "[t]he captain, darting on deck from the cabin, bawled lustily for his spy-glass" (20). The white gaze is presented as an aggressive and corrupting force; although Tommo tells us that the Marquesans remain "very nearly in the same state of nature in which they were first beheld by white men" (21), the "riot and debauchery" that follow when the Marquesans come on board ship speak eloquently of the "contaminating contact" of the white man (26).

It is a mark of the divided nature of *Typee* that Tommo cannot seem to decide whether he wants his island paradise to be seen by the white man or not. On the one hand, he recognizes that secrecy covers abominations: writing of the 1842 French expedition to occupy the Marquesas, he reports that "the secret of its destination was solely in the possession of its commander. No wonder that those who contemplated such a signal infraction of the rights of humanity should have sought to veil the enormity from the eyes of the world" (28). But a few pages later, he expresses a different impulse: "[v]ery often when lost in admiration at its beauty, I have experienced a pang of regret that a scene so enchanting should be hidden from the world in these remote seas, and seldom meet the eyes of devoted lovers of nature" (35). Is the white man infringer of human rights, or devoted lover and observer of nature? Tommo is unsure, and his cultural models do not give him an unambiguous answer to the question. If Typee Valley is an Eden without snakes (252), then who is potential Satan? The French invaders—or Tommo himself? Perhaps the ideal is that such beauty should indeed only be peeped at: enjoyed surreptitiously by a hidden observer who can be enchanted without corrupting what he looks at. But what about his own sense of self? T. Walter Herbert Jr. (1980) has shrewdly pointed out that in *Typee*, "the crisis of meaning is located within Melville himself: he finds his mind radically divided between horror and profound admiration for the islanders, as it is also divided between hatred for civilization and a frantic desire to return to it" (158). My own view is that the strength of the work lies in its (admittedly inconsistent) ability to dramatize and display such divisions. As Herbert puts it, "[a] rarer gift is what Melville displays, a tolerance for ambiguity sufficient to permit anomalous experience to be made available to consciousness, however inconsistent the resulting attitudes and feelings may appear to be" (207).

Once he encounters the Typee, Tommo finds that rather than just feasting his own eyes, he himself has to provide food for the gaze of those for whom his own identity is not self-apparent.

> One of them in particular, who appeared to be the highest in rank, placed himself directly facing me; looking at me with a rigidity of aspect under which I absolutely quailed. He never once opened his lips, but maintained his severe expression of the countenance, without turning his face aside for a single moment. Never before had I been subjected to so strange and steady a glance; it revealed nothing of the mind of the savage, but it appeared to be reading my own. (90)

Here surely is just that experience described by Sartre, in which the white man's normal complacent assumption that he is subject and the "native" is object is reversed. It is *his* mind that is displayed for scrutiny by the other, and by an Other whose own mind is frighteningly inscrutable. If at times it may be true that Tommo's sense of his real self is invisible to the Typee, at other times he feels that it is rather too disturbingly accessible to their penetrating gaze. This process of objectification of the white visitor—described semi-comically in the disrobing of the missionary's wife—is repeated when Tommo and Toby first remove their clothes in front of the Typee:

> During the repast, the natives eyed us with intense curiosity, observing our minutest motions, and appearing to discover abundant matter for comment in the most trifling occurrence. Their surprise mounted the highest, when we began to remove our uncomfortable garments, which were saturated with rain. They scanned the whiteness of our limbs, and seemed utterly unable to account for the contrast they presented to the swarthy hue of our faces, embrowned from a six months' exposure to the scorching sun of the Line. They felt our skins, much in the same way that

a silk mercer would handle a remarkably fine piece of satin; and some of them went so far in their investigation as to apply the olfactory organ. (94)

Tommo and Toby are treated in a manner that calls to mind a reversal of the master–slave relationship: instead of the European eyeing the "native" as object to be valued and priced, here it is the North American descendants of the European who are treated as if they were saleable objects. Tommo is only able to understand the curiosity of the Marquesans in terms of economic metaphors derived from the discourse of shopkeeping (or slavery). But at the same time, Melville allows the reader to draw a distinction: whites evaluate in order to sell, the Marquesan islanders in order to know. The process is repeated when the two white men meet the chief. Revealingly, they initially fail to recognize him as one they have met before; their ability to "see" the Typee is clearly limited:

> This warlike personage, upon entering the house, seated himself at some distance from the spot where Toby and myself reposed, while the rest of the savages looked alternatively from us to him, as if in expectation of something they were disappointed in not perceiving. Regarding the chief attentively, I thought his lineaments appeared familiar to me. As soon as his full face was turned upon me, and I again beheld its extraordinary embellishment, and met the strange gaze to which I had been subjected the preceding night, I immediately, in spite of the alteration in his appearance, recognised the noble Mehevi. (99–100)

Once Tommo asks for permission to leave the valley of the Typee, the unfriendly gazes increase in intensity. He has to contend with chiefs who "had been eyeing us intently" and who grant him "angry glances and gestures" (171) as soon as his request is made known. The "natives" "glanced their eyes suspiciously from Marnoo to me" (172) and signal their suspicion when he talks in a language they do not understand.

As a result of his experiences in Typee Valley, Tommo's own way of looking—"his eye"—changes. Describing Kory-Kory's "outward adornings," he notes that these "were a little curious to my unaccustomed sight, and therefore I dilate upon them" (106). His account of the "strange effigy" of the corpse in the canoe reveals that his ability to see Typee culture has improved: "[t]o the material eye thou makest but little progress; but with the eye of faith, I see thy canoe cleaving the bright waves, which die away on those dimly looming shores of Paradise" (207). And other, once shocking aspects of Typee culture begin to be seen in a new way:

> Raw fish! Shall I ever forget my sensations when I first saw my island beauty devour one? Oh, heavens! Fayaway, how could you ever have contracted so vile a habit? However, after the first shock had subsided, the custom grew less odious in my eyes, and I soon accustomed myself to the sight. (247–48)

It is with the presentation of Fayaway that the work's suspension between realistic and fantasy modes is most apparent. The word "peep" in the full title will have raised expectations that women will be held up to a salacious male view, and *Typee* does not disappoint its readers in this respect. Early reviewers had no difficulty in understanding that Fayaway was Tommo's mistress, and throughout the work she is presented *as object to be seen*. From beginning to end of the work nothing of any moment that she *says* is reported: but what is reported in lascivious detail is what she *looks* like.

> From the rest of these, however, I must except the beauteous nymph Fayaway, who was my peculiar favorite. Her free, pliant figure was the very perfection of female grace and beauty. Her complexion was a rich and mantling olive, and when watching the glow upon her cheeks I could almost swear that beneath the transparent medium there lurked the blushes of a faint vermilion. The face of this girl was a rounded oval, and each feature as perfectly formed as the heart or imagination of man could desire. Her full lips, when parted with a smile, disclosed teeth of a dazzling whiteness, and when her rosy mouth opened with a burst of merriment, they looked like the milk-white seeds of the "arta," a fruit of the valley, which, when cleft in twain, shows them reposing in rows on either side, imbedded in the rich and juicy pulp. Her hair of the deepest brown, parted irregularly in the middle, flowed in natural ringlets over her shoulders, and whenever she chanced to stoop, fell over and hid from view her lovely bosom. Gazing into the depths of her strange blue eyes, when she was in a contemplative mood, they seemed most placid yet unfathomable; but when illuminated by some lively emotion, they beamed upon the beholder like stars. The hands of Fayaway were as soft

and delicate as those of any countess; for an entire exception from rude labor marks the girlhood and even prime of a Typee woman's life. Her feet, though wholly exposed, were as diminutive and fairly shaped as those which peep from beneath the skirts of a Lima lady's dress. The skin of this young creature, from continual ablutions and the use of mollifying ointments, was inconceivably smooth and soft. (108)

This whole description reads to a modern reader like an embarrassing mix of sixteenth-century sonneteer and *Playboy:* what seems utterly lost in the description is anything betokening Fayaway's human individuality or particularity. And indeed, as if half admitting this, Tommo reveals a few pages further on that "[t]hough in my eyes, at least, Fayaway was indisputably the loveliest female I saw in Typee, yet the description I have given of her will in some measure apply to nearly all the youthful portion of her sex in the valley" (110). What for the sonneteer would have had the function of isolating an incomparable uniqueness, here ends up demonstrating the semi-racist denial of particularity: they are all the same. Although Tommo tells us that "[t]his gentle being had early attracted my regard, not only from her extraordinary beauty, but from the attractive cast of her countenance, singularly expressive of intelligence and humanity" (133), no evidence of such singularity, intelligence, or humanity is ever presented.

There is absolutely no doubt that in some of his accounts of Fayaway, Melville/Tommo abandons realism altogether. Take the following passage.

> One day, after we had been paddling about for some time, I disembarked Kory-Kory, and paddled the canoe to the windward side of the lake. As I turned the canoe, Fayaway, who was with me, seemed all at once to be struck with some happy idea. With a wild exclamation of delight, she disengaged from her person the ample robe of tappa which was knotted over her shoulder (for the purpose of shielding her from the sun), and spreading it out like a sail, stood erect with upraised arms in the head of the canoe. We American sailors pride ourselves upon our straight clean spars, but a prettier little mast than Fayaway made was never shipped aboard of any craft. (162)

Robert M. MacLean (1979) has claimed that "Melville's narrative personae are often unredeemed voyeurs" (76), and this is certainly true of *Typee.* But often we also see the voyeur exposed and treated to a dose of his own medicine—except where Fayaway is concerned. Discussing the passage quoted above, T. Walter Herbert Jr. (1980) seems a little loath to speak out too directly, but nonetheless he recognizes the essentially fantasizing, wish-fulfilment—even semi-pornographic—aspect of the description.

> One does not want to place too great a burden of epistemological meaning on this passage, but it is perfectly clear that the central gesture is of the object examined disclosing itself freely to the viewer. There were no lakes in the valley of the Typees, and it is improbable that the islanders would have permitted an exception to the taboo that forbade women to enter boats. Yet Melville's enraptured fantasy crystallizes his interpretation of Typee Valley as an unspoiled Eden: a primal paradise that will reveal its marvelous secrets if man will lay aside his civilized pretensions and enter into the spirit of the savage. (169)

Herbert's judgment can be substantiated by reference to Charles Roberts Anderson's (1930) *Melville in the South Seas,* in which Anderson comments in typically tart fashion that "it is obvious that Melville was romancing with a high-handed disregard for truth when he wrote this piquant episode of canoeing with Fayaway, who had been granted a special dispensation by the priests as a result of Melville's eloquent persuasion" (168). The word "romancing" is peculiarly appropriate in this context, more so perhaps than Anderson intends.

Paradise, we understand, is being able to look freely at a beautiful woman whose returned looks make no demands apart from that one be oneself, that one be what one has already determined one is:

> Whenever she entered the house, the expression of her face indicated the liveliest sympathy for me; and moving towards the place where I lay, with one arm slightly elevated in a gesture of pity, and her large glistening eyes gazing intently into mine, she would murmur plaintively, "Awha! awha! Tommo," and seat herself mournfully beside me. (133)

This, surely, is where we see the archetypal male fantasy finding comfortable lodging in the myths of colonial and imperial conquest. I am irresistibly reminded by this of a Charles Schulz "Peanuts" strip in which Charlie Brown admits to Peppermint Pattie that he would like to marry a girl who would call him "Poor, sweet baby": "If I was feeling tired, or depressed or something like that, she'd cuddle up close to me, kiss me on the ear and whisper, 'Poor, sweet baby.'" "Forget it, Chuck . . . it'll never happen!" he is told, and he has to make do with a kiss from Snoopy (strip from March 8, 1973; reprinted in Schulz 1976). Where Schulz treats the fantasy ironically, Melville indulges himself (and invites his male reader to indulge himself) in it. In *Typee* the woman is beautiful, sympathetic, pitying—and her gaze requires only that one be oneself and take pleasure in her. Not surprisingly, then, Fayaway appears in an "amiable light" "in my eyes" (135): Tommo's (or Melville's) eyes are actually witnessing the product of his own fantasy—and this is so whether or not the description of Fayaway is based on a real Marquesan woman. Little wonder that "when my eye, wandering from the bewitching scenery around, fell upon the grotesquely-tattooed form of Kory-Kory, and finally encountered the pensive gaze of Fayaway, I thought I had been transported to some fairy region, so unreal did everything appear" (162). Its unreality is a function not of perfection, but of a recognition that it *is* unreal: it is Tommo's/ Melville's fantasy. The returned gaze of Fayaway, unlike the gaze of the men of Typee Valley, is unthreatening because it knows and confirms him as he would like to be. For the men, in contrast, Tommo is a blank who has to be given an identity, one which comes to be symbolized by the threatened tattooing, and one the prospect of which horrifies him.

No wonder, then, that parts of *Typee* were very familiar to North American and European readers. They were familiar because Melville was giving them back their own fantasies, attractively packaged with familiar references to all the appropriate Western myths. They remained familiar to readers a century later. Milton R. Stern (1982) includes in his book a short extract from William Ellery Sedgwick's 1944 study *Herman Melville: The Tragedy of Mind,* which contains the following revealing observation:

> As we feel our way into the book, it comes over us more and more that we have all been to Typee, and that under one set or another of associations and images, it lies in all our minds. It is an embodiment of the world as we have all felt it in the glow and rapture of youthful love, whatever the object of that love. (87)

The comment is doubly revealing, yoking as it does what are obviously male fantasies about women with Western fantasies about edenic, unspoiled—virginal—peoples. "We" here is clearly a gendered term: it is hard to believe that Sedgwick is including women readers in this category.

There are repeated references to faces in *Typee,* and the idea that the eyes or the face are windows on the soul, or signs of essential selfhood, is presented on more than one occasion. Thus we are not surprised to learn of the nature of Tommo's objection to being tattooed: "I now felt convinced that in some luckless hour I should be disfigured in such a manner as never more to have the *face* to return to my countrymen, even should an opportunity offer" (259; emphasis in original). The remark is revealing, as it shows how unwilling Tommo is to submit his own identity to the process of change: his face must remain as it is. He will not accept being seen as other than he feels himself to be. If he is to be looked at, he must be seen as he wants to be seen, not as others wish him to be. But he (or Melville) has no scruples in presenting Fayaway in a clearly fictional and fantasized form: she is to be seen as he wants to see her. The unequal relationship between Peeping Tom and observed woman is thus not inappropriate to describe or represent the inequalities of the imperial gaze.

Edward Said (1979) makes much of the double nature of Orientalism. On the one hand, Orientalism "is not an airy European fantasy about the Orient, but a created body of theory and practice in which, for many generations, there has been a considerable material investment" (6), and one which constitutes "the corporate institution for dealing with the Orient—dealing with it by making statements about it, authorizing views of it, describing it, by teaching it, settling it, ruling over it: in short, Orientalism as a Western style for dominating, restructuring, and having authority over the Orient" (3). On the other hand, and at the same time, it is a sort of Foucauldian discourse characterized more by its internal laws "despite or beyond any correspondence, or lack thereof, with a 'real' Orient" (5). Paradoxically, then, "Orientalism" creates an *imaginary* picture of the Orient so as better to be able actually to control and even to produce a *real* socio-historical-economic Orient (and, of course, a real Europe and America that are defined in contrast and opposition to the Orient).

If Said is correct, then we would expect that these opposed aspects of Orientalism—its fictive nature and its power to produce and control a non-fictive reality—would result in a system far less stable and homogeneous than Said suggests, one in which incompatibilities jostle in uneasy proximity. Melville's *Typee* provides suggestive evidence that this is indeed the case. Within one fictional or semi-fictional world, realistic descriptions firmly anchored in precise historical actualities coexist uneasily with what are clearly airy European male fantasies. What I have tried to show in this chapter is that different metaphors of the gaze can be associated with these opposed tendencies: while Tommo's sexual-Orientalist fantasies require the support of a powerful, patronizing, and unchallenged male, European gaze, the returned gaze of the "native other" signals the challenging and disquieting intrusion of specific historical and human realities into Tommo's (and Melville's) preformed Orientalist fantasies. At the level of his artistic creativity, then, Melville clearly recognizes that "being looked at" connotes subservience, while "looking at" connotes power: including the power to mold, form, and even create that which ostensibly is merely being carefully observed and faithfully depicted. This recognition is passed on to the male reader, even in the midst of the very experience of enjoying the rôle of Peeping Tom that the text holds out to him.

What *Typee* does not offer its readers is any depiction of what Kaplan calls a looking relation—that is, an interactive relationship between individuals from different cultures that is based on mutual respect. To this extent Tommo's desire to leave the land of the Typee may well find echoes in especially the male reader's sensation once the final page of the work has been completed. Our non-reciprocal relations with Tommo and the other characters in the work mirror the lack of reciprocity in his relations with those among whom he lives. Oddly enough, if we think back to the interaction between Elinor and Colonel Brandon in Jane Austen's *Sense and Sensibility,* the earlier work seems, in spite of the economic, gender, and cultural inequalities of the world it depicts, relatively democratic in contrast to Melville's work. There seems no room in *Typee* for the sort of humane imaginative reading of others that Austen depicts, no unselfish interpretation of the embodied transparency on the faces of others; individuals in *Typee* are, like the missionary's wife, stripped naked by force, not by the sympathetic but penetrative gaze of well-wishing others.

Turning People into Characters

Henry James's "In the Cage"

HENRY JAMES's "In the Cage" is an exceptionally rich study of the complex interplay between, on the one hand, those new forms of mediated and indirect communication enabled by such technological advances as the telegraph, and, on the other hand, the extremely rigid barriers of class and privilege of late Victorian and early twentieth-century English society. In the world about which James is writing, the world he himself inhabited, it was possible to send a telegram to another continent in a matter of seconds, while being cut off from open communication with the person in front of you by the barriers of social class. As I have suggested earlier, it is with the invention of writing that such paradoxes are born, but the development of forms of electronic communication magnifies those potential ironies associated with the ability to communicate anonymously with others that can be said to have been born with the written word.

An otherwise very mediocre British film entitled *The Magnificent Seven Deadly Sins* (Graham Stark 1971) includes a section entitled "Lust." In it a young man played by Harry H. Corbett, making a phone call from one of a row of telephone booths, accidentally finds himself connected to the pretty young woman in the booth next to him. He knows to whom he is speaking; she does not. After a long and increasingly flirtatious conversation, they agree to meet—but she ends the conversation explaining that first she has to get rid of the creepy man in the booth next to her. This sort of double relationship is yet more familiar to those living in the age of Facebook, Skype, and the cell phone than it was to those living at a time when to make a phone call outside your home you needed a vacant phone booth and coins in your pocket. What is fascinating about the film sequence, though, is the way in which it fixes on an especially asymmetrical relationship: the man and woman communicate freely, and yet the man knows who the women is while she is ignorant of the fact that the man she is speaking to and the creepy individual a few feet away from her are one and the same. Two channels of communication split one man into two quite different people for her, and this is because on the phone she must herself create an image of the man to whom she is talking.

Henry James was clearly fascinated by such asymmetrical relationships, and in "In the Cage" he explores how new technologies and old social barriers combine to produce ironies not unlike those presented in much cruder form in the film sequence. If aspects of the theme can be said to be familiar to readers of James, it is also fair to say that nowhere in his *œuvre* does he confront such ironies more directly. James is not the only one to have been fascinated by such paradoxes: Maurice Merleau-Ponty (1962) juxtaposes the situation of two individuals playing chess by means of the telephone or correspondence, who "are in fact participants in the same world," while

> I, on the other hand, share no common ground with another person, for the positing of the other with his world, and the positing of myself with mine are mutually exclusive. Once the other is posited, once the other's gaze fixed upon me has, by inserting me into his field, stripped me of part of my being, it will readily be understood that I can recover it only by establishing relations with him, by bringing about his clear recognition of me, and that my freedom requires the same freedom for others. (357)

Confirmation of one's "being" requires equality and reciprocity in relations with others, and it is such a "recovery" of the other person in which James's telegraphist is interested, although only so long as the other person is a Captain Everard and not a social inferior. Indeed, her unwillingness to dissolve the class barriers that separate her from those below her on the social scale suggests early on in the tale that she will not succeed. "In the Cage" illustrates how the frustration of natural human impulses by class barriers has its inevitable outcome: fantasy, voyeurism, and even forms of sadistic cruelty.

The first two paragraphs of the novella introduce the reader to the unnamed telegraphist's working space—an area of a grocer's shop from which telegrams may be dispatched. The fact that telegrams can only be sent, and not received or collected here, is significant. In my introduction I pointed out that reciprocity does not necessarily entail full equality between any two individuals communicating face-to-face: the telegraphist and her customers exchange information but the traffic is very much one-way—as it is between narrator and narrative audience.

This opening description explains in part the "cage" of the work's title, and it focuses the reader's attention on the difference between physical and social barriers and boundaries. The corner of the grocer's shop is marked off by a transparent screen, one which

> fenced out or fenced in, according to the side of the narrow counter on which the human lot was cast, the duskiest corner of a shop pervaded not a little, in winter, by the poison of perpetual gas, and at all times by the presence of hams, cheese, dried fish, soap, varnish, paraffin, and other solids and fluids that she came to know perfectly by their smells without consenting to know them by their names.
>
> The barrier that divided the little post-and-telegraph-office from the grocery was a frail structure of wood and wire; but the social, the professional separation was a gulf that fortune, by a stroke quite remarkable, had spared her the necessity of contributing at all publicly to bridge. (James 1972, 9)

The opening is proleptic in a number of distinct senses: although there is a connection in this tale between physical and socio-economic boundaries and barriers, the former are "frail" in comparison to the latter. Furthermore, the ability to divide, to isolate, and to separate that is enforced by social, economic, and professional boundaries is considerably more powerful than the impulses engendered by direct personal contact: class distinctions cancel out the leveling effects of physical proximity, conversation, and mutual eye contact.

At the same time, the many boundaries and barriers encountered by the telegraphist in the tale are always less than absolute. The "cage" is defined by permeable barriers that allow those on one side of them to register what is going on on the other side. "Poison" and "presences" of various sorts drift from one area to another, forcing those isolated or excluded by the barriers in question to acknowledge realities existing outside (or inside) the "cage." But the acknowledgment is incomplete:

just as the telegraphist comes to know of various solids and fluids "by their smells without consenting to know them by their names," so too she comes to be known to various characters who never learn her name. She in her turn knows various individuals who go by a range of different names or pseudonyms, and to know of a number of names without knowing the individuals designated by these names. Not the least of the many ironies uncovered and explored in the tale is that, in common with her customers, the reader never gets to know the name of the telegraphist. Like the governess in James's "The Turn of the Screw," she is designated exclusively by her occupation—an occupation to which she is reduced when in the cage. For Captain Everard and those of his class, the telegraphist is, at least initially, someone who comes to be known as she in her turn knows the solids and fluids of the grocer's shop: through the senses but not by name. She drifts into the world of the rich just as the odors of domestic commodities drift into her cage—sensed but unnamed, unacknowledged, and unwanted.

The smells of food are not the only pollutants that violate the frail physical and more substantial social boundaries inside the shop: Captain Everard's smoke drifts into the cage and in the telegraphist's face. But the telegraphist does not object to this, and indeed when she is asked by the Captain during their meeting outside the telegraph office whether she minds his smoking, she replies, "Why should I? You always smoke *there*" (55; emphasis in original). To understand why smoke is acceptable where the odor of cheese is not, we need to consider the social origins and associations of these varied boundary-transgressing pollutants: such transgression of social distinctions is, for the telegraphist, something to object to only when the transgression is associated with those she perceives to be below her on the social scale.

Although we probably remember the telegraphist of "In the Cage" as a character who spends most of the tale attempting to find things out, she is thus introduced as someone concerned with *refusing* certain forms of knowledge: she cannot avoid becoming familiar with the smells of the items sold by the grocer, but she will not consent to know these items by their names. *Not* knowing certain things, certain people, can be a token of caste or of status, and accordingly those concerned with establishing caste or status may more or less ostentatiously refuse such knowledge. When Cecily in Oscar Wilde's *The Importance of Being Earnest* (1992) tells Gwendolen, "When I see a spade I call it a spade," Gwendolen trumps this by responding, "I am glad to say I have never seen a spade. It is obvious that our social spheres have been widely different" (67). However, although knowledge can bestow power and ignorance can betoken status, there is also a shadowy recognition in James's story that for the powerful, concealment and secrecy are generally unnecessary in the presence of those at the bottom of the social ladder—although there are some significant exceptions to this rule. No one is a hero to his valet in part because it is assumed that no one *needs* to be a hero to his valet.

As a number of commentators have pointed out, however, that leakage of information proleptically and metaphorically signaled by the smells and the smoke *does* become a problem if it goes beyond the poor and the disempowered. For the rich and powerful it is of absolutely no consequence if information about their adulteries and sexual indiscretions should become known to the telegraphist, so long as this information stays with her. But if she chooses to pass it on, that is a different matter. Writing about James's tale, Eric Savoy (1995) has cited Jeffrey Weeks's account in his 1991 book *Against Nature: Essays on History, Sexuality and Identity* of "what became known as the Cleveland Street Affair of 1889–90, a scandal that led to moral panic about 'the upper class corrupting the working class into vice'" (Savoy 1995, 289). As this "affair" involved aristocratic and upper-class clients exploiting telegraph boys as homosexual prostitutes, it has a number of important potential points of contact with James's tale. The affair served to associate telegraph operatives both with illicit or illegal sexuality and with the risk of blackmail. Savoy also draws attention to the historical relevance of the trials and imprisonment of Oscar Wilde:

> [E]ven for the legions of "heterosexual" men who engaged in some form of illicit sexuality which transgressed the boundaries of class, the Wilde trials were bound to have presented a cautionary tale: if Wilde's career had been destroyed on the basis of the court's temporary *empowerment* of the working-class witness, the privileging of his or her *knowledge* of the privileged man's transgression, then some version of Wilde's fate could happen to others, even oneself. (296; emphases in original)

Hugh Stevens (1998) has gone further, and has asked: does the tale's (and much of James's fiction's) "queerness" "consist in this very crossing of sexual scenarios, the radical way in which his sexual scenes endlessly suggest other scenes, so that *In the Cage*, a tale of a heterosexual adulterous liaison, can pass commentary on the fraught secrecy and knowledge characterizing the meeting of Victorian queer subcultures with the public sphere?" (132). Such suggestion is convincingly detailed by Stevens:

> It is interesting to hear from Mrs. Jordan that the "bachelors" are "the most particular" about their flower arrangements, given that the late 1890s saw homosexuality increasingly associated with a public iconography of flowers. We might wonder whether there is indeed "something auspicious in the mixture of bachelors and flowers," a mixture which does not result in a "positive proposal" for Mrs. Jordan from Lord Rye, who makes for his floral arrangements "the most adorable little drawings and plans." (The positive proposal, of course, issues from Lord Rye's "awfully handsome" butler and "loved friend," Drake, who has to leave Lord Rye's service on the occasion of his marriage to Mrs. Jordan, as Lord Rye cannot agree that Mr. Drake should "sleep out.") (130)

The word "cage," we should bear in mind, has long served as both a standard English and a slang term for "prison."

Such contextualizing information helps to bring into relief Captain Everard's uncertainties about the telegraphist when he meets her outside her "cage." On his first seeing her in the street, Captain Everard awaits her with "a hard look" (51), a comment that picks up on the sexual pun built into his surname, and which is not the only half-concealed vulgarism in the tale. James surely knew that "jordan" was a slang term for a chamber pot, and the name Drake, as Hugh Stevens has pointed out (136 n30), may call to mind the name given to another male domestic fowl, especially bearing in mind the prominence given to the name Cocker's. And in the following exchange between the telegraphist and Mr. Mudge, the final bodily reference seems deliberately if coyly planted so as to contrast the telegraphist's romantic dreams with the bodily reality that, Mudge knows, is likely to be all that the sexually predatory Everard is interested in.

> "So you're ready to come?"
>
> For a little, again, she made no answer. "No, not yet, all the same. I've still got a reason—a different one."
>
> He looked her all over as if it might have been something she kept in her mouth or her glove or under her jacket—something she was even sitting upon. (67)

Even after Everard has recognized the telegraphist, his "original attention had not, she instinctively knew, been for the young woman at Cocker's; it had only been for any young woman who might advance with an air of not upholding ugliness" (51). The park which adjoins Captain Everard's apartment is clearly associated with illicit sexuality and prostitution: "The evening had thickened now; the scattered lamps were red; the Park, all before them, was full of obscure and ambiguous life; there were other couples on other benches, whom it was impossible not to see, yet at whom it was impossible to look" (55). Like her earlier refusal to learn the names that go with the smells that invade her cage, the telegraphist here cannot but witness certain things about which she would prefer to remain ignorant.

As Savoy points out, Everard's assumption that the telegraphist may be open to an offer to sell sexual favors soon encompasses another possibility: that she may be interested in blackmailing him. Sex and blackmail represent two crucial forms of "leakage" from class to class: from inside to outside the social cage. The sovereigns which, on later visits to her office, he indicates are available to her could be offered either to ensure silence or to purchase sexual favors, and her fantasies about what a "bad girl" would do with the knowledge she possessed are in typically Jamesian manner both teasingly revealing and frustratingly ambiguous:

> It would be a scene better than many in her ha'penny novels, this going to him in the dusk of evening at Park Chambers and letting him at last have it. "I know too much about a certain person now not to put it to you—excuse my being so lurid—that it's quite worth your while to buy me off. Come, therefore; buy me!" There was a point indeed at which such flights had to drop again—the point of an unreadiness to name, when it came to that, the purchasing medium. It wouldn't, certainly, be anything so gross as money, and the matter accordingly remained rather vague, all the more that *she* was not a bad girl. (42; emphasis in original)

In the 1908 New York edition of the tale the final sentence quoted is punctuated differently: "It wouldn't certainly be anything so gross as money. . ."—here the possibility of gross money being the purchasing medium of choice looms rather larger, and picks up the ambiguity in the unspecified nature of the "it" that the telegraphist considers "letting him at last have." Even the generic classifier, "ha'penny novels," draws attention to the inseparability of money and sexual fantasy. (In this tale, class can be mapped against copper coins: ha'penny novels, penny post, and penny-a-word telegrams.)

The historical contextualization of James's tale offered by Savoy and Stevens is illuminating, although I would argue that for James, allusions (veiled or otherwise) to issues of sexual transgression often open chains of associations that throw light on more profound structural anomalies and tensions in late Victorian society. Savoy's case is also weakened by a failure fully to appreciate the subtleties and complexities of the divisions of social class mapped out by the tale—most glaringly in his description of the telegraphist and Mrs. Jordan as "working-class women." He is not alone in this. Tomas Pollard (2001) also refers to the telegraphist and Mrs. Jordan as "working-class women" (84), while Kate Thomas (2012) refers to the telegraphist as a "working-class heroine" (210). Now, from one perspective it is true that the telegraphist sells her labor power for hire, so that the label "working-class" might be seen to be justified in her case. But at least prior to her marriage to Mr. Drake, Mrs. Jordan does not. She still retains the rank of her deceased clergyman husband, and her income from floral arrangements grants her a marginal existence among the shabby-genteel self-employed, one with all the desired advantages of a close association with the rich. These minute differentiations need to be recognized and understood as crucially important in the tale. It is precisely because both women are desperate to hang on to and consolidate shreds of social status—relics of the past, hopes for the future—that distinguish them from the mass of the working class, that they engage in such a web of deceits and evasions with each other. As a very minor civil servant the telegraphist has a status that places her higher socially than a factory worker or (especially) a servant, and she has realistic aspirations to join the petty bourgeoisie as the future wife of a shop-owning Mr. Mudge.

A key issue here is that of "respectability," something hard to assess by the application of mechanical criteria, but related to such issues as family, residence, work, speech, money, and (especially for a woman at this time) sexual reputation. Some of the telegraphist's most convoluted chains of reasoning are concerned with just this matter. Thus seeking to explain Everard's apparent offerings of sovereigns to her, she speculates: "He wanted to offer her things that he knew she wouldn't take. He wanted to show her how much he respected her by giving her the supreme chance to show *him* she was respectable" (77; emphasis in original). By the end of the tale the telegraphist is willing to view her friend's understanding of respectability in a critical light: "There were indeed tea-gowns that Mrs. Jordan described—but tea-gowns were not the whole of respectability, and it was odd that a clergyman's widow should sometimes speak as if she almost thought so" (89). As the husband of a servant, tea-gowns may become her soon-to-be-discarded friend's highest claim to a fugitive middle-class respectability.

The telegraphist is split between an actual and a fantasized social status, and this split is related to her double standard. She wishes to preserve her actual social superiority over, for example, that servant class that Mrs. Jordan will join by marrying Mr. Drake, while fantasizing a romantic relationship with Everard that transcends class divisions. As the tale develops, we are told explicitly of "the queer extension of her experience, the double life that, in the cage, she grew at last to lead" (21), and on holiday with Mr. Mudge she causes him to chatter while carrying on "secret conversations" with herself (65–66). She finally undergoes that classic experience of the literature of the double: fear of her second self: "to be in the cage had suddenly become her safety, and she was literally afraid of the alternate self who might be waiting outside. *He* might be waiting; it was he who was her alternate self, and of him she was afraid" (76; emphasis in original). But her double life is not just a matter of the public and the private, of the (paid) teller of words and the (illicit) interpreter of those same words, or of the opposition between imaginative life and outward occupation. It is also a reflection and product of a self-interested but finally self-deceiving double standard so far as the divisions of social rank are concerned.

Adam Zachary Newton (1995) has suggested, interestingly, that the telegraphist's shortcomings are related to James's choice of narrative perspective. As he notes:

> *In the Cage* begins in free indirect speech, or narrated monologue. Occasionally it employs quoted monologue—"what [the girl] could handle freely, she said to herself, was combinations of men and women." Usually, however, it renders the girl's consciousness through the narrative mode Dorrit Cohn calls psycho-narration, the focalized reporting of another's thoughts. But presiding over such important distinctions in narrative voice is a pronounced and permanent division in social class and aesthetic sensibility, opening wide the gulf between "authorship," on the one hand, and real authority, on the other.
>
> On a fairly obvious level, the story prohibits translation into figural, first-person narration; the girl simply could not tell her own story, as is not the case for more polished and linguistically sophisticated narrators like those of "The Real Thing" or *The Aspern Papers*. (171)

We could put it another way and say that the telegraphist cannot be allowed to tell her own story because the stories we observe her telling for most of the tale involve the corruption of what she sees by what she desires—and the word "corruption" is not too strong. As in much of James's fiction, though, the provision of incomplete information for the reader means that he or she, in turn, may be tempted to fill in the gaps between what is seen with what is desired. I will argue below that as the tale progresses the reader finds him- or herself doing exactly what the narrative pities or condemns the telegraphist for doing: unable to interact, both character and reader invent.

Those who defend the telegraphist and portray her as the moral center of James's tale allow their concern with her abortive relationship with Captain Everard, and their desire to see love topple class barriers, to obscure the fact that she herself aborts her relationship with Mrs. Jordan for reasons of straightforward social snobbery. Ironically enough, Mrs. Jordan's situation is in one sense exactly comparable with that of Captain Everard: her pending marriage to Mr. Drake, the sobbing widow tells the telegraphist, "has led to my not starving!" (96). A couple of pages later Mrs. Jordan is able to tell the telegraphist that Captain Everard has "nothing," although a few lines further on we learn that this is, alas, not strictly true, as he has "debts." Marriage will be his economic salvation in the same way that it will be Mrs. Jordan's. Even more: just as marrying Mr. Drake will edge Mrs. Jordan down a rung on the social ladder, while marrying Mr. Mudge may promise economic salvation, it will similarly represent a downwards social movement for the telegraphist, who will travel the significant social distance from (very) minor civil servant to "trade," although marriage carries with it the chance to rise into the petty bourgeoisie if and when Mr. Mudge runs his own establishment. Thus the most important division or contradiction in the telegraphist is located on the moral plane: it is one which involves, on the one hand, a sentimental, ha'penny-novel belief in strong personal attraction as a basis for the transcending of class barriers, and, on the other, a refusal to countenance such a possibility in relationships with those socially lower than herself—even if the distance downwards is only marginal. We may assume that none of the novels read by the telegraphist involve relationships between rich women and working-class men. There is, then, clearly an element of sadistic cruelty in the way in which the telegraphist, after it has dawned upon her that Mrs. Jordan is to marry a butler, plays cat-and-mouse with her soon-to-be-abandoned friend:

"Mr Mudge has had great patience with me—he has brought me at last to the point. We're to be married next month and we have a nice little home. But he's only a grocer, you know"—the girl met her friend's intent eyes—"so that I'm afraid that, with the set you've got into, you won't see your way to keep up our friendship." (95)

That this cruel deception is played out while the telegraphist meets her friend's "intent eyes" makes her behavior even more morally reprehensible, while confirming that reciprocal looking is no guarantee of truthfulness or sincerity. Marriage, incidentally, has its own possibilities of incarceration: Laura Hinton (1999) points out that in James's *The Portrait of a Lady* Ralph warns Isabel against marriage to Osmond, telling her, "You're going to be put into a cage" (138).

It is of course true that in the final pages of the tale the telegraphist drops the pretenses associated with her fantasies, recognizes that she shares something of a common fate with the future Mrs. Drake, and grants this lady a certain measure of comfort and solidarity. But the insight and the concession go only so far, and they do not include the prospect of future marital socializing.

> Mrs Jordan, in the elation of it, had begun to revive; but there was nevertheless between them rather a conscious pause—a pause in which neither visitor nor hostess brought out a hope or an invitation. It expressed in the last resort that, in spite of submission and sympathy, they could now after all only look at each other across the social gulf. (97)

As we have already learned on the first page of the tale, the telegraphist is not interested in spanning any "gulf" that separates her from those beneath her in the social order. What gives the closing pages of "In the Cage" a very different sort of strength from those of, say, "The Turn of the Screw" is that both the telegraphist and the reader are returned from oscillation between the seductive alternatives of fantasy and quotidian reality, to a single reality and (for the telegraphist) a single identity. At the end the telegraphist puts aside her rivalry with Mrs. Jordan and recognizes, coldly and fixedly, their common fate.

> Our young lady, at this, dropped into the place beside her, and now, in a rush, the small, silly misery was clear. She took her hand as a sign of pitying it, then, after another instant, confirmed this expression with a consoling kiss. They sat there together; they looked out, hand in hand, into the damp, dusky, shabby little room and into the future, of no such very different suggestion, at last accepted by each. (96)

Their cage is social, and it is economic. And their mutual acceptance of the strength of this cage, and of the unreality of the visions and escapes modeled on "ha'penny novels," is ideologically liberating even if on a realistic level it consists only of a recognition of the impossibility of escape.

The tale thus resists the sentimental view that the artificial divisions of class, economy, and gender dissolve in person-to-person contact, that meeting each other face-to-face, two individuals become purely and powerfully human to each other. Such a view is given strong and by no means to be despised expression in a range of literary works—the encounter between Pierre and General Davoust in Tolstoy's *Anna Karenina* is a classic example—and the French philosopher Emmanuel Lévinas has based a complex humanism on the existential appeal of another's "face." And there is no doubt that the humanity of another person is often most difficult to deny or to escape when meeting his or her eyes. Nonetheless, it *is* a sentimental falsification to suggest that if only we could meet with others face-to-face, then the artificial divisions of contemporary humanity would vanish.

I argued at the end of the previous chapter that the ethically positive process of imaginative voyeurism that we witness in Elinor's reading of Colonel Brandon in Jane Austen's *Sense and Sensibility* makes the society portrayed in Austen's novel seem relatively democratic in contrast to that portrayed in *Typee*. "Relatively," because even within the landed gentry from the ranks of which most of Austen's characters are drawn, there are still very substantial divisions involving money and gender. Nevertheless, many of the key words and terms used by Austen to indicate ethical probity are directly linked to a model of reciprocity in relations between individuals. First among these is perhaps the word "candor," but the qualities that in *Sense and Sensibility* Elinor finds lacking in Lucy—delicacy, rectitude, and integrity of mind (Austen 1995, 122)—are also central to the establishing of that mutual respect that in Austen's fiction is the essential precursor to genuine reciprocity. Henry James's characters communicate with one another incessantly and compulsively, and yet Austen's virtues are often hard to find in these activities. The telegraphist, in a weird way like Melville's Tommo, imposes imaginings drawn from popular literature on the person she encounters. She sees in him what she has extracted from what she has read, rather than what he actually is, in a process not totally unlike the manner in which we see in her what we are reading, not human qualities revealed in responses to our own particularity.

James W. Gargano (1979) has claimed that a "catalog of looks, gazes, stares, and 'regards' in James's fiction would include entries from almost everything he wrote" (303), and he relates this concern with looking and seeing to the high premium placed by James upon being able to look without illusion (306). But whereas for some writers the exchanged look involves direct, unmediated intimacy, for James even individuals facing each other in person have to look out from within cages—social, sexual, cultural—that restrict open human exchange. James, in other words, has the insight to recognize that physical proximity does not necessarily lead to social or moral equality.

Dale M. Bauer and Andrew Lakritz (1987) have usefully suggested that James's telegraphist makes "a fundamental mistake in interpretation: she confuses the intimacy of her knowledge gained as a telegraphist with the intimacy of persons" (63). Another way of putting it is that there is all the difference in the world between violating a privacy and achieving intimacy—although this is an insight denied to the voyeur, the compulsive fantasist, or the Peeping Tom. Intimacy involves the willed sharing of two privacies, not the illicit penetration of one privacy by a person who keeps their own private self well hidden.

Gert Buelens (2006) shrewdly notes that "the power the telegraphist possesses crucially depends on the position in the social sphere that she inhabits: only by virtue of her place in the cage can she achieve such control over those outside the cage" (130). Buelens suggests that true bliss, for the telegraphist, "is found not in any direct, physical intensity such as might result from a sexual relationship with Captain Everard but rather in the oblique possession and command that she achieves from the very exercise of her inferior social role as a P. O. woman" (134). Sometimes you have more power as valet than as officer. Sometimes our relationships with literary characters may seem more blissful than our relationships with our fellows, but the bliss has its limitations.

One of James's sharpest perceptions in the tale is that there is a fearful paradox in the fact that the telegraphist's most direct encounters with others are typically experienced through the shell of her official existence, so that just at that point where most intimacy would be expected—when she is literally face-to-face with other people—she is in a sense least herself. Kate Thomas (2012) has suggested that the establishment of the Post Office produced "commutable relations and intimate strangers" (1), and indeed James's tale depicts a world in which moments of the greatest and most revealing intimacy appear often to take place mediated by telegrams, while direct person-to-person encounters (as is so typically the case in James) involve conventional and ritualized forms of behavior, hints rather than the direct expression of feelings and thoughts, and an apparent determination never to specify or concretize. In her first meeting with Captain Everard we are presented with the contrast between the telegraphist's immediate and her fantasy experience of the encounter.

> He had been there but five minutes, he had smoked in her face, and, busy with his telegrams, with the tapping pencil and the conscious danger, the odious betrayal that would come from a mistake, she had had no wandering glances nor roundabout arts to spare. Yet she had taken him in; she knew everything; she had made up her mind. (17)

He has (rudely) smoked in her face, and she has been unable to exchange glances with him, and yet in her mind she knows everything. He smokes in her face, we presume, because as a person she does not exist for him: she is only her function. It is only later, and unwillingly, that she perceives her essential non-existence for him, a non-existence that is here a matter of her class rather than of her occupation (although of course the two are intimately linked):

> This was one of the questions he was to leave her to deal with—the question whether people of his sort still asked girls up to their rooms when they were so awfully in love with other women. Could people of his sort do that without what people of *her* sort would call being "false to their love"? She had already a vision of how the true answer was that people of her sort didn't, in such cases, matter—didn't count as infidelity, counted only as something else: she might have been curious, since it came to that, to see exactly as what. (53; emphasis in original)

Class and occupation together combine to turn her into something approaching a non-person—a fact which she forces Captain Everard to recognize when they meet outside the cage. When he picks up inquiringly her attribution of "horrors" to him and his fellows, she responds, "Those you all—you know the set I mean, *your* set—show me with as good a conscience as if I had no more feeling than a letter-box" (61; emphasis in original)—a comparison that has indeterminate but insistent sexual connotations of a crude and reductively physical sort. (Eric Partridge [1984, 678] glosses "go and post a letter" as to coït, and dates the slang as midnineteenth to early twentieth century.)

One of the privileges of wealth is that of treating those lower on the social scale as functions or tools rather than as human beings. Even Everard's politeness, when he indulges her with it, has a distancing function:

> There were moments when he actually struck her as on her side, arranging to help, to support, to spare her.
> But such was the singular spirit of our young friend, that she could

remind herself with a sort of rage that when people had awfully good manners—people of that class—you couldn't tell. (20)

To be able to "tell" you have to get beyond a person's official or public self and penetrate to his or her inner reality. It is (no doubt studiedly) ironic that the phrase "face to face" and the word "intimacy" are used in connection with the telegraphist's relation with Captain Everard *not* when she is physically in front of him, but when she penetrates the outer door to the building housing his flat and is able to read his name on the list of occupants:

> What she wanted looked straight at her—Captain Everard was on the third. It was as if, in the immense intimacy of this, they were, for the instant and the first time, face to face outside the cage. Alas! they were face to face but a second or two: she was whirled out on the wings of a panic fear that he might just then be entering or issuing. (44)

As with the governess in "The Turn of the Screw," what starts as "as if" soon becomes a matter of established fact. For the telegraphist, moreover, in an existence dominated by formal and official dealings with unnamed individuals, to discover a customer's name is like intimacy; it resembles the experience of being face-to-face. But the experience of *feeling* face-to-face with him is curtailed by the fear that he might come into the hall-way and meet her, might literally *be* face-to-face with her. At points such as these the telegraphist in some not-fully-conscious sense recognizes that realities of class and economic privilege threaten those experiences of intimacy that can be enjoyed only as fantasies. Like the cyberstalker, she wants to know as much as possible about her target, while exercising a strict control over how much of herself is displayed to him. What she experiences here is not intimacy, but pseudo intimacy.

Early on in the tale, the telegraphist takes the lack of constraints on her fantasy readings of Captain Everard's behavior as a freedom, and as a means whereby intimate fusion with the upper classes may be achieved.

> There came a day when this possession, on the girl's part, actually seemed to enjoy, between them, while their eyes met, a tacit recognition that was half a joke and half a deep solemnity. He bade her good morning always now; he often quite raised his hat to her. He passed a remark when there was time or room, and once she went so far as to say to him that she hadn't seen him for "ages." "Ages" was the word she consciously and

carefully, though a trifle tremulously, used; "ages" was exactly what she meant. To this he replied in terms doubtless less anxiously selected, but perhaps on that account not the less remarkable, "Oh yes, hasn't it been awfully wet?" That was a specimen of their give and take; it fed her fancy that no form of intercourse so transcendent and distilled had ever been established on earth. Everything, so far as they chose to consider it so, might mean almost anything. (39)

As time passes, however, the fact that everything might mean almost anything ceases to seem like a freedom and comes more and more to resemble an impoverishment. The meeting of their eyes—in the world of the clichéd romance of the "ha'penny novel" the moment of a dramatic and erotic fusion of selves and souls—is sadly only the raw material out of which fantasy is able to construct an imagined and, ultimately, an unsatisfying intimacy. Here as elsewhere in the tale the Captain says nothing which signifies or suggests anything that is neither amoral or evidence of thoughtless triviality, although it is surprising how little this fact is remarked upon, especially by critics concerned with insisting upon the fineness of the telegraphist's perceptions. (An exception is Adam Zachary Newton [1995], who comments that "the story unequivocally assigns [Everard] triviality" [165].)

We can compare James Joyce's depiction of the way in which Gerty MacDowell's consciousness is structured and formed by the language and clichés of cheap romance, in the "Nausicaa" chapter of *Ulysses*. The contrast between her vision of Bloom and a more banal and sordid reality is easier for the reader to perceive because Joyce gives us more information about Bloom than James provides about Captain Everard. But what James does provide is consistent and (for James) unusually unambiguous.

Increasingly, in fact, that most intimate of moments, the meeting of another person's eyes, brings with it at best an opportunity for private fantasy or over-interpretation, and at worst disappointment. This sense of mingled power and disappointment is splendidly captured in the delineation of the reactions of the telegraphist when she is confronted with Lady Bradeen in person on the other side of the cage.

"How little she knows, how little she knows!" the girl cried to herself; for what did that show after all but that Captain Everard's telegraphic confidant was Captain Everard's charming secret? Our young friend's perusal of her ladyship's telegram was literally prolonged by a momentary daze: what swam between her and the words, making her see them as through rippled shallow sunshot water, was the great, the perpetual flood of "How much *I* know—how much *I* know!" This produced a delay in her catching that, on the face, these words didn't give her what she wanted, though she was prompt enough with her remembrance that her grasp was, half the time, just of what was *not* on the face. (46–47; emphases in original)

The passage, like the sensations that it traces, is packed, complex, and full of tensions. At the level of the reader's experience within the diegesis there are rich ironies in the description of the telegraphist as "our young friend"; what sort of friendship is it in which our own identity is unknown to the putative friend?

The telegraphist here moves rapidly from glorying in the power of her knowledge of another's secrets, through appreciation of the inadequacy of this sensation when faced with the unknowing face of the person to whose secrets she is privy, to, finally, reassuring herself with the recollection that her "grasp" is, half the time, concerned with what cannot be read from the face in front of her. (As always, such a tracing of meanings crudifies James's ambiguities and indeterminacies by attaching them to specific meanings. Thus the precise force of "on the face" is neither simple nor straightforward: it could mean "on Lady Bradeen's face," or something along the lines of "on the face of it.") Moreover, the telegraphist's remembrance that half the time her grasp is of what is *not* on the face can be read in two very different ways. It might imply that the telegraphist reads gaps and absences so as to penetrate to deeper, concealed truths in the person observed. But a bleaker meaning is that the telegraphist inserts her own fantasies into the space that an absence of expression makes available.

Following this meeting, the telegraphist's direct encounter with the face of Captain Everard repeatedly involves the imposition of a desire-directed meaning onto the gaps and indeterminacies of what is directly perceived:

He looked at her with the kindest eyes and still without saying what she had known he wouldn't. She had known he wouldn't say "Then sup with *me!*" but the proof of it made her feel as if she had feasted. (54; emphasis in original)

It was as if then, for a minute, they sat and saw it all in each other's eyes, saw so much that there was no need of a transition for sounding it at last.

"Your danger, your danger—!" Her voice indeed trembled with it, and she could only, for the moment, again leave it so.

During this moment he leaned back on the bench, meeting her in silence and with a face that grew more strange. It grew so strange that, after a further instant, she got straight up. She stood there as if their talk were now over, and he just sat and watched her. It was as if now—owing to the third person they had brought in—they must be more careful; so that the most he could finally say was: "That's where it is!" (62)

He had, as usual, half a dozen telegrams; and when he saw that she saw him and their eyes met he gave, on bowing to her, an exaggerated laugh in which she read a new consciousness. It was a confession of awkwardness; it seemed to tell her that of course he knew he ought better to have kept his head, ought to have been clever enough to wait, on some pretext, till he should have found her free.

. . .

The look she took from him was his greeting, and the other one a simple sign of the eyes sent her before going out. The only token they exchanged, therefore, was his tacit assent to her wish that, since they couldn't attempt a certain frankness, they should attempt nothing at all. This was her intense preference; she could be as still and cold as any one when that was the sole solution. (71)

It was expressed, in fact, in a larger phrase than ever yet, for her eyes now spoke to him with a kind of supplication. "Be quiet, be quiet!" they pleaded; and they saw his own reply: "I'll do whatever you say; I won't even look at you—see, see!" They kept conveying thus, with the friendliest liberality, that they wouldn't look, quite positively wouldn't. What she was to see was that he hovered at the other end of the counter, Mr Buckton's end, surrendered himself again to that frustration. (73; James revised the "in fact" of the first line to read "of a truth" in the New York edition, thus strengthening our sense of the telegraphist's exaggerated certainty.)

He came back one night with a rush, near the moment of their closing, and showed her a face so different and new, so upset and anxious, that almost anything seemed to look out of it but clear recognition. He poked in a telegram very much as if the simple sense of pressure, the distress of extreme haste, had blurred the remembrance of where in particular he was. But as she met his eyes a light came; it broke indeed on the spot into a positive, conscious glare. That made up for everything, since it was an instant proclamation of the celebrated "danger"; it seemed to pour out in a flood. "Oh yes, here it is—it's upon me at last! Forget, for God's sake, my having worried or bored you, and just help me, just *save* me, by getting this off without the loss of a second!" (80; emphasis in original)

The words "as if" appear no fewer than five times in these passages, and this strengthens our sense that like the governess in "The Turn of the Screw," the telegraphist is indulging in constant and self-interested over-interpretation.

A good example of such meaning-construction can be witnessed in the telegraphist's attempt to extract some sense from Captain Everard's words of mild protest, "See here—see here!" The most likely interpretation of the repeated words is that they represent a bewildered protest expressed through a tired idiom which might more familiarly have been expressed as "Now look here!" or "Steady on!" Captain Everard's limitations are as much intellectual as moral (and economic), and his limited intelligence is effectively indicated by his total lack of any verbal fluency. He is in no way an articulate man. But James has chosen the mild ejaculation carefully, no doubt; in this tale that is so essentially concerned with—even premised upon—the act of looking, it reminds us that seeing is not in itself enough for the telegraphist, because she consistently informs what she sees with what she imagines. And this is exactly what she does once she returns to consider the meaning of the Captain's protest:

"See here—see here!"—the sound of these two words had been with her perpetually; but it was in her ears today without mercy, with a loudness that grew and grew. What was it they then expressed? what was it he had wanted her to see? She seemed, whatever it was, perfectly to see it now—to see that if she should just chuck the whole thing, should have a great and beautiful courage, he would somehow make everything up to her. (72–73)

The movement from puzzlement over what the words expressed, what intention lay behind them, to sudden certainty is representative of the mental processes of a typical Jamesian over-interpreter. Note the extraordinary way in which ignorance and certainty are mixed in the following: "She seemed, whatever it was, perfectly to see it now." On the one hand, the formulation allows for an interpretation that sets past bemusement against present certainty, but it also suggests the imposition of fantasized desire on top of actual ignorance. As Adam Zachary Newton (1995) puts it, "See here" does not possess ethical orientations: "like the interiority which is this text's governing spatial locus, it points down and in, not up and out (and as far as the girl is concerned, it promises more than it delivers, whatever it is she imagines she now 'sees')" (167–68).

James more than suggests that the emptiness of such a world of fantasized communication, and its lack of genuine intimacy and real reciprocity, is productive of a frustration which, eventually, seeks outlet in the satisfactions of a semi-perverted exercise of power. Like one of Emily Dickinson's best-known poetic personae, the telegraphist appears to like (Mrs. Jordan's and Captain Everard's) looks of agony, because she knows they are true.

> "Oh!" said the girl, knowing at this the deepest thrill she had ever felt. It came to her there, with her eyes on his face, that she held the whole thing in her hand, held it as she held her pencil, which might have broken at that instant in her tightened grip. This made her feel like the very fountain of fate, but the emotion was such a flood that she had to press it back with all her force. That was positively the reason, again, of her flute-like Paddington tone. "You can't give us anything a little nearer?" Her "little" and her "us" came straight from Paddington. These things were no false note for him—his difficulty absorbed them all. The eyes with which he pressed her, and in the depths of which she read terror and rage and literal tears, were just the same he would have shown any other prim person. (83)

Her deliberate holding of him in suspense, drawing out the time she takes to give him the information which he so desperately needs (while maintaining eye contact with him as she later does while treating Mrs. Jordan cruelly), seems to be fueled partly by an enjoyment of power and of the pseudo intimacy bestowed by sadism, and partly by a new set of fantasy rôles for herself and for him, rôles which replace the ones that have ceased to gratify her. Significantly, at this point the telegraphist is— for the only time in the tale—exaggerating her lower-class identity by giving her speech a "Paddington tone." If she cannot succeed in escaping out of her cage into Captain Everard's world, she will demonstrate to him that even in her world she can exercise power over him.

Indeed, at one point in the tale the telegraphist is depicted as not wanting to know more about the causes of Captain Everard's suffering:

She caught only the uncovered gleams that peeped out of the blackness, and she wondered what complication, even among the most supposable, the very worst, could be bad enough to account for the degree of his terror. There were twists and turns, there were places where the screw drew blood, that she couldn't guess. She was more and more glad she didn't want to. (85)

But this does not exculpate her from having added to, and taken pleasure from extending, these pains. The metaphorical reference to that same instrument of torture to which James's "The Turn of the Screw" owes its title is worth noting. Both tales involve a female over-interpreter who compensates for her socio-economic disadvantages by building stories out of what she sees. Both heroines believe that their powers of perception and discrimination bear witness to their gentility of the spirit, but both obtain pleasure from the power that their knowledge brings them, a pleasure that is indirectly associated with the pleasures of the torturer even when, as here, this is called up only to be denied.

○

So far so good. But there is one additional reason why the telegraphist's fantasy life seems familiar to us as we read "In the Cage." The tale presents us with a character whose relations with certain of her customers are strikingly similar to a reader's relations with the characters of a novel—indeed, strikingly similar to our relations with the telegraphist. This is in part because she belongs to a long line of fictional characters starting with Don Quixote who themselves perceive real people through the distorting lens of familiar literary representations. The fact that she is a reader of ha'penny novels (we are even given the name of one: *Picciola*—the full title of which is *Picciola: The Prisoner of Fenestrella: or, Captivity Captive* by X. B. Saintine, first published in French in 1839) is crucial to her modeling of the rôle of the reader. Although her own captivity primarily involves social and economic, rather than steel, bars, the telegraphist regularly reverts to the model of her chosen fictional genre to make sense of her world: "She quite thrilled herself with thinking what, with such a lot of material, a bad girl would do. It would be a scene better than many in her ha'penny novels" (42); "That was the hour at which, if the ha'penny novels were not all wrong, he probably came home for the night" (45). But the opening sentence of the tale makes it clear that the "literary" quality of her contact with her more upper-class customers goes beyond matters of plot: "It had occurred to her early that in her position—that of a young person spending, in framed and wired confinement, the life of a guinea-pig or a magpie—she should know a great many persons without their recognizing the acquaintance" (9). Not only does she conceptualize these customers according to the conventions of cheap fiction, but her relation to them is like a reader's relation to a fictional character: one-way and non-reciprocal. Those characters about whom we read, whose lives we discuss, whose emotions we share, whom we know so very well—are similarly unable to recognize any acquaintance with us. While we observe and pity the telegraphist's fantasizing about the rich who live in a world in which she can never have her humanity recognized, we fantasize about her and her life dimly and naggingly aware that our humanity can never be recognized by her. We are in our own cage: the cage inhabited by all readers of fiction.

Kate Thomas (2012) argues that James "affords his humble telegraphist . . . the credit of being an author" (210), while Richard Menke (2008) picks up on James's use in his preface of the word "artist" to describe her, noting that she "fantasizes that she can see into others but that no one really knows her, a situation that echoes the structure of knowledge and insight in third-person narrative, especially the supervision exercised by the narrators of midcentury realist novels" (203). Extending this comparison yet further, Menke suggests that James's tale "cages the soul of an 'authorial' narrator (who 'maintains his own vantage point on the fictional world and its inhabitants') within the figure of the telegraphist," and concludes that "[t]hrough the transparent screen of this narration, James can indicate the 'triumphant, vicious feeling of mastery and power' that may inhere in the one-sided knowledge of a shared reality" (203). One can certainly agree that if the telegraphist's situation in the story is like that of a reader up to that point where the last page has been reached, Captain Everard has married Lady Bradeen, and is "now for ever lost" (99), then some of her customers seem possessed of the multiple identities of an author.

> She had seen stranger things than that—ladies wiring to different persons under different names. She had seen all sorts of things and pieced together all sorts of mysteries. There had once been one—not long before—who, without winking, sent off five over five different signatures. Perhaps these represented five different friends who had asked her—all

women, just as perhaps now Mary and Cissy, or one or other of them, were wiring by deputy. Sometimes she put in too much—too much of her own sense; sometimes she put in too little; and in either case this often came round to her afterwards, for she had an extraordinary way of keeping clues. (14)

The reader too may yearn to seek back through the text and the name of the author to the real life of Henry James, but even when—unlike the telegraphist—we know who the author is, he or she remains forever hidden behind the frustratingly ambiguous clues provided by the words on the page. The duplicity of authors has to be confronted by the interpretive skills of a reader who, like a detective, is capable of paying due attention to clues and able to avoid the perils of over-interpreting and under-interpreting: putting in too much or too little. But detectives, alas, are generally concerned not with interacting with the present lives of individuals but rather with gathering information about lives already lived.

The telegraphist's life is both enriched and impoverished by her wealthy customers (we are told that "she had no interest in the spurious or the shabby, and no mercy at all for the poor" [23]). It is enriched because it offers her a world into which she can escape from the drabness of her everyday life and from the unexciting prospect of marriage to and life with Mr. Mudge: "She was perfectly aware that her imaginative life was the life in which she spent most of her time; and she would have been ready, had it been at all worth while, to contend that, since her outward occupation didn't kill it, it must be strong indeed" (12). An alternative explanation is, of course, that it is precisely the nature of her outward occupation that produces the strength of her imaginative life. The reader who appreciates this may well be led to ask to what extent the nature of his or her own outward occupation drives an interest in the imaginative life lived in the pages of fiction—even fiction that costs rather more than a ha'penny and is written by Henry James.

The telegraphist's imagined life with her rich customers is impoverished because it takes place in a world in which she is almost as ghostly as the narrator of Jean Rhys's "I Used to Live Here Once": she can see these people as they stand right in front of her, but to them "people of her sort didn't, in such cases, matter" (53). The "cases" in question are those involving sexual transgression: the telegraphist is only "almost" as ghostly as Rhys's narrator because, unlike that character, she exists as a possible sexual partner. Physical proximity is not enough.

> Yet if it was now flagrant that he did live close at hand—at Park Chambers—and belonged supremely to the class that wired everything, even their expensive feelings (so that, as he never wrote, his correspondence cost him weekly pounds and pounds, and he might be in and out five times a day), there was, all the same, involved in the prospect, and by reason of its positive excess of light, a perverse melancholy, almost a misery. (18–19)

The misery she feels is that of having no sense that for him she has a human identity as rich as the one she attributes (or misattributes) to him: "the thing in all this that she would have liked most unspeakably to put to the test was the possibility of her having for him a personal identity that might in a particular way appeal" (20).

○

In a fascinating article about James's amanuensis Theodora Bosanquet, Pamela Thurschwell (1999) quotes an entry in Bosanquet's diary for Tuesday, October 29, 1907: "Mr. James away in town so I had a free day. Went round to his house however & carried off an armful of books & spent most of the day reading Turgenev's 'Smoke' and 'In the Cage' by Henry James. It's just the right length for its subject—really awfully good. It makes me feel desperate though" (10). Bosanquet must surely have seen parallels between her situation while in the same room as Henry James and the situation of the telegraphist while in close physical proximity with Everard. Her feeling of desperation, like the telegraphist's "melancholy, almost a misery," can be related to that sense of being reduced to a sort of mechanical receiving device by another, physically adjacent, human being.[1] The lack that both Bosanquet and the telegraphist experience goes beyond an absence of respect or a failure to communicate: it is a lack of *existence*: the telegraphist quivers "on occasion into the perception of this and that one whom she would, at all events, have just simply like to *be*" (23; emphasis in original). The danger in all this, as a succession of authors and social commentators have pointed out, is that an escape into the exotic world contained within the pages of a work of fiction may offer enrichment of a sort, but overindulged it may also reduce

---

1. Like James, Joseph Conrad also used an amanuensis in his later years, although in his case because gout made it impossible for him to hold a pen. In his novel *Under Western Eyes* he has his character Tekla describe the misery of taking dictation, something that bespeaks a leap of sympathetic imagination that redounds to his credit.

the richness of a real and available life: "But if nothing was more impossible than the fact, nothing was more intense than the vision" (45).

In typically Jamesian manner, then, while reading we are given a nagging or subliminal feeling that our relation to the telegraphist mirrors hers to her rich customers: we have a rich sense of her humanity, her situation, and the complexities of her life, while for her we do not exist. When she does make contact with Captain Everard outside of her physical cage, it is for her like entering the pages of a book, but the rôle that she has imagined for herself in her fantasies is not the rôle that the Captain is clearly envisaging for her. She despairs that she cannot, "not even once or twice, touch with him on some individual fact" (40). The more he comes to life for her, the less she exists for him. He raises his hat to her; their eyes meet on more than one occasion; he puts his hand on her hand—but this reciprocity never really rises to an acknowledgment of anything approaching her full humanity.

A further irony in the story is that its scattered clues pointing to a concealed plot of danger and intrigue have encouraged readers and critics to attempt to reconstruct a totality on the basis of fragments in precisely the way in which the telegraphist does.

> The girl looked straight through the cage at the eyes and lips that must so often have been so near his own—looked at them with a strange passion that, for an instant, had the result of filling out some of the gaps, supplying the missing answers, in his correspondence. Then, as she made out that the features she thus scanned and associated were totally unaware of it, that they glowed only with the colour of quite other and not at all guessable thoughts, this directly added to their splendour, gave the girl the sharpest impression she had yet received of the uplifted, the unattainable plains of heaven, and yet at the same time caused her to thrill with a sense of the high company she did somehow keep. (46)

As it turns out, most of her interpretations are wrong: she learns the more pedestrian, more dismal truth about Captain Everard and Lady Bradeen from Mrs. Jordan, at the end of the story. That penultimate word "somehow" in the passage quoted is the kick of the real. The friend who is to marry a butler, it turns out, knows more than she does.

Pamela Thurschwell (1999) comments that the telegraphist "may be trapped but she is also in the position of the Foucauldian panopticon surveyor—she sees (into minds at least) without being seen" (8). There is no doubt that on occasion her panoptical vision grants her a sense of power, but it also condemns her to isolation and loneliness. Mark Seltzer (2000) perhaps overstates his case when he claims that the novel as literary genre "originates as private letters made public, or, more exactly, as love letters designed, or designated, for interception" (197)—after all, the epistolary novel represents only one branch in the novel's family tree. But he is correct to draw attention to the way in which both the reader and the telegraphist intercept other peoples' private messages. If the telegraphist is in the cage then so too is the reader. Should we look pityingly down on her we expose ourselves to the pity of those whose most important life is experienced not in the pages of books but in reciprocal contact with other people. We may wish that we could meet the characters in the fiction we read in our own world, just as the telegraphist wishes to meet *her* "characters" outside of the cage. And indeed when she suggests a correction to her telegram to Lady Bradeen, it is "as if she had bodily leaped—cleared the top of the cage and alighted on her interlocutress" (48). Such an ontological transgression has no optimistic conclusion, however: Lady Bradeen flees in confusion. The only possible relationship that the telegraphist can enjoy with her customers is, like the only possible relationship we can enjoy with the characters in the fictions we read, an essentially non-reciprocal one. At the close of James's tale the telegraphist and Mrs. Jordan exchange goodbyes, but these are not delivered directly. Each farewell is launched into the fog that isolates the two characters, posted into a void like letters sent to a correspondent living in a different country. And indeed the image prefigures the fact that shortly the two friends might just as well be in different countries for all the intimacy they can expect to enjoy, just as the reader too lives in a world from which James's characters may be observed, but from which they can never look back at him or her. Finishing the final page of "In the Cage" we share with the telegraphist a sense of relief that we are abandoning a world in which our own individuality can never be recognized. At the same time, however, the bleakness of the life that awaits James's character helps us to understand the attraction of the fantasies that can be taken from ha'penny novels and imposed on those who never really perceive her humanity.

The Politics of Looking in/at Alfred Hitchcock's *Rear Window*

She could not help believing herself the nicest observer of the two;—she watched his eyes, while Mrs Jennings thought only of his behaviour.

—Jane Austen, *Sense and Sensibility*

People don't always express their inner thoughts to one another; a conversation may be quite trivial, but often the eyes will reveal what a person really thinks or feels. . . . Dialogue should simply be a sound among other sounds, just something that comes out of the mouths of people whose eyes tell the story in visual terms.

—Alfred Hitchcock, in conversation with François Truffaut (1968)

The Narrative of *Rear Window*

Moving from literary to filmic fictional narrative makes some preliminary comment on the differences between these two forms appropriate. Some commentators deny that fiction films can helpfully be understood as narratives. Frank Beaver's *Dictionary of Film Terms* (1994), for example, contains an entry for "narration," which Beaver glosses as "a term for the spoken words of a person who relates information in a film directly rather than through dialogue" (252), in other words, what is commonly known as voice-over. There is no entry for "narrator" or even for "narrative," leaving the reader with the possible impression that a film that does not contain the spoken words of a person who relates information directly rather than through dialogue is simply not a narrative. Clearly a fundamental difference between, say, a novel and a film such as Alfred Hitchcock's *Rear Window* (1954) can be indicated by means of a question: "If *Rear Window* is a narrative, then who or what is the narrator?" Many commentators on *Rear Window* speak of "the camera" as if it is itself capable of a purposive presentation of selected images, but later on in this chapter I will explain why I find such a formulation either incomplete or unsatisfactory.

In his classic study *Narration in the Fiction Film*, David Bordwell (1985) surveys a range of possible candidates for the rôle of narrator in the fiction film. These include the special cases of a character-narrator (such as Marlowe in Edward Dmytryk's 1944 film *Murder, My Sweet*), and an extradiegetic voice-over commentator (such as is found in François Truffaut's 1962 film *Jules et Jim*). Bordwell recognizes, however, that the challenging question is this: "Even if no voice or body gets identified as a locus of narration, can we still speak of a narrator as being present in a film?" (61). He concedes that "in watching films, we are seldom aware of being told something by an entity resembling a human being" (62). Bordwell's solution appears, paradoxically, to involve narration without a narrator: "I suggest . . . that narration is better understood as the organization of a set of cues for the construction of a story. This presupposes a perceiver, but not any sender, of a message" (62). While a minority of fiction films do provide what Bordwell terms a "definable narrator," in other films he proposes that it is better "to give the narrational process the power to signal under certain circumstances that the spectator should construct a narrator" (62). My unease with this solution is twofold. First, if the narrator is a production of the narrational process, then why not wield Occam's razor and rest content with the narrational process? But second, discussion and criticism of films demonstrate time and again that viewers assume that there is a creative and organizing force behind or outside of the narrational process—and as we shall see there is hardly a better exemplification of this than is to be found in critical discussion of *Rear Window*. Now, it could be claimed that the constant personification of the camera in this film by commentators proves Bordwell's point that spectators construct a narrator, but the problem is that commentators personify the camera in wildly different ways. Jakob Lothe (2000) has made the telling point in relation to Bordwell's position that

> it is indeed difficult to imagine that a film is "organized" without being "sent." Film as an effective communication system presupposes some form of "sender" (the fact that this sender is composed of many links

and may be impossible to identify is another matter). Therefore it makes more sense to say, as Chatman does, that the viewer reconstructs the film's narrative than to say that he or she "constructs" it. (29)

As a performance art, film is experienced not as a retelling of that which has already happened but as an encounter with characters as they exist and events as (or as if) they are happening. When Jeff, the James Stewart character in Hitchcock's film, looks out of his window, we experience this not as someone telling us about a character who looked out of a window, but as a man who is looking out of the window. Film does not possess a double chronology (time-of-happening and time-of-telling-what-happened) in quite the same way that a literary narrative does, except perhaps in the special case of the flashback. Nonetheless, fiction films present the viewer with a sequence of events that is in a sense "told"—that is, presented to viewers in an organized and artistically significant manner—and it is this that in part justifies the term "film narrative." "Presented," in the previous sentence, must entail some sort of presenter, someone who, to put it crudely, describes what we see and how we see it.

Some theorists, following the example of French *Auteur* theory, link the director to the author and then assign this "author" or "implied author" an additional rôle as the consciousness understood by the viewer to have aesthetic control over the material presented to the viewer. Following the adherents of *Auteur* theory I do feel that Hitchcock's films—and especially his Hollywood films—present us with something very much akin to an implied author. Those familiar with these films have typically built up a sense of a particular personality with a recognizable sense of humor and a predilection for teasing and shocking viewers, a sense not unlike that sense of "Jane Austen" that readers of the novelist's works build up from title to title. In both cases—Austen and Hitchcock—this sense of a personality with views, quirks, characteristics, is different from our sense of an actual human being. This "Hitchcock," unlike the real Alfred Hitchcock, for example, is ageless, and is no older in *Family Plot* in 1976 than he (or "he") is in *Shadow of a Doubt* in 1943.

There is also the issue of readers and audiences. I believe that my previous claims concerning the ontologically hybrid nature of the reader of literary fiction can be made relevant to the film audience, and indeed may make more obvious sense with regard to those watching a film than to those reading a novel. While watching a film in a movie theater we have both a feeling of immersion in the diegesis through engagement with the lives that unfold in front of us and a strong awareness of the behavior of those flesh-and-blood individuals sitting around us whose gasps, laughter, and nervous tension communicate themselves to us just as our responses may be apparent to them. The hybrid nature of our experience in such a situation is easy to demonstrate by noting the effect on us of inappropriate audience behavior. If someone laughs at the wrong time this drags us out of the diegesis in a way that an "appropriate" gasp does not. In what follows I will make a crude distinction between "audience member" (the flesh-and-blood individual sitting in the cinema) and "viewer" (the consciousness experiencing a film as it is shown or, in retrospect, straddling two ontological states much as I argued the reader as member of the narrative audience does).

Such ontological issues relate directly to certain aspects of film interpretation. In the case of *Rear Window*, for example, we may ask: are we (as members of the cinema audience) *watching* the character L. B. Jefferies's[1] voyeurism, are we (as viewers) *sharing* in it, or (a third possibility) are we (as members of the cinema audience) in some sense watching someone else (a narrator, the camera, Hitchcock) *observe or present* Jeff's voyeurism? Returning to *Rear Window* in his 1977 "Retrospective," Robin Wood (1989) suggested that "the common simplistic association of subjective camera with audience identification . . . needs careful qualification" (217–18). I think that this is true, and the complexities of the audience member's ontological status are deeply entwined in the need for such qualification. I will return to such issues below.

I would like at this point to focus in some detail on the opening of the film, from the beginning of the credits to the viewer's first sight of the sleeping and sweating Jeff. As it happens I have good reason to remember this sequence. Watching the film on its first UK release in the mid-1950s, I found my youthful self irritated by the length of the credits and said aloud "Get on with it!" to the friend I was sitting next to. A man sitting in front of us with his female companion turned around and asked aggressively if I was talking to them, thus adding a more immediate factor to the element of threat built up as the film progressed, and also reminding me that if I behaved as if a reciprocal relationship with the

---

1. Although the character-narrator of Cornell Woolrich's original 1942 short story is named Hal Jeffries, the name scrawled on the film-character's plaster cast is L. B. Jefferies. I will henceforth refer to him as Jeff, the name used by other characters. Woolrich's story was originally published under various titles: "Murder From a Fixed Perspective," "Murder From a Fixed Viewpoint," and "It Had to Be Murder." Following the success of Hitchcock's film it is now published under the title of "Rear Window."

film were possible, my fellow viewers might assume that they were the ones being addressed.

The credits of *Rear Window* continue to tantalize the viewer who wants to "get on with" the film, to the extent that the occasional commentator represses them altogether. Philip Brookman (2010), for example, states that "When the film opens, Jeffries [*sic*] is watching through binoculars as a woman wearing a bathing suit dances in her kitchen, as if in a peep show," thus cutting out not just the credits and the camera pan round the courtyard but also the viewer's encounter with the sleeping Jeff (213). James Monaco (2000) claims that the opening pan and track of the film "tells us where we are, why we are there, whom we are with, what is going on now, what has happened to get us there, who the other characters of the story are, and even suggests possible ways the story might develop—all effortlessly and quickly and without a spoken word! Paragraphs of prose are condensed into seconds of film time" (210). While conceding that the opening minutes of the film do indeed convey a lot of information, what Monaco's account underestimates is the extent to which viewers are forced to reach interpretative decisions on the basis of incomplete and even contradictory information during this sequence. Were the sequence as straightforward a presentation of information as his account suggests, we might expect that commentators on it would find it easy to agree about its force. In fact, however, it is surprising how many disagreements there are both about what the sequence contains, and what effect it has on the viewer—especially bearing in mind how short it is. Miran Božovič (1992), for example, in the course of an argument that the film is about what Jacques Lacan dubs "the appetite of the eye," writes this of the opening sequence:

> The film opens with the camera directly approaching the window, stopping exactly above the windowsill—that is, when the middle frame of a casement window literally covers the screen. This is a moment of complete identification between the view from the room and the view from the audience: we see all that can be seen from the room; whoever was in the room is now, as it were, in the audience and we have, as it were, entered his room. Once the view from the room fuses with our view, the camera slowly surveys the courtyard from right to left—this shot could be said to correspond to our first eye movement as a giant eye which has opened and looked around.
>
> The movement of the camera directly towards the window which results in the coincidence of the window as a giant eye with the "eye" of

> the camera—our own eye—depicts, from behind, a fusion of two looks, ours and Jeff's[.] (161)

This is misleading on a number of counts. As the film opens and the credits succeed one another, from inside what only later the viewer is to learn is Jeff's apartment, the camera statically surveys what we assume is the rear window of the title, which is at this point covered by three roller blinds.[2] As we watch, the blinds roll up—without any apparent human intervention, one at a time, from left to right. When the right-hand blind is fully rolled up (at precisely the same point that the final credit "Directed by Alfred Hitchcock" is displayed), the camera tracks forward and down, stopping just in front of the window sill (we can see the window frame in front of us, opened outward, on screen right). The middle window frame does not cover the screen: the bottom part of the middle frame approximates to the lower cut-off point of the screen. The camera's slow downward movement is not without significance, as it is less easy to interpret it as representative of the movement of a human being: the camera ends up "looking out" through the bottom of the window—a vantage point which, if we assume that we are dealing with subjective camera, is so low as to suggest that of a child's. But the movement downwards to this position rules out a child's point of view. This may seem like hair-splitting, but it is important in terms of the way the narrative situates the viewer and constructs a viewing position, for while the camera *movement* suggests a form of searching by some living being, the camera *position* in front of the window makes it hard to imagine that it is a human being who is doing this searching.

At this point in the sequence there is a cut—ostensibly a matched cut—with the camera seemingly located *outside* of the window, and pointing down (the apartment is not on the ground floor). It pans round, tilts, and follows a cat for some time (mewing noises are twice heard over, or as part of, the background music) until the cat disappears, at which point the camera then surveys different parts of the three visible sides of the inner, facing courtyard. It next appears to track back into the apartment, where it discovers (or reveals) the sleeping Jeff, starting with a view of his head and then panning down to reveal his whole body. I say "appears," because the perspectival clues given on a flat screen are not unambiguous, and it is possible for height to be mistaken for a vantage point outside of the window.

---

2. All descriptions of scenes in *Rear Window*, and presentation of spoken dialogue, are from my own transcriptions from a DVD of the film.

It is worth noting how words such as "follows," "surveys," and "discovers" in the previous paragraph have the effect of personifying the camera. In ordinary usage, the principle of economy determines that "the camera follows a cat" is preferred to "the camera operator causes the camera to follow a cat." But this usage does help to keep the issue of agency unresolved. After all, behind the camera operator and outside the diegesis is the director. Inside the diegesis there is (for the first-time viewer at least) possibly a character, and possibly an implied narrator or author. Beyond the principle of economy, personifying the camera is appealing when we don't know quite to what or to whom agency should be attributed.

This apart, it seems perverse to argue that this sequence involves a fusion of two looks—ours and Jeff's. First, because as the camera scans the courtyard the viewer has not yet met Jeff: certainly the first-time viewer has no reason to attribute the camera eye to any intradiegetic character-viewpoint at this stage. Even when we *do* meet Jeff for the first time, he is asleep; if the looking of any intradiegetic character has been mimicked or enacted by the camera at this stage, it certainly cannot be Jeff's. A second reason can be found in those miraculously self-opening blinds, rolling themselves up behind the opening credits. Such movement suggests that the camera movement may still be part of what Gérard Genette (1998), talking about literary narrative, has dubbed the *paratext*: those framing devices that act as a sort of umbilical cord joining the diegesis to its extradiegetic sources and authorities. (In the original film, and in its latest remastered release, the film ends with the blinds closing—a scene cut from reissues of the film for many decades because it contained a reference to the first distributor, Paramount. The framing of the action between the raising and lowering of the blinds is one of a number of elements which lead the viewer to see the action of the film in stage-theatrical terms.) A film's credits, like the "prelims" of a book, can usefully be seen as Genettian paratext, yet many films blur the distinction between text and paratext in a way that is hardly possible in a book. The credits sequence in *Rear Window* seems more part of the film—of the diegesis even—than do the prelims of a book. In a book, the pages that contain the paratext and those that contain the text are normally quite separate (there is, conventionally, often a change from roman to arabic page-numbering). But in this film the paratextual information (the writing and the self-operating blinds) is coterminous with the setting of the diegesis. But third, Božovič's (1992) claim that the camera represents "our" eye seems perverse because the movement of the camera is something that the viewer *follows* rather than *shares* at this stage, precisely because we don't know what to expect, and we don't know what sort of looking the behavior of the camera *stands for* or *depicts*. It is also of great significance that this opening sequence is not continuous but involves a cut. Had the sequence been continuous it might have made sense to argue that the viewer starts to identify with the camera, but the use of cutting inevitably reminds us that we are not choosing what to look at, but rather are being given things to observe by some deciding intelligence that is not our own—which is why, incidentally, the sequence generates suspense.

Note that in my comments so far I have, like many of those whose interpretations I quote, repeatedly referred to "the camera" which does this or that. There is something odd about this because within the diegesis there is no camera: mention of the camera thus implies a vantage point outside of the story. But for the viewer located inside the storyworld it seems odd to attribute an awareness of a camera moving around the apartment. However, reference to the camera is encouraged by the film's opening precisely because at this stage of the movie the viewer is struggling to relate the camera movement to some possible intradiegetic human origin. John Fawell (2001) comments specifically on the viewer's inability to make such a connection between the camera and a character in the film's opening sequence, and perhaps on this basis refers to director Hitchcock as determining intelligence—although along with others he also personifies the camera:

> When the credits are through, the camera starts to move through the opened middle window but only momentarily. Hitchcock cuts to a shot of a cat climbing the stairs of the courtyard outside Jeff's window. It is interesting that Hitchcock cuts here to the cat rather than maintaining the shot through the window and into the pan around the courtyard. Jeff is not awake yet, and Hitchcock does not seem to feel obligated yet to create the sense of looking with someone through the window. (43)

For the first-time viewer, however, no human character within the apartment has been encountered at this point, so that the possibility that the camera movement gives us the searching of an as-yet unseen character does, I think, remain alongside the sense that we are being given things to see—which is why I suggested above that it was not clear whether the camera *discovers* or *reveals* the sleeping Jeff.

But if we are given things to see—by whom? A more painstaking and tentative account of the same sequence is provided by Seymour Chatman in his book *Coming to Terms: The Rhetoric of Narrative in Fiction and*

Film (1990). Chatman (who, incidentally, agrees that the vantage point for the shots of the other apartments in the block is outside of the window), gives a long and detailed account of the sequence as a way in to arguing for the usefulness of the concept of "implied author" in film narrative. Chatman suggests that the three blinds "roll themselves up" while the camera remains immobile—a form of words that is perhaps unfortunate, as it seems to exclude the possibility of some purposive framing or narrating activity lying behind the rolling-up of the blinds, although there is no necessary contradiction between stating that—say—Hitchcock has the blinds roll up but that for the viewer they appear to roll themselves up. He then goes on as follows:

> When the titles end, the camera moves out through the window to scan the scene. We do not yet know whether we are to understand that the camera is showing us the stage upon which story events will transpire, or that we are seeing these rear windows through the eyes of some as yet unidentified character (though the magically self-rolling blinds strongly suggest the former). To contribute to the puzzle, the camera does not seem clear about what it wants to show. It acts as if it is simply moving about, looking for something of interest. It follows a cat climbing some steps, but the cat disappears off-frame. Then the camera tilts up as if to explore various apartments. . . . The camera next tilts down a bit, revealing a passageway between the buildings and the street beyond, and finally it comes back into the window from which it set forth. (45–46)

In this account, then, we have both blinds that roll themselves up and a camera that is unclear what it wants to show—or a camera that represents a fictional character. Chatman notes that were the film to have continued only in this way, it could have ended up as a documentary about life in a Manhattan courtyard. But we do not expect it to do so, and it does not:

> Inside the apartment, a close-up of James Stewart's face slides into view; but since he is facing away from the window with his eyes closed in sleep, we understand that the camera's meandering look at the courtyard has been its own descriptive act. The description has taken place in "real" time; however; there has been no pause. What was shown was not a frozen moment but one filled with actions. Story time has passed, even if nothing of great significance has happened. A verbal paraphrase might read (retrospectively), "While Jeff sleeps, the courtyard comes to life: cats prowl, husbands put on ties," and so on. Hence it is reasonable to say

that a cinematic describer—the cinematic narrator *as* describer—explicitly presents the opening sequence of *Rear Window.* (46; emphasis in original)

I quote this descriptive analysis at length because it raises a number of crucial questions about how the scene is experienced by the viewer. To start with, Chatman effectively offers an answer to my earlier question—if a film is a narrative, who is the narrator? For him it makes sense to posit a cinematic narrator or describer who forms part, or is the product, of a mediating chain: director—implied author—cinematic narrator—viewer. But paradoxically this does not prevent him from personifying the camera, which is capable of a "meandering look" in what is "its own descriptive act," which might imply that the camera is an aspect or tool of the cinematic narrator. Note that Chatman's "verbal paraphrase" *is* narrated: we are *told* by Chatman what has transpired on screen. Chatman clearly wants a cinematic narrator to be behind the filmic narrative in the same way that a narrator tells about what happens in his paraphrase. It should, I think, be clear that such a narrator, if his or her existence is accepted, is a far more ghostly and fragmented presence than is a typical literary narrator.

This said, I particularly like Chatman's insistence on the extent to which the viewer is presented with *puzzles,* and is forced to work at some sort of provisional interpretative solution to them. There is no way that the first-time viewer can merely sit and passively absorb what is presented in this opening sequence, as some commentators suggest. What is the significance of the blinds that are raised although no one is there (is this some weird part of the story or just a jokey way of presenting the credits)? Does the camera represent a personified and intradiegetic viewpoint? Does it offer a "seeing identity" ("subjective camera") for the viewer, or does it represent a *showing* for which an extradiegetic narrative authority—a director or a Chatmanian "implied author"—is responsible? I agree that the viewer is given the sense that the camera (or, I might add, the viewpoint that it stands in for or represents) "does not seem clear about what it wants to show"—a very subtle characterization that gives us a third alternative between "looking for" and "showing." Another (but importantly different) way of describing this lack of certitude would be to say that the consciousness represented by the camera has not yet found anything worth looking at, that it is engaged in a process of snooping which is only secondarily or even (in terms of the diegesis) accidentally also one of showing. (I can still recall that, fifty-nine years ago, I thought that I was following the movements of an intruder as the camera moved exploringly around.) The camera, in other words, is doing what we will shortly observe Jeff doing—looking for something to look at. But cameras do not have brains: if there is searching going on then it must be searching on the part of a brained entity either directing, or represented by, the camera.

Narratives mimic and plunder familiar and typical ("natural") human relationships and forms of observation, but in so doing they conventionally suppress elements of these. Thus the exploring camera at the start of *Rear Window* builds on a situation in which a human being or an animal moves around in an unfamiliar place, observing and gathering information. But in the non-narrative situation there is never any doubt as to whether we ourselves are doing the snooping, or observing someone else snoop, whereas in this sequence the viewer cannot be sure about this. Moreover, even if the camera were to give the viewer the sense that he or she was actually the searcher, this would be quite unlike a real-life situation in which we search for something. In the real-life situation we have control over our own movements; in a film we are trapped in an exploring consciousness that makes its own decisions. However much we shift uneasily in our seats, we are as powerless to influence characters and events in the diegesis as is the ghostly narrator of Jean Rhys's "I Used to Live Here Once." Indeed, as viewer we have even less power than as reader. A reader can put the book down and the text will remain as it was when we pick it up again. As viewer (at least in the days before home recording systems), if we leave the movie theater the film rolls on oblivious to our departure.

The uncertainties the viewer experiences at the start of *Rear Window* are representative of a more general uncertainty in the film as a whole, during which the viewer seems always to be being thrown backwards and forwards between observing, observing someone else observe, and being shown. The disorientation and unease that such uncertainty creates seems to me to fit perfectly into a film in which spying and surveillance are portrayed as both necessary and unnecessary, as both justified and morally sick. The uncertainty is also appropriate in the context of a society so paranoid that the dividing line cannot be drawn between the law-abiding (for whom spying is always on someone else) and the dissident (who constitute the legitimate target of surveillance). These are matters to which I will return below.

Uncertainties concerning the status of the narrative relate directly, I think, to moral uncertainties in the film. It is for this reason that over-simple and limiting definitions of the film's "point of view"[3] are so damaging to an appreciation of the complexity of *Rear Window*. That recurrent sense we have when watching this film that the looking is both ours and not ours, that we may ourselves be looking but we may only be sharing vicariously someone else's look, that although we want to look there may be times when, like Jeff faced with the first glimpse of the honeymoon couple, we (half) want to look away, and finally that we may suddenly become aware that our securely anonymous looking has suddenly given way to being *looked at*—all of these disorienting and conflicting sensations contribute in an important way to the film's fundamental ambivalence about the morality of spying on our neighbors.

All narrative beginnings have an expository function. In a film, just as in a novel, we need early on to establish at least a provisional understanding of how a story is being told so as to be able to situate ourselves in relation to the telling, and so that crucial issues of significance may be granted some working resolution by the viewer. What does our seeing represent? Someone's telling—or someone's looking? Or perhaps also our own looking? Or perhaps there is a blending of these alternatives: the viewer follows what the camera reveals and attempts to construct a story that matches this looking. Elsewhere (Hawthorn, 2013) I have argued that in the opening of James Joyce's "Eveline" the reader both becomes the character Eveline and is simultaneously aware of her as a separate person, and fictional narratives can provide such blended points of view that cannot be experienced in life.

Are we looking with, or at, one or more of the represented characters—or at this stage of the film are we trying out these alternatives to see which best fits what the camera reveals? Because all narrative beginnings do involve such provisional interpretative decisions on the part of the viewer or reader, he or she is generally much more active at the start of the film or a novel than once these issues have been resolved, even if the resolution is only provisional or incomplete. *Rear Window* does not help the viewer to make speedy or simple decisions of this sort in its short opening seconds. On the contrary, its opening sequence, however brief, forces a succession of rapid and successive *re*assessments onto the viewer.

Chatman claims that the "description has taken place" in "real," or story, time, and by this he appears to be mean that real/story time starts once the camera moves out into the courtyard. I think that it is correct to assume that a shift similar to that which in literary narrative we might describe in terms of the movement from description to narration

---

3. I have more to say about my use of this term in chapter 6 following.

takes place as the opening credits of the film come to an end. Dana Brand (1999) suggests (without actually using the term) that the opening scenes of life in the courtyard perform a sort of iterative function—an interesting suggestion in view of the fact that the dramatic nature of cinematic narrative might seem to exclude such a possibility:

> When we see, in the opening frames of *Rear Window,* the cat, the milkman, the alarms going off one by one, the uncovering of the birdcage, Miss Torso doing her morning exercises, we see a process that we imagine is the same every single morning. We feel we have a handle on such a world, a world that, like the London of Dickens's "The Streets-Morning," goes through the same emotions every day. We are, as with any flaneur's sketch, reassured. And Hitchcock reinforces our sense of clockwork regularity by offering shots of measuring devices, clocks, watches, thermometers. Things are so predictable in the early portions of the film that everything we see appears to be a visual elaboration of the reading we have just made of the measuring device. (125)

This suggests that the shift from the iterative-dramatic to the "real time" of singulative frequency is one that is gradual, and that much of the early part of the film can be seen in terms of a cumulative blocking or denial of the repetitive, the predictable, and the familiar, and their replacement by the unusual, the unique, and the threatening-uncanny. Such an interpretation would tie in with the classic pattern for a narrative concerned with crime detection: that of stable normality invaded by a disruptive and alien element of some sort, an element which then has to be cleansed from the system so that normality can be reasserted.

I agree that the raising of the blinds during the opening credits has to be understood in some way or another extradiegetically. Miran Božovič (1992) suggests that the opening of the three blinds can be compared to the raising of a theater curtain, and this process seems intuitively to indicate a brief period when Genettian paratext and text overlap, with story time starting while the blinds are being drawn up and paratext ending once the director's name has disappeared from the screen. It is worth reminding modern readers that at the time that *Rear Window* was first shown, many cinemas used both decorative curtains and a fire curtain to cover the screen, and that the decorative curtains were opened at the start of a film and closed at its conclusion.

In this context it is interesting to note that in an article entitled "Why 'Thrillers' Thrive," first published in *Picturegoer,* January 18, 1936,

Hitchcock made the following observations about the difference between the theater audience and the cinema audience:

> In the theater we can see things happening on a stage, remote, imper-
> sonal, detached from ourselves. We are safe, secure, sitting in an arm-
> chair and looking at the struggle and turmoil of life through a window,
> as it were.
>
> In order to appreciate what the characters on the stage are going
> through, we have to project ourselves into their consciousnesses; we have
> to receive our thrills vicariously, which is not the most effective method.
>
> Watching a well-made film, we don't sit by as spectators; we partici-
> pate. (Gottlieb 1995, 109)

Accepting Hitchcock's premise here we might, for example, see the whole narrative development of *Rear Window* in terms of a movement from "safe" theatrical observation on the part of both the viewer and Jeff, to a very "un-safe" cinematic participation at the end of the film as a double invasion takes place. The murderous Thorwald looks at Jeff and he looks at us; he then enters Jeff's apartment, and Jeff is ejected out of the auditorium and onto "the stage," from the safety of his (wheel)chair and apartment and into the observed life outside—just minutes before we leave the cinema and go back to our own quotidian, non-fictional reality. That movement from detachment to participation detailed by Hitchcock has a direct connection to the issue of ontology that I have discussed ear-lier. Detached, we retain a strong sense of our real-world self; participat-ing, we are at least partly through the airlock, half in the world of the diegesis.

In such a formulation, however, "participation" is used metaphori-cally. In the real world, when we participate in some situation or event we interact with others, we have the power to change people and things. However much we have the sense of participating in a cinematic narra-tive we remain locked in a non-reciprocal relationship with characters and events. Like Wallace in the 1993 Aardman animated film *The Wrong Trousers*, we do not so much tramp around in the diegesis but we are rather tramped around by a controlling force separate from ourselves.

There is moreover a great difference between seeing the world out-side Jeff's window as a stage, and seeing it as "life." In his article "In His Bold Gaze My Ruin Is Writ Large," Slavoj Žižek (1992) identifies the rôle of the stage in Hitchcock's 1930 film *Murder!* with that of the courtyard in *Rear Window*: "in the latter, James Stewart is able to relate to the woman (Grace Kelly) only in so far as she appears in the court-yard beyond the door and thus enters his fantasy-frame; like Sir John, who can relate to a woman only in so far as she enters the universe of the play he is about to write" (269 n49). (Žižek's use of the names of the actors when referring to *Rear Window* but of the character in *Murder!* is curious and has significance with regard to issues of interpretation and ontology.) At any rate, whereas for some commentators what lies outside Jeff's apartment is "reality" or, as I have suggested, "life," a reality or real life that Lisa enters and engages with while Jeff is limited to the rôle of an observer, and which he rejoins once he is cast out of his window by Thorwald, Žižek in contrast seems to suggest the opposite, that outside the window lies not reality but Jeff's fantasy. Like Melville's Tommo or James's telegraphist he sees things in the real world, but the form his vision molds them into is as much a matter of what he desires as of what they are independent of his gaze.

As one of the defining characteristics of a fantasy is our ability to control it, Jeff's inability to control what happens to Lisa would seem to suggest that what he sees when Lisa enters Thorwald's apartment is no longer a fantasy. The point seems to me to be important because it under-lines the fact that although Jeff is able to make a fantasy out of what he sees through his window, once his agent is actually out there, in the courtyard and in Thorwald's apartment, then the (controllable) fantasy is shattered and replaced by the more recalcitrant actuality of the real world. Action, and interaction, spell death for fantasy. For the audience, the issue of whether what Jeff sees out of the window is his projected fantasy focuses on the question "did Thorwald murder his wife?"; however, Lisa's entering of Thorwald's apartment also helps to convince us that Jeff has seen, not fantasized, something. The voyeur whose gaze is recognized by its object and returned is no longer a voyeur. Tommo's fantasies are challenged once he lives with the Typee, and James's telegraphist is terrified that she might meet Captain Everard when she enters his building. In like manner, Jeff's inability to control what happens when Lars Thorwald discovers Lisa in his apartment mirrors the viewer's inability to control what happens on the cinema screen.

The opening of the film is tantalizing because it leaves so much still to be established in terms of narrative authority. In the final part of the passage which I quoted from his analysis, Chatman (1990) argues that "[a] verbal paraphrase might read (retrospectively), 'While Jeff sleeps, the courtyard comes to life: cats prowl, husbands put on ties,' and so on" (46). Thus far, I agree. But he concludes: "Hence it is reasonable to say that a cinematic describer—the cinematic narrator *as* describer—explicitly presents the opening sequence of *Rear Window*" (46; emphasis in original). Now in one sense this seems justified. The theatrical opening of the blinds suggests a form of *staging*, and staging almost of necessity requires some form of deliberate or explicit presentation. But if we accept that "the cinematic narrator *as* describer" presents the film's opening sequence, then we need to be very careful to avoid identifying such a narrator or describer who makes an explicit presentation, with the camera, which, as we have seen and experienced, exhibits behavior indicative of searching and unsureness. Chatman is quite consistent on this score, arguing that "it is the implied author of *Rear Window* who decides what the 'camera' shows 'on its own,' what it shows as filtered through Jeff's perception, and what it does not show at all" (130).

The failure of critics to agree on what the camera represents in even this short opening sequence from *Rear Window* is worthy of note, and should suggest that attributing a function or representative significance to the camera—the camera seen as agent or focalizer—should be carried out tentatively and undogmatically. Indeed, what I wish to insist upon is that just as *critics* have difficulty in deciding what or who the camera stands for, so too are *viewers* forced to make interpretive decisions about this, however much such decisions are made unconsciously and in a manner that is heavily influenced by filmic conventions. And this is important for three reasons. First, because it makes the viewer unusually *active,* and second because the viewer's uncertainty about such matters ties in with a more general ambivalence that is at the heart of the film's admittedly indirect engagement with key public issues of its moment. Third, because this is a fictional narrative there is no necessary contradiction in claiming both that the camera appears to be *looking for* something, and that by means of the camera's movements a narrative authority such as an implied author *shows* us various things. In *Pilgrim's Progress* Christian is looking for something, but Bunyan is certainly showing or even telling the reader something by means of Christian's searching behavior.

I would, however, like to make a couple of specific suggestions concerning the viewer's awareness of the camera, and his or her attribution of some sort of specifically *narrative* authority to it. To start with, I wish to draw attention to the fact that the viewer becomes aware of the camera in *Rear Window* on two different occasions. The first is when the viewer is not sure what status the camera and its movements have at the start of the film. Once it is clear that the camera is not giving us the movements of an intruder in Jeff's apartment, the viewer may be led to adopt the working assumption that the camera must represent some sort of *extra*diegetic intelligence. Because this assumption is made at the start of the film, the viewer is more attuned to the camera as representative of an independent guiding and narrating intelligence for the remainder of the film, but because this is only a working and provisional assumption there is always this nagging sense that the viewer is not just being shown but is also looking, that we are implicated morally in the activity first of Jeff and thereafter of Lisa, Stella, and Doyle.

The second occasion when we become aware of the camera is when we are somewhat unexpectedly presented with an unusual camera angle— a shot from above at the point when Jeff is writing his note to Thorwald. Here, for the first time, the perspective is unambiguously one that is supra-human, one that could not be adopted by or represent that of a character in the film. (This might also be said of the movement of the camera outside the window in the opening sequence, but this is a less clear example, as an individual might have been leaning out of the window and looking around.) At both of these points the effect of sensitizing the viewer to the operation of an extradiegetic narrative intelligence is to reduce Jeff's authority and, as it were, to objectify him. At the opening of the film it is the camera that moves around, investigating, surveying, while Jeff sleeps—vulnerable and disempowered. And when Jeff writes his note to Thorwald, at just that point at which he seems to be taking charge, no longer functioning as the passive observer but moving into intrusive manipulation of the action, he is seen from above, in an as-from-god shot that suggests his limitations of perspective, lack of authority, in contrast to that of a (literally) superior determining narrative intelligence. This seems to me to be of great importance with regard to interpretations of *Rear Window* concerned with investigating the attribution of impotence to Jeff—of which more below.

So far as "seeing" rather than "showing" is concerned, I have spoken of "a" narrative intelligence, in contrast to Chatman's many-layered chain of narrative mediation. Within the diegesis we further have the intradiegetic looking of Jeff. We also have to fit in the extradiegetic experiencing of the viewer, which may at times merge with Jeff's own "presented" viewing, and at other times "view his viewing." And the viewer's ontological hybridity involves a further layering (when we recognize Hitchcock himself in the cameo scene, we observe as flesh-and-blood individuals in ironic amusement, but without totally abandoning the world of the diegesis within which Hitchcock is actually a clock-repairer). Chatman goes, however, a step further. Basing his analysis on the work of the narrative theorist Ann Banfield, he builds on her suggestion that "the technology of film . . . like that of the telescope and the microscope, 'allow[s] the viewing subject to see, to witness, places where he is not, indeed, where no subject is present'" (Chatman 138, quoting Banfield 1987, 265). Chatman argues, accordingly, that "ordinary moviegoers . . . will interpret the scanning view of the interior of a courtyard as a tour of the courtyard by the camera 'on its own,'" and that when the shades roll up, "we know that what we see is being presented by a 'subjectivity reduced to nothing else but what the instrument can record.'" For Chatman, the visible details of the courtyard, "are not seen or heard but rather overseen and overheard, as the 'impressions' of an impersonal narrative agency" (138; the quotations are again from Banfield's article).

Note here that there is still a tension between a sort of recording without direction or cerebration ("nothing else but what the instrument can record") and some form of narrative *agency,* albeit one that is "impersonal." We may also wonder to what extent this account offers categories of narrative agent additional to those already listed in my previous paragraph: to what extent are "the camera 'on its own'" and the "impersonal narrative agency" equatable with or to be distinguished from Chatman's "presenter" (or "cinematic narrator"), his "implied author," and his semipersonified "seeker"?

As I have already suggested, the reason commentators (including myself) so frequently talk about what "the camera" does in the opening sequence of this film is that viewers have no way of anchoring camera movements and direction with any specific intra- or extradiegetic human consciousness, even though the camera's movements and direction do imply human-like qualities. But taken to an extreme, such a personification of the camera can become absurd. How, for example, can the scanning view of the courtyard be understood as "as a tour of the courtyard by the camera 'on its own'"? Cameras do not have consciousnesses or the power to make decisions: they have to be pointed and operated. They can indeed be pointed or operated in such a way as to mimic the looking and seeing behavior of either a character or some form of extradiegetic intelligence such as the director. But surely no viewer—first-time or filmfamiliar—interprets the movements of the camera in the opening sequence as those of a self-directing *camera.* Are they not rather interpreted *either* as determined by a narrator (Hitchcock, implied author, or even cameraman) *or* as representative of the movements of someone or something that is possessed of a consciousness, not excluding the consciousness-possessing viewer? Or indeed as both of these, simultaneously or successively.

What is, I think, interesting about Chatman's account when taken as a whole is that from it one can distill a sense of the presence of two very different narrative "forces." What distinguishes these forces is the presence or absence of *communicative or demonstrative intent*. It is, for example, clear to me that the raising of the blinds at the beginning of the film—especially when one takes into account such elements as speed and sequence—is both extradiegetic and packed with an overt intent to display. We could even say that we have here the display of a desire to display. The audience member, at this point engaged in becoming the viewer as he or she is starting to be drawn into the diegesis, is meant to interpret the raising of these blinds as purposive, and as indicating something along the lines of "The performance is going to start, you are now going to be allowed to look out of the rear window named in the film's title, and once these blinds are fully raised you will be able to watch out of this window along with the film's characters." The entity which is possessed of this intent can be named as the author or implied author, or Hitchcock (or "Hitchcock"), or whatever, but it is this controlling element that allows us to respond to and interpret the film as a deliberately constructed artifact, as something with artistic/aesthetic import. Once the film proper starts, we assume, blinds will no longer behave in this way, and they don't—at least until the end of the film where the closing of the blinds signals our exit from the diegesis and the movie theater.

But there is this continual and parallel sense of a non-personified searching or discovering "force" in the film that is distinct from this deliberative or descriptive "force," a sense perhaps best exemplified by the camera movements in the opening sequence which seem to mimic unsure, tentative, investigative human movement. It is as if whatever the camera represents is not so much *showing* the viewer things as *discovering* things, things which viewers can also observe at the same time that they observe the act of searching itself. This sense of a double presence in the filmic narrative, one which both shows and discovers, is, it needs to be stressed, already present in the film *before* we get the additional factor of the character Jeff's emergence as a narrative filter. (And Jeff too, we need to remember, both "finds" and "sees"; the direction of information through his supposed consciousness takes place both actively and passively: he both looks—and discovers—things, but he also sees them without having looked for them.) Once again we have to understand that there is a process of "layering" here. Chatman (1990) suggests that "the visible details of the courtyard correspond to what Banfield, following Bertrand Russell, calls *sensibilia*: 'those objects which have the same metaphysical and physical status as sense-data, without necessarily being data to any mind'" (138). However, it is clear that (as Chatman himself concedes) this is only within the film's diegesis: the film viewer is well aware that although the different activities in the courtyard represent on one level what Chatman dubs "Early Morning in a Manhattan Courtyard," they are also elements that, on another level, are *artistically selected and arranged* by some controlling consciousness or according to some structuring principle.

I have gone the perhaps tedious distance of this long account because with a film that is claimed to merge the voyeuristic activity of character and viewer, we need to be very careful in our attributions of narrative perspective and of agency. Merely on the basis of just this opening scene it is apparent that even some of Hitchcock's own comments about the film's point of view are misleading. In "On Style: An Interview with *Cinema*," first published in 1963, Hitchcock writes: "*Rear Window* is purely subjective treatment—what Jimmy Stewart sees all the time. And how he reacts to it" (Gottlieb 1995, 291). Straight away we can see that there is a tension between these two sentences: if the viewer sees "how he reacts to it," then we are going beyond the purely subjective; we are escaping from Jeff's consciousness and looking at him from the outside. And of course Hitchcock's comments in this article and elsewhere on the paramount importance of cutting make it clear that at a different level there is an "objective" organizing consciousness by means of which viewers' responses are regulated. As Hitchcock says of such cutting/montage: "By the changing of one piece of film only, you change the whole idea" (Gottlieb 1995, 298)—and that "you" is a narrative force—as I have expressed it—that has nothing at all to do with Jeff's consciousness. Of course, a fictional narrative can (and typically will) simultaneously both present us with what an author or director wants us to see *and* give us what passes through the consciousness of an individual. But a film that shows us things happening while Jeff sleeps can hardly be said to provide a "purely subjective treatment."

In his discussions with Hitchcock, François Truffaut (1968) suggests to him that in the scene where the owner of the dog protests at its killing, by "simply taking the camera outside of Stewart's apartment, the whole scene becomes entirely objective," and Hitchcock replies, "That's right, that was the only such scene" (326). In one sense it is true that (with the exception of the brief period in the opening sequence, and also the scene immediately after Jeff has been cast from the window) this is the only scene where the camera is placed outside Jeff's apartment. But the claim that this scene is "entirely objective" and that all others are, by implication, subjective (see the comment from Hitchcock quoted above that "*Rear Window* is purely subjective treatment") does less than full justice to the changing narrative complexity of the film. We should trust the tale not the teller.

Most important, I think, is the argument that the impossibility of fixing point of view or perspective in this opening sequence has an ideological force, and relates to the ideological stress-points and fault lines of the film. Let me attempt to make this point by comparison. Charles Dickens's novel *Oliver Twist* is also a work that is packed full of acts of spying and surveillance, but one in which, I have argued, it is possible to draw a relatively neat line between "good spying" and "bad spying." The distinction is simple because spying is good when indulged in by good characters, and bad when engaged in by bad characters. And this distinction is guaranteed by an omniscient narrator whose moral distinctions are equally clear, and which have to be accepted by the reader. The reader is never made to feel guilty about his or her involvement in acts of spying or surveillance, because there is an omniscient narrator who already knows everything anyway, and whose moral judgments are utterly unproblematic. But spying in *Rear Window* is both good and bad, equally so for the characters who engage in it, and for we who associate ourselves with what characters do, and who indulge our interest in the depicted privacies.

Voyeurism, *Rear Window,* and the Cold War

A succession of commentators have associated the activities of voyeurism and surveillance both with the main character of *Rear Window* and with the film's spectators. Thus while Norman K. Denzin (1995) characterizes the film as "an ode to voyeurism" (118), Elisabeth Weis (1982) argues that one of the major, unresolvable issues that Hitchcock dramatizes in the film is the audience's innate voyeurism: "We are implicated in Jeff's voyeurism because we, too, cannot refrain from spying on his neighbors; that is, we cannot distinguish whether we are watching the neighbors because Jeff does so or because we are voyeuristic ourselves" (110). David A. Cook (1996) finds *Rear Window* "a disturbing and profoundly modern film" whose "theme of the moral complicity of the voyeur (and, by extension, the film spectator) in what he watches anticipates both Antonioni's *Blow-Up* . . . and Francis Ford Coppola's

The Conversation . . . to say nothing of Hitchcock's own *Psycho*" (332). Michel Chion (1992) also comments on this identification between Jeff and the cinema audience (in my terminology, the viewer), an identification which he claims is based on a shared voyeurism: "One of the chief difficulties with the scenario of *Rear Window* was, I imagine, that of making the audience share, throughout the film, in the acts of outright voyeurism in which the protagonists indulge" (155).

Rendered immobile by his broken leg, Jeff, it may initially be assumed, is fascinated by the possibility of Thorwald's having murdered his wife in part simply because he is bored and a crime such as this offers an exciting puzzle to solve. This fascination is obviously one that the cinema viewer will find easy to share, as solving such puzzles—or watching others solve them—is one of the reasons why we watch movies. But Robin Wood (1989) has suggested a darker reason behind Jeff's interest in this particular neighbor. Building on Jeff's unwillingness to commit himself to marriage with Lisa, he argues that what happens in the Thorwald apartment "represents, in an extreme and hideous form, the fulfilment of Jeff's desire to be rid of Lisa" (104). To extend *this* interest to the viewer requires that male viewers at least are possessed of dark misogynistic impulses that emanate from a desire to live free from women. For the female viewer things are presumably different: she wants to see Thorwald punished for his crime, Jeff rewarded for his detective work, and Lisa rewarded with a husband who abandons his nomadic life for a more domestic existence.

Like Jeff, then, in Wood's account the male viewer is a Peeping Tom, someone who obtains erotic gratification from watching the private lives of others and who is gratified by observing a scapegoat punished for inflicting the violence on women that he himself wishes for to symbolically avenge or avert his own entrapment by the female sex. Such an account has the advantage of being able to appeal to the testimony of the Master himself, as on a number of different occasions Hitchcock referred to Jeff as a Peeping Tom. In an article first published in 1968, Hitchcock not only makes this charge, but by implication extends it to Lisa:

> If you want to be really mean towards the character in this film you could call him a Peeping Tom. I don't think it's necessarily a statement of morality because it's a statement of fact. You don't hide from it, there's no point in my leaving it out. When Grace Kelly says that they're a couple of fiendish ghouls because they're disappointed that a murder hasn't been committed she's speaking the truth. They were a couple of ghouls. (Hitchcock 1972, 43)

Hitchcock, moreover, has further claimed not just that James Stewart is a Peeping Tom and that he and Grace Kelly are both ghouls (again, the ontological implications of Hitchcock's use of the actors' rather than the characters' names are worth pondering) but that "we" are all "snoopers"—a suggestion that prompts his interviewer, François Truffaut, to bring in the figure of the cinematic viewer.

F. T. Would you say that Stewart was merely curious?

A. H. He's a real Peeping Tom. In fact, Miss Lejeune, the critic of the London *Observer,* complained about that. She made some comment to the effect that *Rear Window* was a horrible film because the hero spent all of his time peeping out of the window. What's so horrible about that? Sure, he's a snooper, but aren't we all?

F. T. We're all voyeurs to some extent, if only when we see an intimate film. And James Stewart is exactly in the position of a spectator looking at a movie.

A. H. I'll bet you that nine out of ten people, if they see a woman across the courtyard undressing for bed, or even a man puttering around in his room, will stay and look; no one turns away and says, "It's none of my business." They could pull down their blinds, but they never do; they stand there and look out. (Truffaut 1986, 321)

Hitchcock's "we" is surely a gendered term (or why should it be a "woman . . . or even a man" and not just a "person" viewed across the courtyard?).

Robin Wood (1989) has warned against the polarization of critical views of *Rear Window,* noting that such views tend to fall into one of two extreme positions: either the film is "a whole-hearted condemnation of curiosity, prying, voyeurism, *libido sciendi* and *delectatio morosa,*" or it is a "corrupt, distasteful film, it shameless exploits and encourages curiosity, prying, etc. etc." (100). Wood (1989) points out that both of these positions are unsatisfactory: on the one hand, the film itself makes the viewer uneasy about the morality of prying by explicitly discussing this issue, by placing the character Lisa in grave danger, and "by our discovery that the murderer is as pitiable as monstrous"; on the other hand, because "the final effects of Jeff's voyeurism are almost entirely admirable"; and had Jeff not spied on his neighbors, "a murderer would have gone free," so that any condemnation of Jeff's spying must needs be qualified (100).

Although I agree with Wood's conclusions, I feel that the polarization of critical views to which he refers is not accidental. *Rear Window* is a film which contains and to a degree even encourages—then attempts to reconcile—both contradictory views. Indeed, it is precisely in the film's oscillation between (or encouragement of) such irreconcilable views that its ideological character needs to be sought. But to explore the film's ideological complexities these need more specific temporal anchoring than is suggested by David A. Cook's characterization of the film as "profoundly modern." My own view is that this is a film that cannot fully be understood unless its radical links with the Cold War and McCarthyism are conceded and explored. For me, it is just because the film suggests *both* that Jeff's voyeuristic activity is perverse and unhealthy *and* that it is necessary that the ideological rôle it performed in the context of the United States of 1954—the date of its first showing—can be exposed. As in the case of Dickens's *Oliver Twist,* this is a work that performs a function of ideological recuperation.

Jeff is certainly not a person who just happens to catch sight of a man or woman across the courtyard and who looks rather than turns away. There is ample and repeated evidence in the film that he is actively searching for information, deliberately observing his neighbors one after the other, long before there is any suggestion that any one of them is involved in anything faintly illegal. Nor can such behavior be explained or excused by reference to his incapacitation: scenes early on in the film insist upon the fact that he is more interested in *looking at* his unaware neighbors than in *interacting with* Lisa—something quite possible even with a leg in plaster. Stella (played by Thelma Ritter) insists to Jeff that "Lisa Fremont is the right girl for any man who can get half an eye open." Jeff is quite capable of getting both eyes open—but only when looking across his courtyard, not when faced with Lisa. What is more, Jeff fixes upon those of his neighbors whose lives offer some salacious or voyeuristic interest, an interest which is not necessarily sexual but which does seem to require that their privacy be intruded upon. He is drawn to those with problems: one apparently happy family across the courtyard seems to be of no interest to him. Perhaps, like Lisa, it is too perfect to interest him. And of course, as many commentators have pointed out, such perverse looking is clearly meant to be related to his profession as a photographer.

At the same time, and, as I have said, paradoxically, it does not seem to me to be correct to claim as does Dana Brand (1999) that "he decides, without any evidence, that someone is guilty of a serious crime" (129). He has, actually, very good evidence: woken up by the heat in the middle of the night, he observes Thorwald leaving his apartment several times with a samples suitcase. Thorwald's invalid wife, who up to this point, although not immobile, has been more or less confined to her bed, disappears, and Jeff soon establishes that she is no longer present in the apartment, though she had been there the previous evening. Subsequent observations—the sight of Thorwald cleaning and packing up a large knife and a saw, for example—strengthen, legitimately, Jeff's hypothesis that something has happened in the apartment and to the wife.

Here then is the paradox: Jeff is a Peeping Tom who seeks to excuse his fascinated observation of his neighbors by means of an excuse that—clearly, as it postdates his surveillance activities—is not the real reason. But at the same time, the excuse turns out to be true: a murder *has* been committed, Thorwald *has* done everything that Jeff suspects he has done, and it is those who have refused to believe Jeff, those who will not think ill of a neighbor, who turn out to be the ones who are wrong. Jeff really is a voyeur; yet had it not been for this activity, a murderer would not have been caught. On the one hand we are encouraged to condemn Jeff's (and, vicariously, our own) voyeurism—and yet this voyeurism appears seamlessly to turn into a form of detective work that is above moral reproach. As in Dickens's *Oliver Twist,* the activity of surveillance is transformed in the course of the work from being the preserve of the outcast to being the useful and morally irreproachable activity of those with a social conscience. Why should the film point so decisively in two directions in this manner?

In my introduction I suggested that surveillance is an activity that is engaged in for political or economic, rather than private or sexual, motives. In the case of *Rear Window* most discussion of Jeff's behavior involves terms such as "voyeurism" or "Peeping Tom," and the element of salacious interest on Jeff's part is certainly justification enough for such terms to be used. But once Jeff suspects that a murder has been committed, his activities become more surveillance-like: significantly, he now draws other people in to his spying activity, whereas when the focus was perhaps more sexual he acted alone (and even excluded others: when Doyle starts to admire Miss Torso, Jeff pointedly asks about Doyle's wife). Norman K. Denzin (1995) has described "the gaze of surveillance, the gaze of power," as "the gaze which unveils the private and makes it public" (2). That Jeff seeks more and more to make public what he sees in Thorwald's apartment, and what he suspects took place there, confirms a shift from voyeurism to surveillance on his part and has important moral implications.

It is revealing to compare *Rear Window* with a film made eight years later: John Frankenheimer's *The Manchurian Candidate* (1962). *The Manchurian Candidate* is undeniably concerned with McCarthyism and the

McCarthy period of national paranoia. The film has its relatively undisguised McCarthy figure—one capable of deciding upon the number of communist agents in government by reading the number "57" off a Heinz sauce bottle. An unreferenced quotation given in the 1999 *Halliwell's Film and Video Guide* has Penelope Houston referring to it as the "UnAmerican Film of the year," and the film is widely seen as Hollywood's making amends for its compromises and dishonesties during the but recently ended McCarthy period.

And yet . . . in Frankenheimer's film it turns out that there is indeed a communist conspiracy, one planned and organized from China, one involving a brainwashed individual who seems like a good American on the surface—like those good Americans in *Invasion of the Body Snatchers*, first shown a year after *Rear Window* in 1955—who really *is* a tool (admittedly unwitting) of the communists. McCarthyism is a bad thing, it is based on the paranoid rantings of a madman—and yet, and yet— what it fears, suspects, and asserts *is true*. The brainwashed victim *is* programmed to kill, Thorwald *has* murdered his wife. Paranoia, voyeurism are bad; paranoia, voyeurism give good results and are thus necessary.

There is surely a strong case for seeing such a struggle of opposing meanings in terms of a fierce struggle between ideological positions in the 1950s and early 1960s. McCarthyism by 1962 is significantly (although by no means completely) discredited in the United States. Many of its wilder claims concerning the communist infiltration of American society and government are by this date understood to be just that, and not a few of its ostensibly not so wild claims are also given less credence by a skeptical public. A film such as *The Manchurian Candidate* can be seen to be performing a classic act of recuperation by selling itself as a critical rendering of accounts with McCarthyism, and in particular by exposing McCarthy himself as paranoid almost to the extent of insanity, while at the same time legitimizing his decade-long effect on U.S. politics by revealing that—mad though he might have been—the menace against which he warned was a real one.

Rear Window was released in 1954, the year that the televised U.S. Army–McCarthy hearings (in which McCarthy was unable to substantiate penetration of the army by card-carrying communists) made explicit the Senator's declining influence and growing political marginalization. A year earlier, in 1953, the high- (or perhaps low-) water mark of that period dubbed "scoundrel time" by Lillian Hellman was marked by the execution of Julius and Ethel Rosenberg for spying and providing the Soviet Union with nuclear secrets. Robert Stam and Roberta Pearson (1986) have focused on *Rear Window* as a film that is as much about surveillance as about voyeurism, arguing that "at times," *Rear Window* "touches on what might be called the political dimension of voyeurism," noting that if the narrative ultimately confirms Jeff's suspicions of Thorwald, it also sensitizes viewers to the danger of political abuse of the power conferred by the look. They continue:

> Like Coppola's *The Conversation* two decades later, *Rear Window* is, among other things, an essay on the nature of surveillance. And if *The Conversation* clairvoyantly predicted the abuses of Watergate and Abscam, *Rear Window* in some ways echoes the historical ambiance of McCarthyite anticommunism. McCarthyism, after all, is the antithesis of neighborliness; it treats every neighbor as potential other, alien, spy. It fractures the social community for purposes of control. Jefferies is an anonymous accuser whose suspicions happen to be correct, but the object of his hostile gaze might easily have been as innocent as Father Logan in *I Confess* or Christopher Emmanuel Balestrero in *The Wrong Man,* to cite two other fifties films with anti-McCarthyite resonances. (203)

This is very tentative ("touches on," "in some ways echoes"), and although this reading has the virtue of reminding us how the McCarthy period effectively politicized private and domestic spaces, my own feeling is that it skates over the tensions and contradictions in the film rather too easily. For if it is the case that one narrative thread in the film offers a *de facto* justification of McCarthyite paranoia, the film also allows for more critical readings of Cold War hysteria.

For Americans watching the film on its first release, a comment made by Stella near the start of the film must, although using a term associated with voyeurism, have had an inescapably political resonance: "We've become a race of Peeping Toms. What people ought to do is get outside of their own house and look in for a change." It is a curiously double-edged comment: on the one hand, the paranoia of the Cold War and the obsessive surveillance of American citizens that it has brought with it have had a corruptive effect, such that an unhealthy prying and probing into citizens' privacies now needs to be replaced by a look *at* ourselves, rather than *for* the enemy in our midst. But on the other hand there is the recuperative suggestion that looking in private houses is still necessary. Many commentators have remarked on the fact that the action of the film is sandwiched between two scenes in which Jeff is depicted sleeping, and this framing represents a relatively conventional narrative device that serves (among other things) to categorize the sandwiched action as a sort of dream—in political terms perhaps the nightmare of McCarthyism. (The sandwiching effect is mirrored within the film, when the actual murder is committed in a period while Jeff is asleep and is thus enclosed by two waking periods. In spite of the reversal, both of these framing effects are able to link the framed action with some sort of dream world.)

In her essay "Melodrama Inside and Outside the Home" Laura Mulvey (1989a) draws some thought-provoking connections between political and private-domestic life in the United States of the 1950s:

> In the 1950s, the Hollywood studio system was faced with three massive crises: the impact of the HUAC (House UnAmerican Activities Committee) investigation, indictment as a monopoly under the anti-trust laws, and the coming of television. The first two provided an ideological and economic background to the third, which broke the genealogical links connecting different forms of popular theatrical entertainment that stretched back to the early days of urban industrialized culture. (63)

Mulvey points out that the success of television broke up the communal audience of the cinema and replaced it with the "home-based mode of consumption" of family television viewing. One of the items that is conspicuously (and, given his housebound situation, oddly) absent from Jeff's apartment is a television. This may well be related to the politics of filmmaking: at least one Hollywood studio effectively banned TVs from movie sets at this time. But there is a sense in which Jeff's obsessive gazing at life through his rear window is representative of a revolutionary new relation to entertainment in the United States, involving looking from within the family home out onto the world, rather than going out of the home to be entertained as part of a collective audience. From thousands of American homes, TV viewers were able to watch such things as the HUAC investigation. But simultaneously, that same investigation directed attention back inwards, attempting to penetrate the larger, metaphorical American home and its putative un-American infiltrators. *Rear Window* can thus be seen to mirror the two-way investigative gazing that dominated American society at this time: *from* the home into the larger, public arena, and also *into* the home in which, it is feared, Un-American activities may be going on.

References to, and images of, seeing abound in the film—and again and again we meet with evidence not only that the looking has become perverted but also that this perverted looking nevertheless uncovers the truth. Even Stella, who certainly at the start of the film expresses the voice of healthy normality in contrast to Jeff's apparently diseased voyeurism, reveals that by observing how many times her patient—a director of General Motors—went to the bathroom, she was able to foretell the slump of 1929. "When General Motors has to go to the bathroom ten times a day, the whole country's ready to let go." Looking is wrong, but looking is sometimes necessary. Our most private and personal behavior, that which it is most taboo for outsiders to observe, can reveal truths about the health (or sickness) of the body politic. Jeff also draws correct conclusions from (among other things) observing the behavior of a man in his bathroom, although this time he is washing away bloodstains rather than relieving a nerve-weakened bladder.

Robert J. Corber's 1993 book *In the Name of National Security: Hitchcock, Homophobia, and the Political Construction of Gender in Postwar America* suggests that this concern with the interpenetration of private and public/political during the McCarthy period also engages reflexively with the film industry's contamination by McCarthyism. Rejecting Lacanian readings of the film, Corber argues that "the film does not so much critique the voyeuristic economy of the cinematic apparatus as try to retrieve the cinematic apparatus from its contamination by the emergence of the national security state" (98). For Hitchcock, Corber contends, the cinematic apparatus had been implicated in the rise of McCarthyism, and "the voyeuristic economy of spectatorial pleasure had been corrupted by the scopic regime of the national security state" (14). Corber thus argues that the film involves more overt criticism of McCarthyism than I have conceded:

> Implicit in the film's "confession" of its own tainted procedures is a critique of McCarthyism. The film pathologizes Jeff's constant surveillance of his neighbors by suggesting that he suffers from an arrested sexual development. Alluding to the McCarthy witch hunts in this way enables the film to repudiate its own fellow traveling. Although it cannot deny that in the past the cinematic apparatus lent its technology to the national security state, it can recuperate that technology for the liberal consensus by indirectly attacking the government surveillance of suspected Communists, homosexuals, and lesbians as a form of psychopathology. (90)

Thus for Corber, in *Rear Window* in "shot after shot, the film tries to restore voyeuristic pleasure to the private sphere by stressing the autonomy of the camera's look" (101). As I have argued, the issue of what "the camera" represents in Hitchcock's film is more complex and less clear than is suggested by granting it an "autonomy" of looking. Indeed, having an autonomous camera exploring a private apartment suggests a worrying form of inhuman invasion rather than a more comforting restoration of pleasure to the private sphere.

Surveillance, Power, Impotence

In a society concerned with the contradictory aims of exposing subversion and protecting the private life, the movements of the observing camera in a film concerned with spying and voyeurism have an inescapably social and political resonance. At crucial points in *Rear Window* we are reminded that the camera eye has the intelligence of a human investigator but that it lacks real human, existential embodiment. *By implication, then, the activity of surveillance too can be directed by an acute human intelligence while there is, at the same time, something profoundly inhuman about it.* It is worth pondering that in the term "The Intelligence Services" (or even the Central Intelligence Agency), that which is most central to being human—intelligence—is disembodied and evicted from its human home: made the inhuman attribute of a soulless corporation or organization. "Intelligence" is both the most human form of rationality and the most dehumanized gathering of information. In the words of Stella at the start of the film: "Nothing has caused the human race so much trouble as intelligence."

Although there is much intrusion into private spaces in *Rear Window*, there is far less genuine intimacy. A one-sided invasion of another's privacy by force or subterfuge does not constitute intimacy, and neither does a one-way and non-reciprocal display of one's own private self. The spy or voyeur may discover what we refer to as intimate details of a person's life, but he or she does not thereby enjoy an intimate relationship with the person whose privacy has been violated; force or the use of deceit constitutes a denial of intimacy—although as the term "pseudo intimacy" implies, such a discovery may temporarily grant the illusion of intimacy. Genuine intimacy, moreover, does not involve an absolute and comprehensive sharing of privacies: to be intimate with another is not to have unfettered or unrestricted access to their privacy. Intimacy respects the right of the other to a seclusion of aspects of the self. The most intimate relationships are between individuals who retain privacies into which the other cannot penetrate, and does not wish to penetrate.

Up in the ceiling looking down, wandering like a ghost around Jeff's apartment, the camera-spy in *Rear Window* appears on occasion devious and all-seeing, motivated and directed by a human-like intelligence, but—much like the intelligence services of a modern society—without an essential human embodiment or moral supervision. I say "on occasion" because although I have argued that cameras are not capable of purposive action without the guidance of some human intelligence, when the film makes it difficult or impossible to establish exactly what that human intelligence is, then the camera can appear to be possessed of some incomprehensible and scarily inhuman form of self-determination. At such points we retain a sense of the extradiegetic control of its movements—the camera moves and points where director Hitchcock wants it to move and point—but within the diegesis it appears to be an intelligent eye without a human brain. Thus just as Jeff's own surveillance activity is associated with impotence and voyeuristic perversion, so too the camera eye in *Rear Window* is at times, we may be led to suspect, all-seeing and cunning, but alien and inhuman. As William Rothman (1982) has perceptively suggested:

> The camera's penetration of its subjects' privacy, combined with this control over accidents, gives the author what I have called godlike power.
>
> But he is also impotent. Insofar as his place is behind the camera, he represents only a haunting, ghostly presence within the world it frames. He has no body: no one can meet his gaze, he cannot satisfy himself sexually, he cannot even kill with his own hands. (103)

Discussing *The Scarlet Letter* I suggested that there is a paradox in the fact that the voyeur or spy who is in some sense seeking power-knowledge has to *disempower* him- or herself by accepting a rôle in which open and frank engagement with the person observed is not possible. In many cases it is a moot point as to whether spying or voyeurism is the result or the cause of impotence. The spy or voyeur makes him- or herself the passive partner, not able to move freely for fear of discovery, forced to react to the subject of observation rather than able to initiate an action him- or herself. Mladen Dolar (1992) has pointed out that although Jeff's observation of his neighbors may remind us of Bentham's panopticon, the difference is that in the panopticon the prisoners live in permanent fear of the ubiquitous gaze which they do not see, but which nothing escapes (and the disposition finally works equally well if there is nobody in the tower); whereas here, the inhabitants live their quiet ordinary lives (eating, sleeping, dancing, partying, making love and killing each other); Stewart, on the contrary, lives in constant fear in his watchtower—the fear that something will escape him. His problem is how to make his gaze ubiquitous (and the murder actually does escape him: he is asleep at the time of the murder). So the inhabitants are not the prisoners of the gaze of the Other, with its inevitable Omnipresence; it is rather the Supervisor who is the prisoner, the prisoner of his own gaze—a gaze that does not see. (144)

I suspect, however, that the difference is less absolute than Dolar suggests. The spy and the voyeur *always* go in fear that something will escape them: even the observer in the panopticon fears that prisoners may be *thinking* something to which he or she has no access. (I find it impossible to cite this passage without registering bemusement at the idea that "killing each other" is a normal aspect of "quiet ordinary lives"!)

Jeff is, appropriately, a photographer, and in order to "catch" a moving object the photographer has to remain still. This lack of mobility renders him or her vulnerable—as Jeff discovers when he photographs the racing-car accident. But the most striking image, or enactment, of the impotence of the camera comes at the end of *Rear Window* when Jeff tries to prevent Thorwald from attacking him by blinding him with the camera flashgun. (See Wood 1989, 377 for a similar view.) The strategy succeeds only in momentarily delaying Thorwald, whose ponderous, lumbering physicality threatens that harm may be inflicted even without sight. And this scene is packed with paradox: Jeff at last leaves his "theater auditorium" and goes out of the window into "real life," but the experience cripples him even further and hints that the hero-as-photographer may be unfit to exist in any world except the world of representations. Robin Wood (1989) has argued that "[d]omination—power/impotence as two sides of the same coin—is clearly the central concern (one might say the driving obsession) of Hitchcock's work on all levels" (360), and it is clear that this obsession is one that follows Hitchcock through a range of different social, historical, and political circumstances. But these changing circumstances stain the obsession and alter its scope and purchase, and I believe that the significance of the linking of the gaze with power and impotence in *Rear Window* can only be adequately understood through a tracing of the ways in which it negotiates and interrogates a very particular socio-political reality.

This is not to deny that logical connections join the components of the triad gaze–power–impotence, connections that are not specific to one culture or historical situation. But the operation of surveillance and voyeurism in different situations leads to different forms of power and different forms of impotence. If *Rear Window*'s nervous and neurotic concern with the activity of surveillance has a social and political resonance, then such a linking of surveillance with impotence in a "nation of Peeping Toms" suggests something historically specific: that there is something sterile and impotent at the heart of witch-hunting and witch-hunted America of the early 1950s. The unhappiness of unhappy families, as Tolstoy reminds us in the opening words of *Anna Karenina*, varies from unhappy family to unhappy family. In *Rear Window* Hitchcock focuses attention on the unhappiness of the America of 1954.

Slavoj Žižek (1991) has written very perceptively of Hitchcock's concern with "the intimate connection between the gaze and the couple power/impotence":

> The gaze denotes at the same time power (it enables us to exert control over the situation, to occupy the position of the master) and impotence (as bearers of a gaze, we are reduced to the role of passive witnesses to the adversary's action). The gaze, in short, is a perfect embodiment of the "impotent Master," one of the central figures of the Hitchcockian universe. (72)

The insight is, I think, central and crucial, but it needs to be set in relation to a view of the specifically non-interactive gaze. Interactive looking—the reciprocal exchange of glances—does not necessarily define the looking participants as master and servant, nor does it doom one or both of those involved to impotence. But using knowledge in the pursuit of power paradoxically condemns one to being disempowered in a human sense—as, I have argued, can be seen in *The Scarlet Letter*.

Jeff is *already symbolically impotent at the start of the film,* and this condition is directly related to his activity as a photographer, a man concerned with images rather than with action, a producer of images on the basis of which someone else can act.[4] John Fawell (2001) draws attention to the hints in the film that suggest that something is wrong with Jeff's sexuality, from his inability to uncork the (phallic) wine bottle that Lisa brings to the apartment to the "huge telephoto lens [that] rests on his lap,

---

4. Steven Soderbergh's 1989 film *Sex, Lies, and Videotape* links the making of images with male impotence in a very different cultural and historical context.

a comic but visually powerful representation of how his voyeurism has replaced sexual activity in his life" (52). Fawell links such hints to veiled suggestions that Jeff may even be a closet homosexual: "Again and again, Lisa and Stella suggest that Jeff is 'abnormal,' that he has a 'problem,' 'something he can't discuss,' something he is 'hiding' from them, something 'too frightful to utter'" (54).

Slavoj Žižek (1991) in contrast claims that *Rear Window* is

> ultimately the story of a subject who eludes a sexual relation by transforming his effective impotence into power by means of the gaze, by means of secret observation: he "regresses" to an infantile curiosity in order to shirk his responsibility to the beautiful woman who offers herself to him (the film is at this point unusually unequivocal for Hollywood in 1954—note the scene where Grace Kelly changes into a transparent nightgown). What we encounter here is, again, one of Hitchcock's fundamental "complexes," the interconnection of the gaze and the couple power/impotence. (92)

On one level this may well seem convincing, but it fails to confront the fact that it is also surveillance itself—the unreciprocated gaze of both photographer and Peeping Tom—which helps to *render* Jeff impotent. The paradox of intimate interpersonal relations is that it is the opening of aspects of one's privacy to another that enables intimacy. Because the voyeur and the spy (and, indeed, the photographer) conceal their own privacy from others, and in the case of the voyeur and the spy even add to it by indulging in secret acts of which they are ashamed, they disempower themselves in terms of the achievement of human intimacy.

Positioning the Viewer

Robin Wood (1969) cites and gives qualified assent to Jean Douchet's equation of Jeff with the cinematic viewer: "Douchet's interpretation of the film roughly equates Jefferies (James Stewart) with the spectator in the cinema, the flats across the court with the screen: what Jeff sees is a projection of his own desires" (62). By implication: what the spectator sees too is a projection of their own desires, and by watching Jeff punished they are able to indulge their fantasy wishes while ensuring that it is Jeff the scapegoat who is punished rather than them. In a neatly interlocking argument, Stojan Pelko (1992) argues that Hitchcock typically is revolutionary not "in *involving the spectator with on-screen characters, but mainly in making the very character a spectator!*" (109; emphases in original). Murray Pomerance (2013) notes that Thorwald's sitting-room window (and other windows in the apartment complex) is modeled after the size ratio of Cinemascope: 2.33:1 (38 n18). He also lists a succession of commentators who have seen Jeff's wheelchair as a surrogate of the director's chair (38 n17). Together, these observations argue for a chain of associations linking the director (Hitchcock), the viewer, and Jeff—all of whom stare at what is going on inside rectangular frames from a position of fascinated detachment. Hitchcock has of course much more power to intervene in what he sees than Jeff, who in his turn has more power than the completely impotent viewer. Although both Jeff and the viewer are in a sense confined to one seat, Jeff has far more choice over what is looked at: he can choose to look out of the window rather than at Lisa, for example, and he does. It also seems clear that the cinema viewer (or at least the heterosexual viewer, whether male or female) is likely to be frustrated by Jeff's initial lack of sexual interest in Lisa, and that this also serves to distance the viewer from him.

Laura Mulvey (1989c) argues that the position of the cinema audience in the individualizing darkness of the auditorium "helps to promote the illusion of voyeuristic separation." She goes on to suggest that

> [a]lthough the film is really being shown, is there to be seen, conditions of screening and narrative conventions give the spectator an illusion of looking in on a private world. Among other things, the position of the spectators in the cinema is blatantly one of repression of the exhibitionism and projection of the repressed desire onto the performer. (17)

Male viewers are, accordingly, enabled and encouraged to identify with male characters and take part vicariously in their voyeuristic activity, while women are able to locate their exhibitionism within female characters. So far as *Rear Window* is concerned, Mulvey claims that

> Lisa's exhibitionism has already been established by her obsessive interest in dress and style, in being a passive image of visual perfection: Jeffries' [*sic*] voyeurism and activity have also been established through his work as a photo-journalist, a maker of stories and captor of images. However, his enforced inactivity, binding him to his seat as a spectator, puts him squarely in the fantasy position of the cinema audience. (23–24)

Jeff thus both *represents* the male cinema viewer and also *offers* this viewer the possibility of vicarious or displaced voyeuristic pleasure, although at the same time, as I have suggested, his early lack of sexual interest in Lisa introduces a potential point of tension in the (male and female) viewer's identification with him. Moreover, there is obviously a sense in which Jeff's incapacitation has the effect of shifting familiar, conventional gender rôles in the film: it is Lisa who is brave, mobile, and active, and Jeff who remains in the home and passively observes her. Indeed, Tania Modleski (1988) has proposed that "even some of those films which seem exclusively to adopt the male point of view, like *Murder!, Rear Window,* or *Vertigo,* may be said either to have woman as the ultimate point of identification or to place the spectator—regardless of gender—in a classically 'feminine' position" (4–5). This is so, Modleski, argues, even though both *Vertigo* and *Rear Window* seem "to confine us to the hero's vision of events and to insist on that vision by literally stressing the man's point of view throughout"; thus the "[t]he film spectator apparently has no choice *but* to identify with the male protagonist, who exerts an active, controlling gaze over a passive female object" (73; emphasis in original). Modleski justifies her view by reference to the fact that in *Rear Window* "the *woman* is continually shown to be physically superior to the hero, not only in her physical movements but also in her dominance within the frame: she towers over Jeff in nearly every shot in which they both appear" (77; emphasis in original). This dominance is symbolically confirmed in the final scene of the film:

> As important as this gesture [picking up her magazine] is, even more important is the fact that the film gives her the last look. This is, after all, the conclusion of a movie that all critics agree is about the power the man attempts to wield through exercising the gaze. We are left with the suspicion (a preview, perhaps, of coming attractions) that while men sleep and dream their dreams of omnipotence over a safely reduced world, women are not where they appear to be, locked into male "views" of them, imprisoned in their master's dollhouse. (85)

The seeing-activity of men in *Rear Window* is not always to be relied upon, does not always represent an objective gathering of information from the outside world. On the one hand, the song composed by the songwriter in one of the apartments facing Jeff's tells "Lisa" that "I see you all the time"; on the other hand, this seeing takes place "in the same old dream tonight." Recall that the action of *Rear Window* is sandwiched between opening and closing shots of the sleeping (and presumably dreaming) Jeff. It is certainly the case that Jeff and Doyle seem to spend a lot of time looking at women, but this does not mean that they always *see* them clearly. In three scenes in the film Jeff is pictured sleeping. In two of them Lisa is awake and alert, and in the third Jeff fails to see the "woman in black." Generalizing about Hitchcock's films, Laura Mulvey (1989c) has claimed that in them, "the male hero does see precisely what the audience sees" (23). But in *Rear Window* this is not always the case: we see Jeff *not* seeing things while women are looking or doing. This suggests that Robin Wood is right to detect a subversion of gender stereotypes in *Rear Window,* one that is active on more than one level. The viewer's identification with Jeff is always under threat, is never more than partial and provisional, and may indeed cause the male viewer to recognize that such an identification carries with it the risk of what is conventionally seen as feminization.

The Expressive Face

Cornell Woolrich's 1942 short story on which the film of *Rear Window* is based[5] lays much stress on the ability to read many things from an individual's facial expression. It is not just in the light of our familiarity with the film that certain passages from the story seem possessed of a strikingly *cinematic* quality. This, for example, comes from the third page of the story:

> He was looking slightly out, maybe an inch past the window frame, carefully scanning the back faces of all the houses abutting on the hollow square that lay before him. You can tell, even at a distance, when a person is looking fixedly. There's something about the way the head is held. And yet his scrutiny wasn't held fixedly to any one point, it was a slow, sweeping one, moving along the houses on the opposite side from me first. When it got to the end of them, I knew it would cross over to my side and come back along there. Before it did, I withdrew several yards

---

5. Keith Williams (2007) has suggested that Hitchcock's film may also owe a lot to H. G. Wells's 1895 short story "Through a Window," in which a journalist with a broken leg similarly observes various dramatic events through his window. As Williams points out, this story also involves a quarreling married couple, a nurse who regularly visits the invalid, and a "killer, who abruptly transgresses [the hero's] frame of spectatorial immunity by climbing into the room" (44).

inside my room, to let it go safely by. I didn't want him to think I was sitting there prying into his affairs. There was still enough blue night-shade
in my room to keep my slight withdrawal from catching his eye. (Woolrich 1998, 7)

The narrator (the story is told in the first person by "Hal Jeffries") comments interpretatively on this careful scanning:

> It was just a little oddity, it failed to blend in with his being worried or
> disturbed about his wife. When you're worried or disturbed, that's an
> internal preoccupation, you stare vacantly at nothing at all. When you
> stare around in a great sweeping arc at windows, that betrays external
> preoccupation, outward interest. (7–8)

In contrast, when Thorwald later on glances out of his window, the narrator is quick to distinguish a new quality in this act:

> Something about it struck me as different from any of the others I'd seen
> him give in all the time I'd been watching him. If you can qualify such an
> elusive thing as a glance, I would have termed it a glance with a purpose.
> It was certainly anything but vacant or random, it had a bright spark of
> fixity in it. It wasn't one of those precautionary sweeps I'd seen him give,
> either. (29)

What such passages bring to the foreground is the potentially reflexive
nature of looking: the more we search for information, the more we risk
revealing things about ourselves.

Although Hitchcock's film changed so much in Woolrich's short
story that one almost hesitates to accept the categorization "adaptation"
(most dramatically, the rôle of Lisa, who does not appear in the short
story, was added), it retained and developed the story's concern with
the deep significance of facial expression and looking behavior. As my
opening quotation demonstrates, Hitchcock was a director who from
the start understood that film is not primarily a verbal medium—but he
also understood that film is a narrative form. He also understood better
than most that the human face—and in particular the eyes—holds enor-
mous potential for storytelling, character display, and character interaction. Donald Spoto's (1983) biography of the director is one of the best
sources of information and discussion concerning Hitchcock's own life-
long concern with eyes and seeing. Spoto points out that films as far

apart as *Young and Innocent, The Birds,* and *Psycho* are replete with images of looking and seeing, backed up in many cases by verbal references to the eyes and to seeing, both literal and metaphorical (165, 463). Spoto counts forty occasions in *The Birds* when characters say "I see" or "You see," most of them additions made by Hitchcock in the second draft of the script, and he compares the empty eye-sockets of the mummified Mrs. Bates in *Psycho* with the pecked-out eye-sockets of the dead farmer in *The Birds.* (Stella comments to Jeff at one point in the film that the punishment for being a Peeping Tom used to be to have one's eyes put out.) Spoto reports Anne Baxter's impression that the director was "very quiet, and he kept his hands in repose, but he commanded a great deal of respect with his mesmeric eyes" (338). Hitchcock's obsession with Tippi Hedren, according to Spoto, involved his staring at her all the time, on and off the set (456). What is common to all these forms of looking is a lack of reciprocity, and a paradoxical sense that the more the look insists upon its power (and thus becomes a stare) the more it locks out intimacy and thus condemns itself to impotence. Staring—that is, looking fixedly at another person rather than engaging in a reciprocal exchange of glances intercut with looking away—generally puts pressure on the person stared at to avert their gaze. The stare is the non-reciprocal gaze of power and impoliteness.

Hitchcock seems not to have wanted actors with extremely expressive and mobile faces: Spoto (1983) quotes Gregory Peck to the effect that when he asked Hitchcock about mood or expression, the director "would simply say that I was to drain my face of all expression and he would photograph me" (276). Writing specifically about *Rear Window* in his 1963 essay "On Style," Hitchcock confirms that although the look and the face are of supreme importance to him in this film, their richness of communicative potential is not something intrinsic but something that is contextual, something that is exploited by means of cutting:

> Mr. Stewart is sitting looking out of the window. He observes. We register his observations on his face. We are using the visual image now. We are using the mobility of the face, the expression, as our content of the piece of film. Let's give an example of how this can vary, this technique, with whatever he is looking at: Mr. Stewart looks out. Close-up. Cut to what he sees. Let's assume it's a woman holding a baby in her arms. Cut back to him. He smiles. Mr. Stewart likes babies. He's a nice gentleman. Take out only the middle piece of film, the viewpoint. Leave the close-ups in—the look and the smile. Put a nude girl in the middle instead of

the baby. Now he's a dirty old man. By the changing of one piece of film only, you change the whole idea. (Gottlieb 1995, 289)

According to Hitchcock, then, there is no dictionary of the look in *Rear Window,* no evidence of an essentialist belief in fixed meanings for particular facial expressions. But if there is no dictionary of the look there is a grammar of shots in this film, one in which the meaning of a particular facial expression is fixed—by selection and combination, as in human word language—by the director-speaker.

The filmmaker thus uses the eyes of characters in a different way from the writer of literary fiction, and this one can confirm by contrasting my two opening quotations—from Hitchcock and from Jane Austen. The Austen quotation is given to us as the conscious thought of Austen's character Elinor, and its intradiegetic status in a classic realist novel is important. The meanings that Elinor reads are generated from within the characters whose eyes she observes: they are *expressive* meanings. This is not of course to exclude a level of conscious artistic organization on Austen's part: *Sense and Sensibility* is also a work packed with references to eyes and to (literal and metaphorical) seeing, and these references have a cumulative force and build up a significance that goes beyond the level of individual character expression. But the component units of this system are expressive and realistic. The meanings generated by eyes and looking in Hitchcock's films in general, and *Rear Window* in particular, are, according to Hitchcock himself, as much contextual as expressive; they are the meanings generated in part from outside the level of character-experience by means of a grammar of shots; *they are simultaneously Hitchcock's meanings and also the meanings of his characters.* That sort of doubleness is an essential part of the richness of fictional narratives. In Austen's novel the reader responds to Elinor's observation of Colonel Brandon's eyes; in *Rear Window* the viewer responds directly to the eyes of the characters.

Donald Spoto reports that in directing Tippi Hedren, Hitchcock "began to take unusual care in the rehearsal and preparation of every shot—directing her 'down to the movement of an eye and every turn of my head,' she remembered" (456). Hitchcock himself confirmed to a London journalist:

I controlled every movement on her face. She did purely cinematic acting of very fine shadings all the time. She wasn't allowed to do anything beyond what I gave her. It was my control entirely. (quoted in Spoto 470)

It is not surprising that such accounts have led commentators to see evidence of a Svengali-like male control in the use of female facial expression in Hitchcock's films—and a control that is well funded with a disturbingly perverted sexual element. Hitchcock on the set of *Rear Window* communicated with actors by means of concealed radio receivers, monitoring and controlling his performers much as the prison superintendent in Bentham's panopticon imposed an authority on inmates.

Donald Spoto also reports Evan Hunter's account of working with Hitchcock on the script of *The Birds;* although their discussions were tape-recorded for future use, the recording was stopped while Hitchcock described the rape scene in *Marnie.*

> "I didn't want to write that scene for him, and I told Hitchcock so. I thought it would break sympathy for the character of the man, and it's totally unmotivated. But Hitch said he wanted it in the film, and he insisted that at the exact moment of the rape he wanted the camera right on her shocked face." (469)

The expressive face in Hitchcock is—especially when it is a female face—one that assumes an observer, and typically a male observer who is in some way separate or cut off from the individual observed. Unlike the film *Peeping Tom*—a film that is often compared to *Rear Window*—the crucial observing that is done in Hitchcock's films in general and *Rear Window* in particular is done by someone whose observing is not observed within the diegesis. It is not the rapist who observes the shocked face in *Marnie,* but the camera, the director who controls its movements, and those for whom it observes. The power and desire that are involved in rape or murder are closely related to male powerlessness or impotence. The act of rape is itself an admission that the rapist is incapable of obtaining consensual sex with the victim. *Rear Window* does not involve rape—although it does portray what might be seen as the beginnings of two potential rapes: the scene in which Miss Torso shuts her door while physically struggling with her companion to prevent him from entering her apartment, and the scene in which the young man brought home by Miss Lonelyhearts starts to impose himself on her sexually against her will. The threat of rape is thus a continual presence in *Rear Window* and is one of a number of possible forms that male violence directed against women can take—the most extreme of which is murder. Many commentators have noted the repeated references to dismemberment in *Rear Window,* and while Miss Torso and Miss Lonelyhearts are given names suggesting a symbolic objectification and dismemberment, Mrs. Thorwald is literally dismembered by her murderous husband.

In the concluding section of his collection of Hitchcock interviews, written after the director's death and entitled "Remainder," François Truffaut (1986) writes:

> I knew all these movies by heart, but upon seeing the excerpts isolated from their contexts, I was struck by the sincerity and the savagery of Hitchcock's work. It was impossible not to see that the love scenes were filmed like murder scenes, and the murder scenes like love scenes. (533)

It is curious and not a little disturbing to see the reversal described by Truffaut categorized as "sincerity and the savagery": how does the filming of love scenes as if they were murder scenes, and the filming of murder scenes as if they were love scenes, in any way suggest *sincerity?* At the same time, Truffaut's sense that there is something important to be explored in the reversal to which he draws attention is surely sound. It is tempting to wonder whether Hitchcock was drawn to Joseph Conrad's novel *The Secret Agent*—which he filmed in 1936 as *Sabotage*—because of the overtly sexual way in which the murder by stabbing of the character Verloc is described. Donald Spoto (1983) provides the fascinating information that Hitchcock actually saw Conrad's own stage adaptation of *The Secret Agent* in London; according to Spoto the performance was a "theatrical event that apparently made so strong an impression on Hitchcock that he persuaded Balcon to let him film it, in 1936" (62).

The most dramatic eye contact in *Rear Window* undoubtedly occurs at the end of the film when Thorwald, after having observed Lisa's signaling to Jeff behind her back and indicating to him that she is wearing Mrs. Thorwald's wedding ring, suddenly looks out of his window and straight towards Jeff. In a survey for the journal *Sight and Sound* in which film directors were asked which for them was Hitchcock's most definitive scene or moment, Andrew Bergman (1999) cited this scene. (Yet again, the comment involves a striking shift between character-names and actor-names.)

> The murderous husband Thorwald (Raymond Burr) discovers Grace Kelly in his apartment and then discovers that Jimmy Stewart is watching the both of them. Jimmy, the helpless voyeur in his wheelchair, becomes us, the audience—passive, frightened, unable to act. It is literally a nightmare moment—a man unable to move, immobilised, terrified—and also

the delicious nightmare of a moviegoer, happily unable to predict the outcome. The scene terrified me at age eight and terrifies me still. (21)

It is, curiously enough, hard to be sure whether the look is straight at
the camera; after having looked at the scene a number of times I feel that
it seems directed slightly to one side of the camera—by which means
(if I am right) it both unites us with and separates us from Jeff. Thorwald's look is, however, clearly the look of threat, a threat increased by
the leaden expression on his face and the fact that his eyebrows are not
raised to indicate "I wish to communicate with you." At this point in the
film Jeff presumably exchanges a look with Thorwald for the first time.
But this visual interaction and reciprocity denote and promise not intimacy but violence. If elsewhere in the film Jeff is, on occasions, the viewer's *alter ego*—and there is still an element of such identification in this
final scene—Hitchcock chooses at this point not to stress this relationship
by having Thorwald look at us the way that suggests or invites reciprocity. (William Rothman [1982] has commented interestingly on a scene in
Hitchcock's early British film *The Lodger,* in which the lodger "looks right
at the camera, a smile on his lips" [29].) Having Thorwald return our
gaze would give us precisely that contact and interaction which voyeurism
excludes. The viewer is even cut off from the pseudo intimacy of threatened violence.

It would be wrong to suggest that Jeff's face is without expression in
the film, however. It is revealing that the first extended sequence in which
Jeff's facial expressions are varied and expressive is that, early on in the
film, in which Stella has gone to fix him a sandwich and he is looking
out of the window. To start with, his face displays mainly eagerness to
see as he strains to amass information about his neighbors. But once the
newlyweds arrive in their apartment, Jeff's face offers us a running commentary on the scene that unfolds opposite him, cutting from curiosity to
bewilderment, and thence from amused understanding to embarrassment
and shamed observation. That last sequence of emotions is unrolled for
us at some speed: Jeff gives us a smile of enlightenment as the newlywed
husband re-enters their apartment carrying his wife so as to be able to
"cross the threshold" in the conventional celebration of marriage. Then,
as the couple kiss, Jeff averts his eyes with an embarrassed look on his
face, but cannot resist turning them back with a guilty look on his face.

But are these expressions "there," or are they, as Hitchcock has suggested, dependent upon cutting and on meanings that the observer generates on the basis of the contextual clues that Hitchcock provides? Well,

Jeff's expressions do contain certain conventional elements which help us to assign meaning. As the couple leave their apartment so as to be able to re-enter it, Jeff's eyebrows are lowered, his head dips slightly as if he is concentrating on the scene, and his mouth opens slightly. All of these elements conventionally denote puzzlement or a search for meaning. When they re-enter the room he leans back (suggesting that he is no longer searching for information), and he mouths the word "Oh!" A very slight smile comes on his lips at this point. The couple are then pictured as they begin to embrace, and Jeff turns his face away from the window, and looks away and slightly down, an action that immediately to me connotes embarrassment. Michael Argyle and Mark Cook (1976) tell us that as long ago as 1872 Charles Darwin noted that people who are ashamed or embarrassed look down, and that this observation was repeated by Erving Goffman in 1956 (77). In an article entitled "The Cultural Dimensions of Nonverbal Communication," Michael L. Hecht, Peter A. Andersen, and Sidney A. Ribeau (1989) have suggested that such signals are of different significance in different cultures (174), but Jeff's aversion of gaze here seems clearly to indicate an embarrassed recognition that he is infringing on the privacy of the newlyweds by continuing to look.

Almost immediately after averting face and gaze, however, Jeff throws a quick look back *but without turning his face all the way back towards the window.* His eyes as he observes the couple embracing are pointing leftwards because his head is facing away from the couple and downwards, and this mismatch of facial and eye direction—his pupils are on the far left of his eyes, which results in a large amount of the whites of his eyes showing to our (the viewer's) left—is a classic sign of a look of guilt, evasion, or indirection. Most Western people asked to characterize this look would, I feel, describe it as "shifty," "furtive," or "guilty"; it attempts to gather, but not to display, information—but display information it nonetheless does.

In contrast to those of other primates, the whites of human eyes play a key rôle in signaling or disclosing eye direction, and they are thus extremely rich in communicative potential (Cole 1998, 209). Their rôle in *Rear Window* is absolutely crucial. Norman Bryson (1983) has distinguished usefully between the gaze, "prolonged, contemplative, yet regarding the field of vision with a certain aloofness and disengagement, across a tranquil interval," and the glance, "a furtive or sideways look whose attention is always elsewhere, which shifts to conceal its own existence, and which is capable of carrying unofficial, *sub rosa* messages of hostility, collusion, rebellion, and lust" (94). Important in our discussion is the fact that although we are to assume that Jeff knows rationally that he is not observed, nonetheless his body language and gaze behavior are of a sort that have a clear significance in an interpersonal context. His guilty glance has a powerful expressive force, and it provides an important moral commentary on his voyeurism and, by extension, on all forms of non-reciprocal looking that involve forcing another person's privacy and integrity. (Jeff provides us with a look that is some way comparable with this later on in the film when, telling Lisa about the songwriter, he says, "he lives alone: probably has a very unhappy marriage." As he delivers the line he turns his face away from her—she is serving the meal—while screwing his eyes back round in her direction. Again the tension between facial and eye direction suggests a conflict, this time between a desire to observe her response to the tart comment, and a wish to avoid giving away this desire to her.)

Norman K. Denzin (1995) has noted how the activities of the voyeur are at variance with what he terms "the concept of the free, interacting, autonomous individual" which is reproduced and inscribed by "the ideologies of capitalism and democracy" (6). He insists that "[t]his individual, and his or her private spaces, are central to the mythologies of the capitalist-democratic society," and that "[t]he voyeur simultaneously challenges and protects the spaces this individual inhabits" (6). Voyeurism thus exposes but simultaneously attempts to conceal a fault line running through the dominant ideology of 1950s America: privacy must be respected and protected, which requires that this privacy be violated.

Jeff's vacillation between looking and averting his gaze enacts in miniature this paradoxical challenge and protection. He wants to know, to enjoy the power that invasion of another's privacy can bring with it, but at the same time he does not want to know, because he does not want to experience the shame that illicit observation will cause him. And he does not want to know because he is aware that such knowledge is inimical to both intimacy and (self-) respect. Like America, Jeff is portrayed as one who believes in the sanctity of individual privacy, but who feels a compulsion to violate it. Perhaps too there is a sense that by looking he invades private territory, but by keeping the subject of his gaze unaware of his surveillance he simultaneously protects this same private territory. Moreover, so far as their *own* private territory is concerned, Jeff and other snoopers take very good care to ensure that it remains inviolate. In this double movement, I would argue, Jeff enacts the contradictory message of *Rear Window* as a whole: surveillance is pathological and perverted (Lisa initially refers to his use of the binoculars to spy on his neighbors as "diseased," and even Jeff asks rhetorically whether it is "ethical to watch a man with binoculars and a long-focus lens"), but at the same time it is necessary if freedom is to be preserved. Jeff goes on: "Is it ethical even if you prove that he didn't commit a crime?" The question is slightly unusual: we might expect, "Is it ethical even if you prove that he did commit a crime?" It would seem that spying can always be morally justified: either you exonerate someone (the innocent should have nothing to hide), or you discover a crime (the guilty have no right to privacy). We shouldn't spy on our neighbors—but if they are proved to have done nothing wrong then maybe it's ethical, and it is only as a result of such spying that the murderer is caught. Indirectly, then, Jeff's hesitations mirror the hesitations of, as Denzin puts it, "the ideologies of capitalism and democracy," which have personal freedom and individual privacy as fundamental constitutive elements, but which also (and especially at the time that *Rear Window* was made) insisted on the need for comprehensive surveillance to fight the perceived menace and inner corruption of subversive communist infiltration. At the same time, the film bespeaks a recurrent nervous fear (a fear not expressed in *Oliver Twist*) that the loss of a respect for privacy may be a cure that is worse than the disease it is meant for. After the killing of the little dog, its owner charges the members of the community with not being proper neighbors, asserting that real neighbors "like each other, speak to each other, care if anybody lives or dies: but none of you do." She asks whether they killed the dog because it loved everyone, but we know that it was killed because it was snooping. Snooping, digging for buried clues, is not something one does because one loves those on whom one is spying.

The movement of Jeff's gaze away from and then back to the couple, and the clear tension between direction-of-face and direction-of-eyes, suggests an inner tension, a clash between desire and conscience. At this point the newlywed husband draws down the apartment blind—picking up and echoing the *raising* of Jeff's blinds during the credits, and conceivably linking the window with the eye via the connotations of the implied word "blind." But at this point it is very striking that Jeff's gaze remains directed at the window, his face expressionless and his attention apparently fixed on the now-covered window. We assume that fantasy has now taken over, that he is picturing what is going on behind the lowered blind. (Later on in the film Miss Lonelyhearts's blind is lowered when she returns with the younger man, although it remains transparent.) At this point Stella returns, although he is unaware of her presence until she comments ironically: "Window shopper!" He blinks with apparent surprise, turns his head to her, and the scene ends. A window shopper is, of course, a person who looks at goods in shop windows but cannot (or does not) buy them, and in the context of what Jeff has been looking at, and his previous conversation with Stella about not wanting to marry Lisa, the comment has an inescapable suggestion of either voyeuristic perversion or of impotence. (As a good dictionary of slang will confirm, male sexual potency and activity are frequently conceived of in financial or economic terms.)

This is not the only time that Jeff smiles to or at an unaware person across the courtyard—he also smiles as he toasts Miss Lonelyhearts, and when the composer returns home drunk and sweeps his papers onto the floor. These smiles are actually slightly odd. In my introduction I suggested that the smile we make while reading a novel "comes from that overwhelming sense we have that we are in the presence of another person or people capable of witnessing our facial movements" (p. 4). A similar point can be made about Jeff's smiles in *Rear Window*. Adam Kendon (1990) has noted that in normal human interpersonal interaction, "smiling, in each partner, is closely related to smiling in the other," and he concludes that smiling "is a symmetrically reciprocated emotional response" (79). Jonathan Cole (1998), too, has drawn attention to the fact that people normally smile only when others are there to witness the fact: "Children smile not when they open a present but when they turn to their parents; adults' joy at a strike at tenpin bowling is shown not when they are pointing downlane at the pins, but when they turn to their friends" (59). Jeff is responding in the one case to Miss Lonelyhearts's smile at her imaginary dinner companion, but he does not smile at Lisa when she is actually dining with him. Of course actors may have to display emotions in situations in which they would not do so in ordinary life (Doyle smiles the first time that he sees Miss Torso—although Jeff wipes the smile off his face by asking about Doyle's wife). The fact that many people gesture energetically when on the telephone confirms that our communicative behavior is not always logical, and indeed the one time that Thorwald is pictured smiling is while he is on the phone. (The first time Jeff smiles in the film is when he too is on the phone, talking to his boss.) Nonetheless, Jeff's smiles to the unaware and the unresponding do half suggest that in the early part of the film his fantasy relations with his spied-upon neighbors are almost more real (or felt to be more intimate) than are his relations with the flesh-and-blood individuals in his apartment—Lisa in particular. Such smiles betoken both understanding and a sense of superior, if well-disposed, detachment. Jeff *exchanges* smiles with Lisa for the first time when she starts to support his theory, when she states that the woman who left Thorwald's apartment with him at 6 a.m. cannot have been Mrs. Thorwald—"at least, not yet." Genuine and reciprocal intimacy between Jeff and Lisa appears to start at this point.

Another evocative use of eye aversion on Jeff's part takes place the first time Jeff sees Thorwald leaving his apartment with a samples case in the middle of the night. The cloudburst has awoken Jeff, and he sees and laughs at the couple opposite who have to leave their balcony in a hurry because of the rain. Immediately afterwards, Jeff notices Thorwald leaving the apartment. The following sequence of head and eye movements then takes place.

> Jeff looks down and away from window (our left).
> He bends his head down.
> He shifts his eyes to our right back towards the window, without moving his head.
> He shifts his eyes to our left, without moving his head.
> He moves both head and eyes to our right.
> He continues moving head round slowly to our right.

At this point there is a cut to a shot of Thorwald disappearing along the passage opposite, and we surmise that Jeff has moved his head to take in this information. Finally, Jeff's head and eyes move down and there is a cut to his watch. Fade out. Then fade in to the watch again, some time later. As Jeff observes Thorwald again leaving his apartment with his case, Jeff's head and eye movements are again out of sync, suggesting a man trying to make sense of what he sees.

Although this is hard to convey by means of a verbal transcript, the total effect of these movements is to signify puzzlement and the attempt to think through a problem; human beings typically break eye contact and stare at something neutral if they want to devote mental energy to solving a problem. The response seems to have a dual purpose: it shuts off the intake of potentially distracting visual information, and (in circumstances where others are present) it communicates the information that one is thinking and does not want to be disturbed.

The use of averted gaze is quite different here from its occurrence earlier, in the scene during which Jeff and Lisa talk over their meal, and the conversation becomes increasingly heated; Lisa signals annoyance, opposition, and anger by turning her face and her gaze away from Jeff while he is talking and by keeping her arms folded. Although it is normal for Caucasians in the United States to look at an interlocutor less when listening than when speaking (Argyle and Cook 1976, 106), to look away continually when a conversational partner is actually speaking generally denotes the desire to demonstrate opposition or antagonistic emotion. Revealingly, Jeff has stared straight at Miss Lonelyhearts prior to this meal, and has smilingly raised his glass in response to her toast to her imaginary guest. The two are thus linked as individuals locked in relationships with imagined or unaware others; the difference is that Jeff seems happy with such an at-a-distance relationship, whereas Miss Lonelyhearts cannot maintain the pretense and collapses in tears on the table. He smiles: she weeps.

○

For much of *Rear Window* reciprocity takes place far more in fantasy than in reality—in Jeff's smiles across the courtyard, in Miss Lonelyhearts's conversation with her imagined dinner partner. Until Lisa is pulled half unwillingly into his obsession, Jeff displays far more bodily and facial signs of intimacy in fantasy interaction with those upon whom he spies than he does with Lisa. He can be intimate only at a distance, only when his personal privacy remains barricaded to others. Jeff gains an illusory sense of intimacy through his voyeuristic forcing of the privacies of others, but this intimacy is as unsatisfying for him as it is for Miss Lonelyhearts when dining with her imaginary lover. Jeff thus stands as an appropriate symbol of any society that claims to have the inviolability of its citizens' privacies as a cornerstone, but that assumes and demands the right to force these privacies in the interest of defending them.

This might imply that Jeff is an unattractive character, but for most viewers it appears that he is not. Indeed, for most viewers I suspect it is the perception that both Jeff and Lisa are grappling with intractable problems, that they are trying to reconcile opposing interests and conflicting values, that helps to make them admirable characters. On the personal plane their seeming willingness to compromise (more apparent, it is true, on Lisa's part than on Jeff's) helps to establish viewer sympathy for them. This sense of development extends to each character's recognition of previously unremarked strengths in the other: Jeff understands that Lisa is able to act bravely and decisively in a physically challenging situation, and Lisa has accepted that Jeff's observations of his neighbors have had a beneficial result. On the plane of personal relationship, then, the film shows two characters maturing and adapting to the needs of the other. It is true that not all of their differences have been settled, but given good will we can assume that they have some chance of facing a positive future.

On a more symbolic plane, however, the picture is far more murky. As is often the case, the ideological implications of the film are to be found more in its second-level meanings, where contradiction and inconsistency can more easily be concealed. In one sense the film ends in conventional fashion, with a return to normality, a normality that no longer demands continued surveillance. Jeff's back is now facing the window, and he is asleep. But it is worth comparing this ending to that of a film that appeared three years later: Sidney Lumet's *Twelve Angry Men* (1957). If the political subtext of *Rear Window* consists of hints and of parallels which an alert viewer has to work hard to draw, that of *Twelve Angry Men* is far more overt. What goes on in the jury room is clearly presented as a model of American society at large, and the message of the film is pretty obviously that the efforts of one courageous individual who is prepared to stand against the majority and to fight for justice and against prejudice can be successful. When Henry Fonda's character "Mr. Davis" leaves the courthouse at the end of the film—a set that is if anything even more claustrophobic than is Jeff's apartment in *Rear Window*—he walks out into bright sunlight. The political allegory here seems direct and unconcealed: American is emerging out of a dark night of prejudice. Three years is a long time in politics, of course, and McCarthyism was far weaker and more discredited in 1957 than it had been in 1954. Those watching the film—who themselves are by this point in the narrative probably thinking about their own imminent departure from the darkened room they have shared with the same people for a couple of hours— can associate themselves with this movement as they too prepare to walk out into open public space and fresh air.

This is not to suggest that *Twelve Angry Men* is a better film than *Rear Window*; indeed, the somewhat clichéd and unqualified optimism of its ending seems crude in comparison to *Rear Window*'s more nuanced view of opposing forces—on both the personal and the political plane— which have moved together in gestures of reconciliation and compromise, but which have by no means been finally and unproblematically resolved. It is not always happy endings that make great art. Although *Rear Window* as a whole involves an attempt at recuperation, at simultaneously condemning the invasion of privacy and the voyeurism of McCarthyism while half suggesting that maybe they were necessary, it leaves enough questions in the minds of viewers to help them engage with these crucial issues. If Robin Wood is correct to argue that the film subverts an ideological system based upon incompatible gender rôles—and I think that his argument is persuasive—then it may also be possible to praise the film for exposing other incompatibilities in the then dominant ideology. The recuperation, in other words, is far from complete.

At least one strong and politically charged association in Hitchcock's film does not resonate for present-day viewers in the way it quite possibly did for many who saw the film in the United States on its first release. Elise Lemire (2000) has pointed out that the book that Lisa is reading in the film's final moments—*Beyond the High Himalayas*, by William O. Douglas—was a real book, published by Doubleday in 1952. As Lemire reports, Douglas

> was not only an avid naturalist but was best known, for the 36 years he served, as a champion of civil liberties on the U.S. Supreme Court, where his term as associate justice is still the longest to date. In June 1953, he faced impeachment charges when he granted a stay of execution to Julius and Ethel Rosenberg, who had been convicted of passing atomic secrets to the Soviet Union. The Rosenbergs were executed on June 19, 1953. Hitchcock received the first treatment of *Rear Window* in April 1953 and is listed as a producer of the film as early as May of that year. (90n39)

As Lemire adds, it would be interesting to know at which point Hitchcock decided to feature Douglas's book in the film (if, indeed, the decision was Hitchcock's own). It is of course possible that the book was chosen merely because its title suggested those remote and inaccessible places that Lisa is preparing herself, or pretending to prepare herself, to visit. But for some viewers, the book may have been a reminder of a tradition in American politics that was opposed to all that McCarthyism stood for.

Writing about *Rear Window*, Jeanne Allen (1988) has argued that Hitchcock's subject in this film "is the struggle between partners for privacy *and* intimacy," a subject to which she claims female spectators and feminists are particularly sensitive (40; emphasis in original). Her reading of the film has Jeff and Lisa achieving an intimacy that respects each other's privacy. And it is true that Jeff's final dreams are his own, just as Lisa can read while Jeff sleeps. But the fact that Lisa feels free to put aside the travel book and read her fashion magazine only when she is sure that Jeff is asleep suggests that the establishment of a secure private domain for a woman is something that still requires not a little subterfuge. More than one commentator on the film states that by the final scene Lisa and

Jeff are engaged. Thus Robert J. Corber (1993) states that, to be sure, "Jeff finally agrees to marry her" (109), while Robin Wood (1969) refers to "the fact of their engagement" at the close of the film (70), and repeats this comment in his later book on Hitchcock. But I see no evidence that this is the case: Lisa certainly has no engagement ring on—and this is a film very much occupied by rings and their significance. It seems that viewers of the film want to impose a closure on it that has no textual justification. It is, surely, part of the strength of the film that its tensions are still active as the bamboo curtains descend for the last time. Privacy, in other words, is still under threat at the end of the film—just as it was in the America of 1954. And it may be this insight that is the film's greatest virtue.

Can You Guess How You'd Look?

Michael Powell's *Peeping Tom*

I HAVE a lingering affection for that outmoded term "point of view."
Recent narrative theorists have disliked the term because it obscures distinctions (for example between perspective and voice in literary narrative), and because its reliance upon a visual metaphor seems ill-suited to
the various ways in which a narrator or reader is positioned by and in
a literary text. But its reliance upon a visual model carries with it certain advantages so far as the analysis of film is concerned, and it has the
important virtue that, in contrast to the alternative term "perspective," it
perhaps draws more overt attention to the possibility of a link between
technical and ideological positioning. I find both terms useful; their purchase clearly overlaps, but "point of view" draws rather more attention
to this link between the technical and the ideological, a virtue that is of
paramount importance when one's concern is with ethical issues—with
how a text encourages its readers or viewers to situate themselves with
regard to matters of moral discernment and conduct. "Camera perspective," however, has a sharper and more specific meaning than does perspective in verbal fiction. There is always the possibility of doubt as to
where written words are coming from, and through. But (at least in the
days prior to digital image manipulation) a camera is a physical object
that, notwithstanding issues of focus, movement, zoom, and so on, can
only be in one place and pointing in one direction at one specific moment

of time. When discussing camera position I accordingly prefer the term "perspective."

Morality is intimately concerned with the point of view we adopt when considering events, and with how we act in response to what we learn as a result of adopting such a point of view. It is impossible to survey events and the issues they potentially raise from all perspectives; our very choice of one point of view over another may thus have a crucial moral dimension. In the non-narratological sense of the term, our point of view on things has thus a moral dimension, affecting such matters as empathy, involvement, and judgment. Action, in the sense of an involvement that will influence the course of those events that have triggered an ethical response, is not an option when we are reading a book or watching a film, but to the extent that imaginative involvement in art hones our powers of moral discrimination, the form of our metaphorical positioning with regard to what we read, or view in the cinema, has moral significance. A scene in a film involving the murder of a woman by a man can be experienced by a male viewer in very different ways. Is he led to feel the horror of the event and to experience vicariously the terror and suffering of the woman? Is he, alternatively, invited to experience the perhaps perverted pleasure attributed by the film to the murderer? Or is he perhaps encouraged not to empathize with either character, but to follow the scene in a more distanced and intellectual manner? Through whose eyes are we encouraged to witness events? These are crude alternatives, but even expressed in such an unsophisticated manner one can see that the choice of a technical point of view, a proffered narrative perspective, has major implications of a moral character. Where the camera is positioned bears upon the wider perspective from which we observe, and this perspective has moral implications.

Michael Powell's 1960 film *Peeping Tom* raises these issues in a stark way. A movie about a man who films women while murdering them and while they are faced with their own mirror reflection, but which seems more concerned with directing the audience's sympathy towards the murderer than towards his victims, could hardly be expected to escape censure, and indeed it seriously damaged its director's career and destroyed that of its writer. Publicity for the film unambiguously invited the audience to indulge a salacious voyeurism in watching the film: one publicity poster pictured the doomed first victim, Dora, staring at the camera/murderer, and viewer, accompanied by the text: "Can you see yourself in this picture? Can you see yourself facing the terror of a diabolical killer? Can you guess how you'd look? You'll live that kind of excitement, suspense, horror, when you watch 'Peeping Tom.'" The publicity text is clearly concerned with preparing viewers to adopt unusual points of view, but this particular formulation involves some very odd twists. Although it is ostensibly addressed to a victim ("you" are facing the killer), imagining how "you" would look instantly switches the point of view to that of the murderer—a switch that, in the actual film, the murderer's use of a mirror perhaps invites. The words "excitement, suspense, horror" also seem to offer the viewer the chance vicariously to experience emotions associated with both crazed killer and terrified victim. The one emotion that a woman facing imminent death can more or less be guaranteed *not* to be experiencing is "excitement," while the striking absence among those emotions listed is "pity." This curious shuffling of points of view leads me to suspect that the man looking at the poster is invited not so much to imagine what the threatened woman is experiencing, but rather to imagine the murderer imagining what the threatened woman is experiencing.

In the texts that I have considered so far, male violence towards women represents an extreme form of non-reciprocity, a logical conclusion perhaps to the process of treating another person not as human being to be interacted with but as object to be used. Such violence is there as a real threat in *The Scarlet Letter,* in which a possible punishment for adultery is execution, and is shockingly actualized in Sikes's bludgeoning of Nancy to death in *Oliver Twist.* In *Typee* and "In the Cage" violence lurks unactualized in the margins of the text, but in *Rear Window* and *Peeping Tom* not only is the violence horrifyingly actualized, it is also obsessively observed by characters in the diegesis and by the viewer.

There is a sense in which *Peeping Tom* is a title that suits Hitchcock's film better than it does Powell's. The Peeping Tom is, traditionally, one who attempts to watch while remaining hidden. In *Peeping Tom* the murderer wants his victims to know that their killing is being witnessed, and indeed takes this element a stage further by presenting them with an image of how they look to the man about to kill them. In a bizarre twist, then, murderer and victim share a view of the victim's final moments. In such a case the viewer is presented not so much with a lack of reciprocity based on the ignorance of the person spied upon that he or she is being observed, but more with an absence of human reciprocity based on an ignoring of the victim's human needs and rights. There is interaction between murderer and victim, but it is not an interaction based on the mutual recognition of and respect for the other. Even so, I believe this film is also concerned with exploring non-reciprocity, albeit of a different sort from those examined in previous chapters. In this film the power granted by concealed observation is replaced by the exercise of power in its most brutal and direct form. If the Peeping Tom looks but does not act, then at the time that the murders take place the killer is not a Peeping Tom—that rôle is reserved for the viewer.

In the film non-reciprocity takes a number of forms. At the most important level a succession of women are denied agency and free interaction in the most fundamental way, by being murdered. And while being murdered they are forced to observe not their murderer, but themselves. Furthermore, the fact that the killer films his murders allows him at a later stage to revert to a more conventional voyeuristic position. Watching the films he has made, he is now cut off from the living victim's gaze, but he is seeing what the dying woman saw—herself. And he is, moreover, doing exactly what the viewer in the movie theater is doing: looking at a film of a murder. As a result he observes his own acts of violence not as a perpetrator but as a spectator, positioning himself in relation to these acts in a manner disturbingly like the position of the member of the cinematic audience. There are, in addition, other scenes in which the murderer does act more like a voyeur: filming the police as they investigate one of his murders; hiding in the ceiling of a film set; spying on tenants in his house by means of concealed cameras.

There is all the world of difference between what Lisa Zunshine (2008) terms the "embodied transparency" of a look that allows another person to read off inner states from the expression of an individual that have been generated by "trying emotional situations" (66) not caused by the second person, and those expressions that have been prompted by the expression-reader him- or herself. In the passage from *Sense and Sensibility* that I discuss in the introduction, Elinor's skill at reading the embodied transparency of Colonel Brandon's expression allows her to penetrate to truths about the colonel's preferences that pre-exist her inquiry and that have nothing to do with her. In contrast, when Mark, in *Peeping Tom*, is reading the expressions on the faces of the women he has murdered which he has registered on film, he is reading a terror that he himself has created—observing a performance for which he has written the script. Unable to gain access to the interiority of a woman not threatened with violence and death, he reads off from the faces of those he is killing the inner states that he himself has ensured the women are experiencing. His voyeurism is (among other things) solipsistic and egocentric. He knows that the woman's look of agony, to cite Emily Dickinson again, is true: he himself has caused it.

The film's screenwriter, Leo Marks, referred to Mark, the murderer, as a voyeur, and he even has a psychologist in the film discuss Mark's "scoptophilia" [*sic*]. Marks, who had been a coding expert during the Second World War and who wrote a book about his wartime activities (see Marks 1998), was fascinated by the work of Sigmund Freud (who once visited his parents' bookshop in London's Charing Cross Road), and originally proposed to director Michael Powell that he make a "biopic" of Freud (Christie 1994, 85). According to Marks, "The greatest code of all was the unconscious, and Freud appeared to have deciphered it. Perhaps not accurately, altogether, but what an attempt he'd made!" (Marks 1998, xii). For Marks, "whilst psychotherapy is the study of the secrets a person keeps from him or herself, codes are the study of secrets nations keep from each other" (xii). The film and the published screenplay are full of references to "keys," and there is no doubt that the film does at times attempt to get the viewer to adopt the perspective of sympathetic analyst of the murderer in the film; his homicidal voyeurism is at one point explained through a conventionally Freudian view of the effects of childhood trauma.[1]

One unfortunate aspect of this is that readings of the film can easily slip from interpretation to decoding, uncovering precisely those Freudian meanings that screenwriter Leo Marks put into his script, in a circular cycle of transformations that ends up—like any good process of decoding—precisely where it started. In such a case, Mark, and Leo Marks, have in common that they encode in a film expressions on the face of a woman that they themselves have scripted. But to bring a critical and morally alert intelligence to bear on the film we need to go beyond decoding to interpretation. We must proceed beyond the clues to be found in the film's screenplay, and consider the complex and shifting positioning of the viewer by the whole range of filmic techniques of which the director makes use.

The Opening Scene

The opening of *Peeping Tom* (including the credits) is cinematically highly crafted. First we are presented with the names of the producers against a neutral background, and then with a realistic archery target colored like

---

1. Writing of Samuel Richardson's *Clarissa*, Laura Hinton (1999) notes that the scene of Clarissa's departure with Lovelace is full of references to a key, adding: "This view of Clarissa perceives her body as key*hole*. The key is Lovelace's phallic weapon in a masculinist economy, wielding his power over Clarissa's body. The keyhole is his fetishistic substitution, his voyeuristic medium" (64; emphasis in original).

a Royal Air Force roundel with concentric circles of red (outside), white, and blue (center), into which a number of arrows have already been fired. ("The Archers" was the name given to the production company formed by the collaboration of Michael Powell and Emeric Pressburger, so that this shot has iconic and extratextual-generic significance.) The brief sequence opens as a close-up with only the center of the target visible, but the camera then pans backwards to reveal the whole of it. The twang of a bowstring and the swish of the arrow then accompany the image of an arrow fired into the center of the bull. After a few seconds the words "A Michael Powell production" appear on screen bottom left. After a half fade we then cut suddenly to the image of a closed right eye. Almost immediately it jerks open, filling the screen as did the target. The pupil of the eye is blue, like the center of the target into which the arrow has been fired (a duplication that reinforces a sense of the eye's vulnerability, and that will be picked up in the subsequent murder scene when the killer's knife-tipped tripod leg is moved towards the open-eyed victim). The sudden opening of the eye suggests surprise or fear—a suggestion underwritten by a dramatic double chord on the film's soundtrack. The first chord is struck while the eye is closed; the second, which modulates upwards, after it has been opened. In spite of the expectations raised by the film's title, this brief opening shot strongly evokes a sense of the eye of the observed rather than that of the observing person. Something has shocked the possessor of this eye, perhaps something represented by or simultaneous to the first dramatic chord on the soundtrack: the eye is not narrowed in a manner suggestive of surveillance, but widened in the manner of a scared potential prey. It appears too to be the eye of a woman: something that suggests not a male sexual aggressor but his conventional victim. As Carol J. Clover (1992) aptly remarks, "In case we doubted which of the eye's two operations *Peeping Tom* wishes to privilege in its analysis of horror cinema, this opening minute spells it out: not the eye that kills, but the eye that is 'killed'" (181). At the same time, the opening sequence clearly implies a male beholder, at once the source, and perceiver, of the woman's terror. And this male beholder sees—exactly what the theater audience sees.

There is a sense in which this very brief scene (which, like the film's final shot, is never given intradiegetic anchoring or correlated with the rest of the film's action) serves as a sort of ideological establishing shot. Traditionally an establishing shot is, as Frank Beaver (1994) has it, "[a] shot that establishes the location of a film story or scene" (134). Here, however, it is not so much physical or geographical location as ideological positioning or point of view that is established. The viewer is put into the place of the male murderer facing his terrified female victim—much as the advertising blurb promised.

The eye appears to be looking into the camera, although it is hard to be absolutely sure; ascertaining eye focus and direction is hard when one is faced with one eye rather than two, and without being able to correlate eye movement with head inclination. Indeed, it is not easy quickly to establish whether it is the right or the left eye on the screen; in the cinema this may be impossible. The pupil also makes small flickering movements, suggesting that it is not fixedly focused upon one stationary object. So that although the eye does indeed seem to be focused upon the camera, it is not necessarily the case that the effect is, as Reynold Humphries (1995) claims, that of making spectators "suddenly finding themselves being looked at" (40); the primary effect is that of allowing us to observe the eye of a woman frightened by something that is both us (our narrative positioning) and not us (we are not the character in the film threatening the woman). It is worth asking why Powell focuses in on one eye rather than on a pair of eyes. The immediate answer is that this enables him to establish a parallel with the archery target, but more generally, however, this sense of not being sure whether we are being looked at helps to establish the ambiguity at the heart of voyeurism: the voyeur both wants to be invisible *and* to have his identity confirmed in interaction. Thematically, then, this opening sequence introduces an economy of gazing which is asymmetrical: the implied (and arguably inscribed) male viewer observes from a position of power, no threat is directed against this viewer, but the person observed expresses a fear which we assume he has inspired. At the same time, no recognition of the viewer's or our own humanity is vouchsafed by the observed eye. At its most extreme: we are invited to enjoy observing a fear from the perspective of an individual who both has and has not caused it: to the extent that we occupy the position of the murderer it is we of whom the victim is terrified; to the extent that we are sharing the murderer's viewpoint but not responsibility for his actions, it is someone else who has inspired the fear. But whatever the case, we are unable to alleviate the fear: we are as powerless as is the victim, while remaining safely insulated from the danger facing both her and the man threatening her.

This curious mix of power and impotence, a mix present in the dramatic scene of the first murder but given an extra twist in the subsequent scene in which the murderer watches the film of this murder, serves as a sort of motif that runs through the whole film. The murderer is both active agent and impotent victim of his own perversion—and, like the cinematic viewer, he keeps watching films depicting the murder of women.

Following the opening credits the film moves directly into the first dramatic scene in which Mark encounters, then murders, the prostitute Dora. After a brief shot showing an amateur movie camera concealed at chest level behind the duffel coat of the (as yet anonymous) Mark, we switch to something akin to subjective camera as we follow what we assume is being filmed by this intradiegetic camera. I say "something akin to," because we see the cross of the viewfinder imposed on what is in front of us, so that although Dora in one sense appears to look at, and talk to, "us," "we" are looking through the viewfinder of a camera she has not as yet seen, and through which no one is actually looking. The effect is thus like subjective camera but with a weird distancing effect. The viewer cannot sink into the fantasy that he or she is in the world of the film, being addressed by Dora, because we are presumably seeing something that the still anonymous Mark is not seeing in quite the same form, as we know that he is not looking through the camera's viewfinder. This particular ciné camera has to be held at eye level for the viewfinder to be used; Mark cannot be looking through the viewfinder at the start of the encounter, otherwise Dora would notice this and not be shocked later on when she becomes aware of the camera. Thus although Kaja Silverman (1988) is correct to state that Mark's relation with the women he murders is mediated by his camera, she is in error when she states that "from the moment that he first sights one of them as a bridge to phallic identification, he never looks away from the view finder" (33)—both with regard to Dora and, subsequently, to his later victims Vivian and Milly.

Once the two have reached her bedroom and she has started undressing, Dora does notice what Mark is doing after he has turned to his bag, retrieved something, and has started to project a light onto her face, and we may be expected to assume that at this point he is holding the camera up to his face. It is worth stressing that prior to Dora's awareness of what Mark is doing, this opening sequence places the viewer in what, were the scene to be treated as "realistic," is a disturbingly double (or ambiguous) relationship to what is displayed. Our point of view is in one sense human: Dora appears to be looking at and talking to Mark/ us, but "we" are represented by a lens of which she is at least initially unaware. In another sense, however, our point of view is non-human (we are seeing through a viewfinder through which no one is looking, so that when Mark projects his film later on we see the captured events for the second time, but he sees them *in this form* for the first time). Discussing *Rear Window*, I noted how many commentators on the film personified the camera. In parts of *Peeping Tom*, Mark's intradiegetic ciné camera is indeed "seeing" things that, at the moments the film is being exposed, no human being is observing from that perspective. Later on in the film we do have shots which appear to show what is visible to Mark through the ciné-camera viewfinder, but they represent what Mark is actually seeing; at no other point in the film following this opening sequence is the camera producing a record of "what happened but no one saw in quite this way at the time." This opening, then, sets a particular distantal tone: we follow Mark's watching, but without feeling a close identification with him. The cinematic viewer is not placed fully in the position of the murderer: it is as if he or she is a camera, a recording device with no human feelings, thoughts, or ethical responsibilities.

This sense of seeing from someone's perspective without seeing through their eyes is one of the experiences that makes this opening sequence so very disturbing. On the one hand it invites the use of words such as "vicarious" and "voyeurism," but on the other hand it does have a defamiliarizing effect, forcing the viewer to, as it were, *see* the voyeur while *being* the voyeur. Dora's bemusement followed by terror is offered up to "us" to witness and experience, and "we" indeed appear to be addressed as the source of her fear, but at the same time "we" are not Mark, so we are not accountable for what she suffers. We are offered the chance to be surrogates for Mark, without responsibility for what he does. "We," in fact, are not even a person (Mark) at the start of the scene; we are only a camera, filming with no one looking through the viewfinder (it is again tempting to compare the effect to the effect induced by the apparently searching camera at the start of *Rear Window*, especially as both sequences come right at the start of their respective films). What then this opening sequence does, among other things, is to combine and confuse points of view so as to present the viewer with the voyeuristic experience in its impossibly purest form. We see without being there, in a manner that recalls Chatman's (1990) citation of Ann Banfield's claim that film technology "allow[s] the viewing subject to see, to witness, places where he is not, indeed, where no subject is present" (see p. 146). We are both the murderer causing Dora to react in terror and also the empty space behind the viewfinder. We are powerful and feared, and absent and impotent.

Reynold Humphries (1995) has interpreted this opening sequence in a slightly different manner. He has argued that because Dora looks the viewer straight in the eye (in his words, "the woman's look is on the same level as that of the camera, whereas we know from Shot 3 that the camera is hidden on the level of the man's waist," and because Dora is unaware of the existence of the camera, "only one interpretation is possible: it is the camera of *Peeping Tom* and not the man's camera which allows this exchange of looks, which is thus an exchange between spectator and prostitute" (44). But if the camera is, as he suggests, "the camera of *Peeping Tom* and not the man's," then why do we see the cross of the viewfinder imposed upon the screen? And why, when Mark replays his film, is Dora looking straight at him/us as she does while Mark is filming? I agree with Humphries that this scene presents the viewer with an interpretative problem: on a realistic level, it provides us with contradictory information. For if Dora were unaware of Mark's camera, she would not be looking at it (i.e., at Mark's chest or stomach rather than at his eyes). But this is not the only such contradiction in *Peeping Tom:* as I will argue below, another one is when we appear to be watching Vivian seconds before her death through Mark's camera, at which she is looking, although this time we do *not* see the viewfinder cross even though what we see during this second murder sequence shares an identical camera point of view with Mark's later projection of his filming of this scene.

Realism and the Conventional

"Contradictions" such as this have of course to be understood at least in part in terms of filmic conventions. When we move from shot to reverse shot of a dialogue between two people we can work out that the scene must have been shot twice, because we never catch sight of the "other" camera. But this is not how we read, or are meant to read, such a scene. Similarly, when Dora looks us in the eye, in a frame that includes a viewfinder cross, I suspect that few spectators respond "That's impossible!" How viewers read this scene can only be guessed at on the basis of one's own responses, but I surmise that most first-time viewers (who while watching the film have little time to ponder the issues I have mentioned) feel that they are being given Mark's experience of the scene through its filmed record, while retaining a shadowy and disturbing-defamiliarizing half-sense that it *is* impossible. After all, we are looking from a concealed viewpoint but we are simultaneously being acknowledged, interacted with. And it is this contradiction that is precisely the impossible wish of the voyeur: to combine invisibility, invulnerability, and power with human interaction. It is important for director Powell to place the viewer in the situation of experiencing being looked at by Dora, placed in a position in which we appear to be recognized by Dora and sharing what we assume to be *Mark's* rather than *his camera's* viewpoint, while at the same time enjoying the security and voyeuristic privilege of being given access to what the eye of a hidden camera "sees." The important point, I think, is that the film offers members of the cinema audience exactly that illusory and unattainable combination of perspectives for which the Peeping Tom yearns: on the one hand anonymity and symbolic power through undetected observation, and on the other hand interaction and existential recognition. The offer is made only to be rescinded, however. It is clearly revoked later on during Mark's screening of the film, when we are placed behind Mark's back, watching the film (remember that when the film was first shown almost everyone in the cinema will have had someone behind him/her, able to watch *them* watch Mark watch the film).

In the earlier of his two articles on *Peeping Tom,* Reynold Humphries (1979) demonstrates that the unacknowledged conventions that guide and construct our viewing are defamiliarized and foregrounded at crucial points in the film. One particularly important insight in Humphries's account of the film involves a brief moment in the opening sequence of the film when Mark approaches so close to the extradiegetic camera— what Humphries refers to as "the camera of the *énonciation*"—that his screen image is blurred. As was the case with *Rear Window,* when the extradiegetic camera seems to enter the diegesis, then this has ontological significance: the blurring of the image is also a blurring of the boundary between the extra- and the intradiegetic worlds. This blurring of Mark's image draws the attention of the viewer to the existence of an extradiegetic camera, and this, along with the sense that we the viewer can now be looked at by Mark's intradiegetic camera, unsettles our sense of voyeuristic invulnerability. What we see is no longer the result of the observation of an invisible eye, but of the operation of a very material camera, one subject to the laws of optics. Because our point of view is thereby physically anchored in the film's diegesis, it can be observed, and as Humphries notes, we "are now looked at by Mark's camera, i.e., our look is no longer safe, we are the object of a look and our unity is disrupted" (194). This unsettling of our sense of an invulnerable, invisible extradiegetic perspective continues, according to Humphries, throughout the film. In the scene during which Mark films the police as they take away Dora's body, for example, Humphries shows how the cutting between intra- and extradiegetic cameras again makes the viewer aware of the existence of the normally "invisible" camera. As I will argue below, such disorienting and defamiliarizing effects are compounded in the long scene with Vivian, where we are shown an additional intradiegetic camera as well as Mark's. Humphries's conclusion contains some useful summarizing points:

> Thus the film achieves three things here: it reinforces identification (Mark's point of view = the spectator's point of view) and undermines it on another level (Mark's point of view ≠ that of the director of *Peeping Tom*). Given these two elements, a third comes into play: when the spectator does not see via the camera of the *énoncé*, he/she cannot but see via that of the *énonciation*. There are therefore two cameras involved, but they are not filming the same thing all the time and one "depends" on the other. (195)

Building on these points, I would suggest that by undermining the audience's voyeuristic activity the film draws attention to the contradiction at the heart of voyeurism itself: the simultaneous desire for both distance and involvement, for invisibility and human recognition and acknowledgment. Moreover, presenting the cinematic viewer with such contradictions also highlights ontological issues. As an individual member of the cinematic audience (the equivalent of Peter Rabinowitz's "actual reader"), we observe events over an ontological gap: distanced, apart, watching that which is not real. As viewer (the equivalent of Rabinowitz's and Phelan's "member of the narrative audience"—see p. 10) we watch characters who belong to our world, for whom we feel those emotions that in the real, extradiegetic world prompt to involvement and action. In one of these worlds there are cameras recording events; in the other, there are not.

Reynold Humphries (1979) draws attention to another unsettling effect during the screening of Mark's father's film, when in the film the young Mark turns his newly acquired movie camera (the gift bestowed by paternal authority, with which he will later film his murders) on the movie camera of the father, and thus on Mark's tenant Helen (who is watching the projected film), and on us, too.

> For her, it is too much and she asks Mark to stop the film. Her voyeuristic status is even more clearly revealed to her than at the point where he started to set up his camera to film her. Now the screen is doing what it

is not meant to do: it is looking back at her/us, returning her/our look, showing itself to be the Real that is beyond our grasp, outside the realm and reach of desire, what we thought we could grasp in reality and quite unproblematically; that imaginary unity into which we re-inscribe ourselves anew with every film-going experience is split apart. (198)

The "Real that is beyond our grasp" summarizes neatly what both the sexual voyeur and the viewer as member of the narrative audience observe: something real but untouchable. In both cases the relation between the observer and the observed is non-reciprocal.

The viewer's complex and contradictory experiences during the film's opening sequence are founded upon assumptions that have to be established very rapidly as this opening scene develops. The shot showing the camera inside Mark's duffel coat is not included in Leo Marks's screenplay, and had the film not included this shot then the viewer might be led to assume that Mark is filming while looking through the viewfinder. Moreover, the control of the camera suggests the guiding hand of someone able to see what he is filming—especially in its final zoom forward closer and closer to Dora's face, a movement which even on first viewing we may assume accompanies some sort of threat. (The final shot in the "live" scene is of Dora's face filling the screen with her eyes almost shut in terror, but when we watch the same events in Mark's replayed film immediately afterwards, the final shot is of Dora's open, screaming mouth, which this time fills both Mark's and our screen: her eyes are not to be seen.)

As I have already pointed out, there is a point at which realistic assumptions cease to be appropriate to this sort of analysis. In "real life" a camera with no eye at the viewfinder just could not film as accurately as does the camera in this scene. However, to object to the film on this basis would be to ignore the way in which cinematic conventions guide and govern the way in which the audience reads this scene. The typical viewer responds to this scene, one suspects, just as he or she was presumably intended to: vicariously sharing Mark's experience of first meeting the unsuspecting Dora and then observing exactly what *she* is observing: her terror as she is murdered (a terror that seems aimed at and caused by the observer)—while also knowing that Mark is capturing this sequence of events on film. Nevertheless, the contradiction that exists at the diegetic level in this scene (Dora is—impossibly—looking at her own reflected image, at the camera, and at Mark's face) is crucial to the film's exploration of the experience of voyeurism, for this impossible blending of the unseen camera and the seen eyes represents the impossible dream of the voyeur: to watch while hidden and unperceived and at the same time to be interacted with, to exchange intimate and mutual recognition of self with another. Most important: this uniting of mutually exclusive points of view has a defamiliarizing effect on the audience, and this, it seems to me, is of *ethical* significance.

Up to the final few moments in this scene (that is, those following Mark's turning away from Dora and then turning back as he plays a light on her face), Dora certainly seems unaware of the camera, so that the effect of the scene is partly that of making the viewer a concealed observer of *both* Mark and Dora, an effect confirmed when we immediately proceed to a scene subsequent to the murder in which we are placed behind Mark, watching him watch Dora's projected image on screen. At the same time, because we know that no one within the film's diegesis can be seeing, or could see, exactly what we are seeing (Dora *and* the viewfinder cross) because the viewfinder cross would not be visible when the film is projected, there is a strong sense of *staging* in this scene, one buttressed by the urgency of the soundtrack music, about which more will be said below. This is a *performance* arranged for us; as with the raised blinds during the credits of *Rear Window* its artifice reminds us, makes us conscious of the fact, that we are watching a film, not just in the sense that in the film's diegesis we are observing a process of filming, but more importantly that what we see and hear is being controlled and metaphorically orchestrated for us. We are invited to enjoy being a camera through which no one is looking, we are invited to sink into the safe and surrogate fantasy world of the cinema, while having these experiences defamiliarized, deconstructed, laid bare. We are invited, in short, to luxuriate *in* the sensation of being a Peeping Tom while looking *at* the hopelessly impossible desire of the Peeping Tom. The film gives and the film takes away—but we retain a knowledge and understanding of what we have been both granted and deprived of.

Reynold Humphries (1995) has also drawn attention to the fact that the projected film of Dora's murder which Mark is shown watching has been edited down from the film we see being made as we look at a screen containing the cross of Mark's viewfinder. As he notes, although the film lingers on the trash can, it does not include a shot of the film packet being discarded, and the sequence on the stairs where he and we meet with a second woman who is coming down the stairs is also missing. Humphries argues that it cannot be Mark who is to be taken as the film's editor:

If he removes the sequence on the stairs, why keep the shot of the bin? As I have insisted, the shot remains held for several seconds, despite the fact that we do not see the box of film. There is no reason for this on the level of the *énoncé,* but once we foreground the role of editing as part of the *énonciation,* a coherent explanation is possible. (48)

Humphries's "coherent explanation" falls into two parts: first, that the experience of being treated as an object of contempt by the woman descending the stairs is removed for both Mark and for us, and second, that "it is redundant so far as the story goes: reaching the victim's bedroom and killing her are paramount. The spectator's desire to get to the essential thus has alarming repercussions for his/her viewing position(s)" (48).

The cinema viewer is unlikely to be aware of these cuts on initial viewing, and is perhaps not intended ever to be so: in a personal communication to me, Reynold Humphries has suggested that we are dealing here with the working of unconscious coding: as a result of eliminating certain materials between the filmed and the projected scene, "the film brilliantly gives the spectators what they want and what they are there for: to see the gory details and to *enjoy* them." Thus the cuts are important not in spite of the fact that they may not be noticed by the audience, but precisely *because of this fact:* they focus on Mark's and the (male) spectator's desire. The speeding up of the sequence as projected by Mark helps to emphasize an element of sexual excitement, clearly displayed in him as he watches the film. And as has been noted, the projected film gives us both less (the cuts) and more (the final shot of Dora's screaming mouth) than the "live" sequence. As to whether it is reasonable to assume that Mark may have edited his own film, I think my primary response is that, like the question of how many children Lady Macbeth has, this is not something the viewer is encouraged to think about, as he or she is unlikely to notice the cuts. (Which does not, it should be stressed, mean that he or she is unaffected by them.) Nevertheless, the lingering shot of the trash can does have thematic force, and Mark's interest in it could be given an intradiegetic explanation.

Comparison of Powell's film with Leo Marks's screenplay is interesting at this point. In the screenplay the woman descending the stairs (described by Humphries as a prostitute) is presented as follows:

A Woman with hair like a two-toned car comes down the stairs, winks at

> *Dora—looks at us for a moment with great curiosity . . . winks . . . then*
> *passes out of camera.* (Marks 1998, 7)

The description actually gives greater backing to Humphries's description of her as a prostitute than does the filmed sequence, in which the viewer is likely to take her expression of distasteful impatience to extend to Dora's profession and her assumed client. Again in the screenplay, the cuts in the sequence are achieved by the screen's being obscured by Mark's head, but importantly the sequence of the woman on the stairs *is* included. Powell's compression of the sequence creates a greater urgency and suggestion of sexual excitement, and Humphries is certainly right that the exclusion of the sequence on the stairs—whether as a result of the editing activity of the intradiegetic Mark or of the extradiegetic Powell—has the effect of removing those elements which are unconnected to the murderous sexual chase and also the descending woman's contemptuous gesture, a defamiliarizing challenge to Mark's camera which threatens both his and our voyeuristic enjoyment. Before moving on from this quotation, it is worth noting Marks's use of "us" rather than "Mark."

Watching Watching

A foregrounded playing around with reflexive processes of double observation recurs throughout *Peeping Tom*. Mark's father films the young Mark watching a couple embrace (and the young Mark is played by director Michael Powell's own son—so that the representation of a father filming his son involves . . . a father filming his son); Mark wishes to film Helen watching a film of himself ("wanted to photograph you watching"); Mark explains to Vivian that he is "photographing you photographing me"; Mark is watched by a detective as he himself observes Helen leaving work; and as he arranges his own death he goes so far as to personify the cameras he has set to film his own death: "Watch them Helen, watch them say good-bye!"[2] The repetitive pattern cannot but remind the viewer that he or she is *also* watching someone watching someone. Kaja Silverman (1988) has suggested that on a general level, "obsessive self-referentiality works to uncover the pathology of male subjectivity," and that

---

2. As the film diverges significantly from the published screenplay, citations of film dialogue are based on my own transcription from a video version.

Peeping Tom gives new emphasis to the concept of reflexivity. Not only does it foreground the workings of the apparatus, and the place given there to voyeurism and sadism, but its remarkable structure suggests that dominant cinema is indeed a mirror with a delayed reflection. It deploys the film-within-a-film trope with a new and radical effect, making it into a device for dramatizing the displacement of lack from the male to the female subject. (32)

Certainly those scenes of the film which take place in a fictionalized film studio during the production of the intradiegetic *The Walls Are Closing In* have a strongly reflexive quality, allowing us to observe the intradiegetic director Arthur Baden watching the scene that he is creating for an intradiegetic audience, a scene that composes part of another scene which is what the actual director Michael Powell has created for us. Like the players' scene in *Hamlet* the reflexive quality of such strategies of duplication has a sort of Brechtian alienation effect, causing us to be aware of the artifices of the genre. As a result, it is possible to isolate two opposing forces in *Peeping Tom*. On the one hand, we have filmic conventions that from the first shot of the jerked-open eye onwards encourage us to situate ourselves with regard to the depicted action as uninvolved observers, allowing and even encouraging us to slip into the rôle of voyeur. But on the other hand, we also have a set of self-reflexive elements that make us conscious of our own voyeuristic activity and of the existential impoverishment and potential violence it carries with it, and that make it impossible to sink into this rôle undisturbed by sensations of guilt and inadequacy.

The challenges to the audience's voyeuristic enjoyment in *Peeping Tom* are generally indirect and implicit rather than overt and explicit. If for example we compare the film's final scene with that of Alfred Hitchcock's *Rear Window*, we can note that although there are clear parallels between the two scenes—the main male character's space is invaded, a camera is used as or mistaken for a weapon—the manner in which the viewer is situated with regard to the diegesis in the two works is quite different. In *Rear Window* it is as if murderer Lars Thorwald is threatening us, invading the space (first visually, then physically) which stands for the cinema auditorium. When the door bursts open, the viewer is facing it from Jeff's perspective; Thorwald is bearing down upon *me*. When the door is battered down by the police in *Peeping Tom*, the camera is filming from one side, allowing us to watch Helen and Mark as the police rush over to them. We witness the scene neither from the perspective of the police nor from that of either Mark Lewis or Helen. The camera at this point is like the teacher of languages in the confession scene in Joseph Conrad's *Under Western Eyes:* an unobserved observer. But if the viewer of *Peeping Tom* is repetitively situated as unobserved observer, he or she is also repetitively reminded of the fact. Thus at the very end of the film, the shot of the blank screen-within-a-screen, a shot which comes just prior to the cinema audience being faced with an actual rather than a depicted blank screen, causes us to recognize parallels between our situation in the cinema and Mark's situation in the diegesis. Time and time again we are granted the experience of being a voyeur, only to be forced to observe our own observing. And "being observed" is irreconcilable with "being a voyeur."

The scene in the film studio leading up to Vivian's murder is also worthy of note in this respect. If we follow this scene from Vivian's attending to her makeup alone in the dressing room, we can follow a series of shifts of perspectival positioning. In the dressing room the soundtrack is strictly intradiegetic: natural noises, voices from outside, and the music which ostensibly emanates from Vivian's portable tape recorder. The camera pans and cuts to follow Vivian as she hides from the security guard, then slips out along the corridor and into the studio, but our attention is focused on her and not on camera technique, which is such as to render itself invisible to the non-technical spectator. Then as she enters the studio the camera cuts from a close, sideways-on angle, to a high shot down. In retrospect (and perhaps in prospect, as hypothesis) we may see this particular shot as representative of Mark's viewpoint, as he eventually appears high up on a hoist. But there is no sense at this point that camera angle and movement, or cutting, have any intradiegetic anchoring; technique does not draw attention to itself, but encourages the viewer to concentrate on Vivian and her situation from a spectatorial and uninvolved position. We are encouraged to adopt the familiar role of cinematic viewer/voyeur. As Vivian moves into what appears to be an inner studio, she starts to call Mark's name. He does not answer, but arc lamps are switched on, one at a time. As each lamp is switched on, a jarring chord on the soundtrack—clearly this time *extra*diegetic—signals "surprise," and Vivian looks appropriately shocked and disturbed. The conventional element in this use of the soundtrack to accentuate suspense represents a significant transition here, from a soundtrack that is ostensibly intradiegetic to one that is clearly extradiegetic (the chords have no realistic source within the world of the scene). It is at this point that our sense of staging is strongest: the film at this point conforms to the conventions of a thriller, in which sudden and unexpected sounds and images cause the viewer to duplicate that tension and fear that is being experienced by one or more characters. The sudden chords may of course be conventionally interpreted as transpositions or displacements of the successive shocks experienced by Vivian as one by one the lights are illuminated, but they also serve as strong generic markers, causing the viewer to entertain expectations appropriate to the genre suspense/horror film. And of course in shocking the audience, they evoke empathy between viewer and Vivian: we experience (admittedly in a reduced and safe form) what she is portrayed as experiencing.

Sound and Diegesis

Familiar cinematic conventions work so as to cause the viewer automatically and unconsciously to interpret particular aspects of a film soundtrack as overt markers of the subjective experience of characters, and indeed there is one fine example of this elsewhere in the film. When Mark is watching the film of Vivian's murder, the urgent background piano music already associated with the building up in him of murderous sexual and voyeuristic excitement is played, but when he hears a knock on the door (it is Helen) and switches off his projector, the music stops abruptly at exactly the moment that he switches off the film, as it does, too, in a later sequence when Helen makes Mark switch off the projector. It seems clear at this point that this music is the objective correlative of sexual excitement in Mark, one which displays rather than comments upon his subjective state. Thus the viewer's understanding of the significance of this music develops in the course of the film; it is first heard during the film's main credits, which are run after the scene in which Dora is murdered, beginning as Mark watches the film that he took of Dora. The sense of urgency, crescendo, and climax in the music, accompanying Mark as he watches the film (as Reynold Humphries [1995] points out, "The fact that the man rises from his chair as the woman undresses and sinks back into it as she dies is an obvious moment of *jouissance*" [49]), and the strong culminating chords suggestive of closure as the film ends on Dora's open mouth, all encourage the viewer to read the music as a depiction or "objective correlative" of Mark's increasing sexual excitement and climax. Then when Helen first enters Mark's darkroom, and she asks to see the film that he has just been watching, Mark picks up the film which, the viewer knows, shows the police removing Dora's body, and the recognizable piano music starts in a slower, more reflective form, but stops when Mark on second thoughts returns the film to the cupboard. On its first use in the film, then, this piano music is given a double identity: accompanying the credits and so extradiegetic, yet associated with Mark's voyeuristic replaying of his film and so betokening his perverted sexual excitement, and thus in a sense interpreted by the viewer as member of narrative audience as intradiegetic. Following this point, as scene follows scene, and especially after the music stops when Mark switches off the projector subsequent to hearing the knocking on the door, the music increasingly tends to be read more as a marker of Mark's dark subjectivity and less and less as extradiegetic accompaniment.

To a much more limited extent this can also be said of the dramatic chords that accompany the switching on of the arc lights in the deserted film studio—they represent subjective shock experiences in Vivian while at the same jolting us and thus allowing us to empathize with her. But their more familiar and conventional nature also brings a greater sense of staging to the scene, more of a sense of an extradiegetic controlling organization, which is not there in the scene in which Mark is watching his film. The question of who is responsible for the staging is again complex. As each chord accompanies Mark's switching on of the arc lamps, this is a scene that he is staging. But as the chords are clearly not intradiegetic, the staging must be attributed to the film director. Once again, then, we have a sense of ontological blurring or instability, as the chords oscillate between the intradiegetic and the extradiegetic.

The scene in which Mark shows Helen his father's films of himself falls in between these examples: the piano music comes to a sudden dramatic climax on two occasions: first when the lizard is dropped on the young Mark's bed, and second when the adult Mark shocks Helen by revealing that the woman whose arms are seen in his film is his (dead) mother.[3] In both cases it can be argued that although the mood-changes signaled by the music represent an objectification of subjective experiences, first those of the young Mark and subsequently those of Helen, the music has more of an extradiegetic feel to it than it does in the earlier scene where Mark is watching his film alone. The music is repeated again while pictures of the development of the film of Vivian's murder are

---

3. Mark's gift of an "insect" brooch to Helen seems intended to replay this horrifying scene in a revised form that renders it safe and thus undoes the previous trauma. The brooch is, however, shaped not like a lizard (as Kaja Silverman [1988, 35] claims) but like a dragonfly.

being shown—pictures which are cut to, and imposed as double expo-
sures upon, the pictures of Mark and Helen at the restaurant. And the
music is again repeated when Mark projects this film depicting Vivian's
horrified face in the presence of the blind Mrs. Stephens (leading to one
of the most striking visual effects of the film when that part of the frame
projected onto Mrs. Stephens's body produces an image which resembles
a skull, the clearest point at which the association between representation and death is made).

Blindness and Insight

Linda Williams (1984) has noted that "many of the 'good girl' heroines of
the silent screen were often figuratively, or even literally, blind," and she
suggests that one of the ways that female blindness functions in classical
narrative cinema is to allow "the look of the male protagonist to regard
the woman at the requisite safe distance necessary to the voyeur's pleasure, with no danger that she will return that look and in so doing express
desires of her own" (83). In Chaplin's *City Lights* (1931), for example,
the Tramp approaches the flower girl when she is blind, but he attempts
to avoid contact at the end of the film when she has regained her sight.
Blindness, in other words, appears to offer a straightforwardly literal
barrier to full interpersonal reciprocity. The tramp is *safe* with the blind
flower girl, who cannot see that he is a tramp, and this security mirrors
and represents the safety of the viewer in the movie theater, who cannot
be seen by the characters on the screen.

Mark does not kill Mrs. Stephens, although early on in this scene it
appears that he is preparing to do so, and we are led to surmise that this is
because he cannot see fear in her eyes, nor can he reflect her own terrified
eyes back for her to witness. Thus although Williams's point seems essentially correct, Mark's need for his victims to see is partly a need for them
to be able to perceive the threat to their life and to exhibit fear, and partly
a perverted recognition of the fact that their inability to see him would
(and does) ignore his existential needs and rights just as he ignores theirs.
Generally speaking one would assume that a blind woman would represent an ideal target for a Peeping Tom, allowing more extensive unobserved observation than in the case of a sighted individual. The fact that
Mark's psychosis cannot operate with the blind Mrs. Stephens suggests
that he is portrayed as more than simple voyeur.

Cameras and Points of View

In the climactic scene immediately prior to Vivian's murder there are at least three anchor points which serve to determine the viewer's perspective. First there is (i) the extradiegetic camera (actually camera*s*, as we cut between different angles), filming first Vivian and then Mark and Vivian, ostensibly invisible to them and representing no intradiegetic presence. Next there is (ii) the studio camera through which Vivian looks, and through which on occasion the viewer may imagine that he or she is looking. And then there is (iii) Mark's own movie camera, the one with which he actually films Vivian's death. In the closing seconds of this scene it is not always clear whether we are being given the information recorded by (i) or by (iii). Shots of Mark filming are clearly from the perspective of (i), as we see his own camera from an angle incompatible with that of the observed studio camera. And early shots of Mark filming Vivian are clearly seen "through" the lens of his own camera, as we see the cross of the viewfinder. But later head-on shots of Vivian give the impression of being seen from the perspective of Mark's camera, although Vivian is actually looking (I think) very slightly to our left. As the knife-ended tripod leg is held in Mark's left hand, we may assume that it is this that fixes her gaze, and that this is why her eyes are not pointed directly at the lens. We can indeed see the shadowy tripod leg along with what we may later assume is the attached mirror, the "something else" mentioned by Mark, although side-on shots of the blade-carrying leg do not reveal it. But, paradoxically, although we do not see the cross of his camera viewfinder as we have earlier in this scene and in the film's opening sequence, our perspective seems so close to that of Mark's own camera that although logically the perspective would seem to be (i), the viewer does, I think, assume that it is actually (iii). Although the cross disappears from the viewfinder in this reading, Mark's chalking of a cross on the floor to mark the spot on which he wishes Vivian to stand may be taken as some sort of wish to transfer that reality that he observes through his viewfinder onto the world outside the camera. When she does stand in the allotted space, Vivian obscures the cross (which is proleptically the cross marking her grave); her presence thus deletes the reminder that we are seeing through Mark's viewfinder, so that the subsequent absence of the viewfinder cross seems oddly appropriate. This invisibility of the viewfinder cross captures Mark's subjective experience of the scene: for him the camera is invisible, just as it will be when he views the film he is taking. Also important is the fact that in the closing seconds of this scene, after Mark has said "There's something else," the soundtrack restarts the "dramatic" music, warning the audience of the impending climax and increasing our sense both of Mark's growing sexual excitement and of the managed nature of the presentation.

It is hard to be definite concerning the precise results of such a mix of elements, but my own response to the film suggests to me that during this scene the viewer as member of narrative audience never simply feels either that they are seeing and experiencing from the perspective of one of the characters, or alternatively that the scene has been staged for them. Generally the sense is of a transparent narrative that allows the viewer to observe from a neutral and extradiegetic position, but this sense is on occasion colored by an impression of staging which is undoubtedly called up by the dramatic chords, the extradiegetic music, and the final climax shot of a blood-red arc light. Only at the close of the scene is the viewer placed precisely in Mark's position, looking with him through his viewfinder. My assumption is that the absence of the viewfinder cross is something of which the audience is unaware given the dramatic nature of the sequence, and Powell may indeed have chosen to omit the cross so as to increase the dramatic impact of the scene, so as to focus on Vivian-being-frightened-of-Mark rather than on Vivian-being-filmed. It is also the case that the film's relentless and repetitive portrayal of processes of reflexivity produces a constant sense of multiple meaning that is in tension with our experience of being an uninvolved observer of a realistic sequence of actions.

All of these elements *prior* to the final shots of the terrorized Vivian release strong generic expectations that dilute the viewer's sense of a realistic scene and thus cause viewers to distance themselves from the characters and lessen their involvement with the fate of these characters. Another way of expressing this would be to suggest that these elements heighten the voyeuristic element in our experience of the scene, because the generic markers increase our sense that "it is only a film." The scene also invites voyeuristic engagement because our looking does not mirror anyone's looking in the film's diegesis—which would counter our sense of unobserved watching and give us a greater sense of vulnerability—but neither do we feel the strong presence of an organizing intelligence with a design upon us, something that again would reduce that sense of privacy and secrecy central to the experience of the voyeur. (The organizing intelligence is of course there, but because it is dissolved into the fluid movements of the extradiegetic camera to which our attention is not drawn, its conventional nature renders it invisible to us.) However, I am very conscious that the actual viewer's gender cannot be ignored at this point: there is no ideal and asexual "viewer as member of the narrative audience" in such cases; there are men and women who doubtless move in and out of the diegesis in different ways.

At the end of the scene the viewer's placement changes: the viewer is in the scene, being looked at and responded to by Vivian, under pressure to fill the persona of Mark. How the viewer responds to this pressure will doubtless vary according to—among other things—the actual viewer's gender. Such an oscillation between invisibility and non-existence, on the one hand, and object of fear, on the other, brings together the two aspects of the Peeping Tom's desire: to be safe, invulnerable, private, and to be responded to. The fact that these two aspects are irreconcilable is *not* foregrounded to the same extent at this point; indeed, because the viewer is allowed to experience them successively rather than simultaneously, it is concealed.

In this scene, then, the film presents the (male) viewer with a double sense of invading a privacy. We are first positioned to invade Vivian's privacy by voyeuristically observing her when she believes herself to be alone, and then we both watch and partake in Mark's invading of Vivian's privacy in the most brutal manner possible when he kills her.

Defamiliarizing Voyeurism

I propose, then, that *Peeping Tom* is filmed in such a way as to encourage especially the male viewer to become more aware of his voyeuristic tendencies in some scenes, and less in others. But even in scenes in which the defamiliarizing process is less apparent, the *cumulative* force of the shifts of point of view is generally destabilizing. The viewer is made a self-conscious voyeur while watching a film about a self-conscious voyeur, and thus experiences the paradoxical sense of being both hidden and stripped bare to the gaze of others.

Such reflexive parallels might be felt to underwrite the attempt to garner sympathy for Mark Lewis, especially as little attempt is made to evoke the viewer's compassion for either Dora or Milly—although some such attempt is perhaps made in the case of Vivian. Interviewed by Chris Rodley, screenwriter Leo Marks (1998) denied that the similarity between his name and that of Mark Lewis was deliberate or significant. From a man who used to set newspaper crosswords, this claim is not wholly convincing, especially as the name Marks gives the director *in* the film—Arthur Baden—is obviously an in-joke, suggesting a link with the director *of* the film Michael Powell through the name of founder of the Boy Scout movement Lord Baden-Powell. Marks (1998) does, however, link Mark to the cinema viewer in a manner that is reminiscent of Hitchcock's claim that we are all Peeping Toms (see p. 151):

> I believe that the cinema makes voyeurs of us all. And I wanted to write a study of one particular voyeur, from a little boy to the time that he died. I wanted to show, visually, what made him a Peeping Tom, and scatter throughout that as many visual clues as I could find, in the hope that the audience would want to discover the clear text of this man's code for themselves. (xx)

The comment seems oddly divided against itself. In the cinema, we are all voyeurs. But there is something special about Mark Lewis's upbringing that has turned him (but not most people) into a Peeping Tom. Being a voyeur is an experience that all film viewers have, but it is also an experience that needs a very special set of circumstances in one's upbringing to take place. The film will help viewers to understand why Mark has become a voyeur, but although it will impart this knowledge to viewers who at the time are themselves behaving as voyeurs, Marks does not here suggest that in watching a film about a voyeur we will all become aware of our own voyeurism as film viewers. In like manner, I feel that *Peeping Tom* is a film divided against itself. Aspects of the film are such as to encourage the viewer to relate his or her own cinematic watching to Mark Lewis's scopophilia, but other aspects discourage such a drawing of parallels. If the viewer recognizes her- or (especially) himself in Mark Lewis, then coming to terms with this shared experience of being a voyeur should mean that understanding Mark Lewis will cause the audience to have greater insight into its own voyeuristic impulses and, conversely, that confronting the voyeuristic element in our cinematic experience will help us to understand—and sympathize with—Mark Lewis. But conversely, if we see Mark Lewis as an isolated oddball, the one-off result of his father's perverted treatment of him in childhood, then we are unlikely to see similarities between his scopophilia and our cinematic viewing.

One way of reconciling these apparent contradictions is to argue that the film shows how a traumatic childhood can cause a man to become a voyeuristic murderer, and to behave in real life like a member of a cinema audience. Such an approach to the film would imply that the viewer is encouraged to compare her or (again, especially, his) non-reciprocal relationship with film characters to the non-reciprocal relationship experienced by the voyeur-murderer with his victims.

Our choice of interpretive strategy has, I think, much to do with the extent to which we recognize the ways in which *Peeping Tom* engages with what Elisabeth Bronfen (1996) has described as the "perverse economy of gazing" (71) in our society at large. For in spite of what I believe are its serious moral and aesthetic lapses, the film does uncover the violence implicit in the trade in representations of women's bodies. Although in one sense Dora, Vivian, and Milly are on the margins of society, in another sense their trades symbolize structurally central elements in the Britain of 1960. I find it interesting to compare the tobacconist's shop in which Mark takes his pornographic photographs with the shop in which Mr. Verloc, the title character in Joseph Conrad's *The Secret Agent,* uses as front for his political spying. Both shops display pictures of naked and semi-naked women, and both shops—because they *are* shops, open to the general public—serve as points of contact between the taboo, the marginal, and the perverse on the one hand, and the public, the normal, and the respectable on the other.

The male viewer's intermittent identification with Mark Lewis is crucial, for it draws the men of a whole society into Mark's perverse economy of gazing. Even the way in which the film divides women into those who "ask for it" and "good girls" like Helen is deconstructed by the way in which Mark is connected to both: he is both charming dinner companion and shy conversationalist with Helen, and also murdering pervert with Dora, Vivian, and Milly. The four women all play different parts in the same system, just as the prostitute in William Blake's poem "London" is related to "the marriage hearse." It would be bizarre to categorize *Peeping Tom* as a feminist film, and yet it makes available insights that were central to that second wave of feminism that was to flourish at the end of the decade in which it was first shown. Before the arguments of second-wave feminists gained currency, the idea that prostitution, pornography, or even the work of the glamorous female film star were linked both symbolically and directly to structures of violence in society would have seemed absurd. And yet such a link is to be found clearly delineated in *Peeping Tom.* In this film, that a man filming a woman is *literally* involved in violence against her has crucial *symbolic* force. We can note in passing that this same association of filming and violence is picked up in a work for which the term "feminist" does not seem in any way inappropriate—Margaret Atwood's 1972 novel *Surfacing,* in which a husband who abuses his wife also forces her to perform naked while he and his partner film her.

Moral Decisions

In an interview first published in 1989, the American film director Martin Scorsese comments at length about the effect that *Peeping Tom* had on him when first he saw it in 1962. Summing up his view of the film, he states:

> I have always felt that *Peeping Tom* and *8½* say everything that can be said about film-making, about the process of dealing with film, the objectivity and subjectivity of it and the confusion between the two. *8½* captures the glamour and enjoyment of film-making, while *Peeping Tom* shows the aggression of it, how the camera violates. (Thomson and Christie 1996, 18)

How is it, then, that unlike Hitchcock's *Rear Window*, the film caused such outrage on its first release? Even Hitchcock's *Psycho* (1960), which also attempted to explain why a mad murderer had become as he was, and which included a graphic murder scene, did not inspire the level of indignation prompted by *Peeping Tom*.

The answer may not be simple. On the one hand, there seems little doubt that the film does offer the male viewer the possibility of vicarious enjoyment of a voyeuristic observation of acts of violence against women. On the other hand, the film's implicit association of this violence with patterns of what was at the time a widely accepted objectification of women seems to have challenged a conventional view of the murderer as other rather than as an extreme version of the normal and accepted. And the attempt to *explain* the leading character's murderous second self certainly would have aroused the ire of those who believed that evil was *sui generis* and not accessible to analysis or explanation. I believe, too, that the very success of the film in allowing the male viewer (for a while) to voyeuristically experience the sadistic murder of women also came with a sting in the tail: the final view of Mark as pathetic and impotent carries the implication that the empathizing male viewer was equally pathetic and impotent. The extremely complex movements of point of view in the film thus betray the male viewer into a knowledge of things about himself that he would rather not know.

A changed view of the film must also in part relate to a changed cultural context. Seen by viewers familiar with the arguments of feminists in the 1970s and later, the film is less sympathetic to a murderer and more critical of a culture. And that reminds us that actual audiences will always assess their experiences of point of view and perspective in relation to multiple extrafilmic contexts and influences.

What's Bugging Harry?

Francis Ford Coppola's *The Conversation*

He talked and I listened. That is not a conversation.
—Joseph Conrad, *Under Western Eyes*

FRANCIS FORD COPPOLA's 1974 film *The Conversation* is an unrelenting indictment of the self-destructive nature of a life devoid of genuine interaction with other people. The main character in the film, Harry Caul, is a surveillance expert, a man paid to secretly record the conversations of others. Harry's life as depicted in the film is a perfect exemplification of what Arthur Dimmesdale in Hawthorne's *The Scarlet Letter* (1983) knows: that "to hide a guilty heart through life" (93) and to violate "the sanctity of a human heart" (212) are activities that go against the grain of healthy and natural human impulses. Furthermore, the downward spiral of Harry's life confirms what Dimmesdale learns, that to the untrue man, "the whole universe is false,—it is impalpable,—it shrinks to nothing within his grasp" (166). By the end of the film Harry's world has shrunk to the confines of his stripped-down apartment. Like Dimmesdale, Harry is incapable of opening himself up to others, and like Chillingworth in Hawthorne's novel, Harry is guilty of attempting to penetrate the secret of a human heart—many human hearts, in fact. As the film progresses, the viewer's initial fascination with Harry's power, with his ability to access the private and secret lives of those he is bugging, increasingly gives way to a pitying sense of Harry's impotence, an impotence that has largely been brought about by the exercise of this power.

Unlike Dimmesdale, though, Harry is not split between a knowledge of the wrongness of what he is doing and an inability to find the courage to stop doing it. At the start of the film Harry is less reflective and less self-analytical; he senses that many things are wrong with his way of life, and he experiences promptings from his conscience that are healthy, but he lacks Dimmesdale's clear insight into the source of his problems and the ability to formulate what he should do to resolve them. Moreover, while Dimmesdale reaches a sort of equilibrium in relationship to his sin and his concealment, which bit by bit have become part of what he is, Harry's situation gets less and less tolerable and increasingly unstable as the film progresses. The more isolated he becomes, the more unable he is to open himself to others, the more he cuts himself off from genuine interaction with others, the more desperately he tries to hang on to a diminishing private sphere. Discussing *The Scarlet Letter,* I quoted the narrator's summary of one of "the many morals" of Arthur Dimmesdale's miserable experience: "Be true! Be true! Be true! Show freely to the world, if not your worst, yet some trait whereby the worst may be inferred!" (271). This, Harry Caul is unable or unwilling to do: the furthest he gets is to reveal something to the priest in the confessional.

The Conversation is, then, a film that underscores many of the lessons that, I have argued, can be drawn from the other works on which I have focused attention in previous chapters. But in this final chapter I would like to look at the effect on the members of the movie-theater audience of the film, those individuals who have been compelled to witness and in part share Harry's progressive alienation from other people. At the end of the film, Harry is trapped in his denuded apartment, playing his saxophone alone as he apparently experiences a paranoid alienation from the social world. Those who have followed his story escape from their claustrophobic imprisonment in the film theater and rejoin the flow of their daily lives. What do they take into these lives from their experiences of this film?

The Conversation—as its title suggests—is a very verbal film. It is language that presents itself as the route to reciprocal relationships with others, while increasing isolation leads to a loss of mastery of language. But, as I will argue, reciprocal relationships are also the key to understanding language: listening to words that have been uttered in the context of a complex relationship can easily be misunderstood when studied without an awareness of the nature of this relationship. The title of Coppola's film is fundamentally ironic: a real conversation is the ideal example of genuine interaction between two human beings, but as the quotation from Joseph Conrad's *Under Western Eyes* with which I open this chapter makes clear, for a real conversation we need more than one person listening to another person talk. For those watching the film, who have themselves been listening to the talk of others without themselves conversing, this lesson has a special force. In Conrad's novel the young student Razumov, called to meet the Czarist official Mikulin and to explain his relation to the captured (and by this time executed) terrorist, Haldin, whom he has betrayed, seeks to downplay the importance of the discussions that he has had with Haldin by claiming that they were one-way and non-reciprocal, and thus bear no witness to any identity of views or shared attitudes on the part of the two. A real conversation, by implication, involves give-and-take; it requires that each utterance in some way or another respond to the previous utterance made by one's interlocutor. The etymology of "conversation" is revealing. The word gathers a specific association with talk only in the late sixteenth century, having originally the sense of "living together" (which is how it comes also to mean "sexual intercourse" from at least the early sixteenth century). It is presumably because verbal interaction between two individuals in some way or another resembles living together that the dominant modern meaning has arisen.

By calling his film *The Conversation*, then, Coppola focuses the attention of his audience on that most intimate, humanity-defining of activities: the reciprocal exchange of views and opinions in direct person-to-person verbal interaction. As the film develops, however, this ideal is more honored in the breach than in the observance. The actual conversation to which the title most directly alludes is indeed a frank exchange of views between two individuals, but Harry and the viewer eventually learn that it is one concerned with the planning of a murder, and it is conducted in a crowd of people to make it more difficult for anyone to overhear what is being said. Other discussions between individuals follow in the film, but in no single case can it be said that the audience is allowed to witness a frank, open, and honest exchange of views between two or more individuals. In the ideal sense, there is not a single real conversation in this film, only a discussion about the need to kill someone.

The film makes a strong case for the view that however easy it is to distinguish the activities of the spy and the voyeur in theory, in practice the two activities tend to bleed into each other. Harry Caul, the main character in the film, is a surveillance expert whose conscience starts to give him problems once he begins to experience a human affinity with the people on whom he is spying—although he is already suffering from the guilty knowledge that a previous assignment of his may have resulted in the deaths of those he bugged. But in spite of this increasing sympathy for those on whom he is spying, Harry is not a voyeur: as he becomes progressively more concerned with the lives of those on whom he is spying, his interest is less a matter of voyeuristic self-gratification and more a genuine concern for the well-being of his targets. It is true that, like the character Seymour Parrish in Mark Romanek's 2002 film *One Hour Photo*, his strongest emotional attachments are to people unaware of the nature of his interest in them. But unlike the classic male voyeur, neither he nor Seymour Parrish has a primarily sexual interest in a female "target"; both become gripped by a disinterested concern for the humanity of those who are observed, a humanity they are both eager to protect because it mimics something they want in their own lives but are unable to obtain. This concern, along with the knowledge of private and secret aspects of the lives of those he observes, grants Harry a feeling of pseudo intimacy, a feeling he values because his life is devoid of the real intimacy that genuine, reciprocal interaction with other people might provide. At the same time, the film makes it clear that this sensation *is* that of pseudo intimacy, and it does not prevent Harry from experiencing a steadily increasing sense of isolation and existential impoverishment.

To what extent, then, is Harry—like Jeff in *Rear Window* and Mark in *Peeping Tom*—an analogue to the man or woman sitting in the cinema auditorium? We do not look out of a window with him and share his interest in the neighbors upon whom he spies, and neither do we watch him sitting in front of a screen watching a projected film. But the cinema audience listens as well as looks, and as Harry attempts to understand the conversation that he has recorded, so too do we. In the early part of the film we share his obsessive need to work out exactly what the two young people are saying, and what it means, and his misunderstanding is also our misunderstanding. However, an equally if not more important link between Harry and us involves the experience of pity. Just as Harry grows to pity those whose conversations he is bugging, so too are we led to pity him as we observe him through the one-way glass of the cinema screen. And just as he is unable to help those he pities, so too are we unable to help him. His powerlessness becomes ours.

Even if the average member of the cinema audience is not a surveillance expert or a voyeur, he or she has very likely faced the same problem with which Harry must contend: that of living in a society based on two conflicting systems of value. Coppola's film can be associated with a tradition of moral exemplification in literature and film that stretches back at least to the nineteenth century, a tradition that explores the impossibility of neatly dividing one's life into the two realms of, on the one hand, the personal, and on the other hand, the commercial or professional. Within this tradition "the personal" is based on human values such as love, disinterestedness, solidarity, and openness, while "the professional" operates according to a set of business ethics in which human values and feelings have—or are meant to have—little or no place. The difficulty or impossibility of making and maintaining such a neat division in a life is a theme that runs through much canonical literature of the last two hundred years: Dickens's fiction reverts to it time and time again, although perhaps most directly in a novel such as *Great Expectations,* in which a number of characters—Wemmick, Jaggers, and even Pip himself—attempt with varying and limited degrees of success to straddle (or, better, to oscillate between) two opposed systems of value. Harry Caul, like Wemmick, initially believes that he can live one set of values at work and another in his private life. But he is no more successful than is Wemmick in Dickens's novel, although his failure is more comprehensive and its results are more destructive.

At the start of the film Harry sees no contradiction in going straight from a job which requires him surreptitiously to record the private conversations of the young couple to objecting to the fact that his landlady has a key to his apartment. The recording is his job, his apartment is his home. It is not coincidental that *The Conversation* shares with *Peeping Tom* a concern with keys and locks. Harry's landlady has entered his apartment in order to leave him a birthday present, thus disobeying his order that she maintain a strictly business relationship with him and leave his private space unviolated. Wemmick, too, attempts to keep his private life private, by modeling his house on a medieval castle complete with moat and drawbridge. Harry does not go this far, but the multiple locks on his door are there for the same reason. Like the characters in Dickens's *Great Expectations,* and like the telegraphist in "In the Cage," he discovers that dividing one's life into two separate domains, each run according to different principles and values, is not easy. These two parts of a single life have a tendency to leak into each other just as the smell of cheese drifts into the telegraphist's cage in James's story, and geographic or spatial separation is not enough to preserve a clean distinction between them.

At the start of the film, Harry claims a complete lack of concern for who is paying for the information he is trying to obtain, or why they want it. When his partner Stanley asks who is interested in the couple under surveillance, he responds brusquely, "Don't know for sure," adding a little later, "I don't care what they're talking about. I just want a nice fat recording."[1] This response contains a slightly unexpected element, inasmuch as commodification in his case involves not cash but technical excellence. Where we might expect a reference to the nice fat fee, we actually get one to the nice fat recording: Harry grants the products of his technological expertise an animate identity, almost as if he projects his biological and emotional needs into electronic commodities. (Indeed, the only time in the film that Harry appears spirited and natural is when he is talking about the technology of his work to his professional colleagues or to competitors at the convention.)

At the start of the film Harry's success in his work leads him to assume that he can be a seeing eye (or a hearing ear) without being a seen (or heard) person in either his private or his professional life. And indeed there is some justification for his confidence: it is not Harry who gets "burnt" as the team films and records the young couple at the start of the movie, it is the younger Paul. "I got burnt, Harry, she looked at me. Sorry." The trick is to be the sort of person no one would look at, and Harry fills this rôle better than most. But by the end of the film it is Harry who has been most emphatically burnt, and it is Harry who is most comprehensively looked at. The mime artist's mimicking of Harry in the opening scene is proleptic: as the film develops, the hunter becomes the hunted, the surveillance expert becomes the target. The spy ends up as the pure object of surveillance, being seen but seeing nothing of his observers or of their instruments. *Rear Window* and *Peeping Tom* end with the private spaces of Jeff and Mark being invaded; *The Conversation* too ends with Harry convinced that his apartment is bugged. But there is no rush of other people into Harry's apartment at the end of the film: in this closing scene he remains utterly alone and devoid of any human contact. Of the three endings, I personally find that of *The Conversation* the most frightening.

Discussing *The Scarlet Letter,* I quoted again from Joseph Conrad's *Under Western Eyes* (2003): "A man's real life is that accorded to him in the thoughts of other men by reason of respect or natural love" (11), and I suggested that if the thoughts of others are directed towards a self that is knowingly constructed as a "front" rather than one that is a real expression of personhood, there is a sense in which the man or woman concerned has no real life. In *The Conversation* the fact that no one notices Harry is a professional advantage but an existential disaster. Harry's very

---

1. Quotations from the dialogue are from my own transcriptions, taken from a DVD of the film, but I have checked them against the published screenplay (Coppola, 1999).

ordinariness, we understand from the opening sequence, helps make him invisible. We recognize that were we to encounter a man like Harry in a crowded street, we would pay him little or no attention. A man whom no one notices and who will not open himself up to others—indeed, who actively prevents others from making human contact with him—is a man engaged in a process of existential suicide. Those activities that Harry sees as forms of self-protection are actually processes of self-destruction.

All of this would suggest that productive links might be drawn with the situation of the member of the cinema audience, spying on the young couple with Harry, engaged in a process of non-reciprocal observation of the fictional characters on screen, and failing to enrich his or her "real life" by engendering thoughts in other men "by reason of respect or natural love." Discussing *Peeping Tom,* I noted that the film seems divided against itself. On the one hand, the character Mark's behavior is explained in terms of his having been damaged by his upbringing. On the other hand, however, repeated portrayals of Mark as a man watching a film seem designed to underpin the claim made by the film's scriptwriter Leo Marks (1998) that "the cinema makes voyeurs of us all" (xx). Mark is one of a kind, and he is all of us. Something similar can be said of Harry. He wants to be able to observe the young couple and his other targets without having to make any commitment to them or their lives, just as we want to be able to leave the cinema without having incurred obligations that follow us out into the street. But just as the effect of a film can be hard to shake off, so too Harry finds it impossible to reconcile his conscience with the possible results of the recording he has made. Moreover, while Harry's work as a surveillance expert makes him very different from the average member of the cinema audience, his unfulfilled need to balance the demands of conflicting systems of value represented by work and home renders him a character in whose life the viewer may see some of his or her own problems magnified.

The viewer's frustration with Harry's inability to perceive the self-destructive nature of his refusal of real intimacy becomes more intense as the film progresses, and this increasing frustration eats away at the viewer's initial excitement at sharing Harry's ability to invade the privacies of those upon whom he is spying. While being with Harry at the start of the film is experienced as a privilege that carries with it some of the power-exhilaration that goes with the ability to penetrate unobserved into the private lives of others, by the end of the film being with Harry means being incarcerated in a claustrophobically stripped-down apartment, searching for something that cannot be found and believing that it is one's own privacy that has been invaded—feeling, in fact, that one has no privacy left.[2] To this extent the film deglamorizes the rôle of spy and voyeur and shows impoverishment and imprisonment where previously we might have seen freedom and power. Thus while the viewer does not feel that his or her space has been invaded in quite such a dramatic and threatening manner at the end of *The Conversation* as it has been at the end of *Rear Window* or *Peeping Tom,* the fact that the invasion that may have taken place is technological rather than immediately human makes it more worrying. While at the end of their respective films Jeff and Mark are in contact with other human beings, the suspected invasion of Harry's apartment offers no promise of relief to the desperate isolation of the character with whom the viewer identifies. In many ways Harry is like the prisoner in the panoptical jail, believing that he may be being observed at any time, but never sure when or whether he actually is. And in both cases, the concealed observer is finally located in a place from which he or she can never be expelled: inside the mind of the prisoner.

Coppola certainly knew about the buzz that spying by means of new technology could bring with it. He has himself reported that

> when we were making *The Conversation,* the news on the Watergate break-in happened. I remember we were shooting, and we said, hey, isn't this weird? This is sort of what we're about. But I didn't approach it that way. Wiretapping and surveillance were, quite honestly, something that appealed to me. Partly because I was paralyzed as a kid, and I was very good at technology and science, so I knew how to plant microphones in things and hear what people were saying. I remember we threw a party once and we bugged the bathroom so we could hear the girls talking. [*Laughs*] And this was in 1952! I was a friend of technology. And surveillance, I think, is another aspect of remote control. When you're paralyzed, remote control is everything. That's why boys like Lionel Trains. (quoted in Nocenti 1999, 63; italicized parenthetical word in original)

Even here, we may note, the "friend of technology" is also "paralyzed": Coppola's and Harry's recording equipment, like Jeff's telephoto lens, is a substitute for a lack rather than an extension to the power of a man who is already whole.

---

2. David Thomson (1978) claims of the film's ending that "[t]he double meaning in 'bugger' is never forgotten in *The Conversation* and part of the final humiliation is of a suppressed homosexual being magically raped" (186). I find little if anything in the film to support this reading.

Many commentaries on *The Conversation* relate its central theme to America's traumatic living-through of the Watergate scandal. Not only did both the film and the political *cause célèbre* involve the invasion of privacies by means of advanced forms of electronic surveillance, but both involved an ironic reversal whereby the would-be spy was himself spied on and exposed—Harry Caul in the film and Richard Nixon in the Watergate scandal. According to Annie Nocenti (1999), however, the film was completed before the Watergate scandal broke; she reports that "[b]y the time the film was released, the Watergate scandal had hit, making the project surprisingly timely" (61). Whatever the case, it seems likely that such things as the mention in the film of a would-be presidential candidate whose candidature is destroyed by the results of surveillance are more likely to be an afterthought or an accident than the deliberate presentation of a commentary on contemporary politics. Coppola does, however, concede to his interviewer that "when you work in a theme, when you're writing and utilizing stuff, whether it's from your life or from other work that you like and want to appropriate, there's a reason why you're choosing that. You're choosing what somehow feels right to you. That's creation, basically" (64). In choosing what feels right, a filmmaker may be influenced by events and relationships in the larger social and political world as well as by his or her own private history. If the lack of a full context leads Harry to misinterpret the words he records, placing the words of the film in the new political context provided by the Watergate scandal generates new meanings for viewers.

While *Rear Window* presents Jeff's fascination with his neighbors (and his initial lack of fascination with Lisa) as clearly in some sense unhealthy from the start, in *The Conversation* the more rational understanding that spying on others is a perversion of natural human behavior is, initially, to a certain extent in tension with this "Lionel Trains" fascination with the technology of surveillance. Thus while the natural reaction of the viewer to Jeff in the early part of *Rear Window* is something along the lines of "Put the camera down and look at Lisa," the reaction that *The Conversation* encourages us to foster with regard to Harry at the start of the film is that of sharing his fascination with his surveillance and of dying to decode exactly what the young couple are talking about. It is only as the film develops that we become progressively less interested in the couple and more interested in Harry (whereas in *Rear Window* we become less and less irritated with Jeff and more and more interested in finding out what has happened in Lars Thorwald's apartment). This shift of interest is, I think, allied to the subtle manner in which *The Conversa-*

tion causes the viewer to be increasingly uneasy about his or her initial desire for Harry to decode and explain the recorded conversation.

It is certainly true that the focus on those (at the time) almost unbelievable technical possibilities made available by electronic surveillance certainly fed in to fears as well as fascination—fears about the real possibility of an Orwellian Big Brother state which had an apparently limitless ability to invade the privacy of its citizens. (The film was released only a short decade before the resonant date of 1984.) But to see the film as Orwell plus electronics is arguably to misrepresent the thrust of its narrative and the concerns that it raises in the viewer. The film's overt socio-political comment seems directed more at the growth of powerful corporations than at the political dirty tricks best represented by the Watergate scandal. As the film progresses it becomes clear that although Harry is the most skilled surveillance agent measured in terms of personal skill, his tiny organization is doomed to fall by the wayside in competition with bigger outfits such as that run by Moran, who later succeeds in poaching staff from Harry. Business corporations are less vulnerable than individual craftsmen when it comes to such things as conscience and ethics; we are led to assume that Moran would never develop the scruples or the guilt that come to plague Harry—or allow them to develop in his employees. And Harry's outfit is and will remain small, presumably, because of his inability to trust others.

Perhaps linked to this view of Harry's anachronistic rôle as independent craftsman in a world increasingly dominated by the corporation is the film's implied critique of a society in which the anonymity of the city on the one hand, and the split between work and home, business ethics and personal relationships on the other, combine to destroy Harry. As the film unfolds, we learn that this split between two systems of value precipitates a crisis for him as surely as it does for Dickens's Wemmick. Not only do human concerns—conscience—seep into his work attitudes; work habits seep into his private life, making it impossible for him to reveal himself to others, to abandon his secrecy. From one perspective this could be taken as a criticism of an individual unable to divide his life in the way society urges. But few viewers of the film can fail to respond to such failures other than as moral successes.

Particularly interesting in this respect is the link made in Coppola's comment between surveillance and disability—in his own case a physical disability resulting from childhood polio. The intratextual link between a loss of mobility and a recourse to surveillance that is fixed in *Typee* through Tommo's injured leg and in *Rear Window* through Jeff's broken leg is thus in the case of *The Conversation* an extratextual one. The later film certainly draws a connection between Harry Caul's activities as a surveillance expert and his disabled emotional and personal life. If physical paralysis led the young Coppola to make use of bugging devices and remote controls, his film about an expert in bugging portrays this character as emotionally paralyzed and stunted by his work. One of the most haunting aspects of *The Conversation* is its depiction of Harry Caul's woes as unknowingly self-inflicted. He remains unaware that in securing (or attempting to secure) his privacy by erecting impenetrable barriers he is simultaneously impoverishing it.

The big city brings with it a historically unique degree of personal privacy. As Wemmick tells Pip in Dickens's *Great Expectations* (1965), if one wishes to hide "there is no place like a great city" (384). Anyone who has lived in both a large town and a small village knows that it is in the latter that one has fewest secrets and least privacy. But this much greater potential for developing and protecting personal privacy in the modern city is double-edged: it is accompanied by the permanent risk of isolation, loss of significant human contacts, and acute loneliness of a sort more or less impossible in a small village. *The Conversation,* then, mixes some very modern and some very old issues. The paraphernalia of surveillance in this film is extremely modern. The depiction of a character who wants to invade the privacies of others while securing his own from scrutiny, and who ends up by impoverishing himself, is by no means new. But the degree to which it is possible to cut oneself off from other people in a big modern city exceeds the degree of isolation one can achieve in a small village, where even the rôle of "hermit" is a paradoxically public one. We have a word to describe a hermit because this chosen lifestyle could hardly be kept secret in a small community. There is no comparable word to describe a character such as Harry because the Harrys of this world are invisible and can even die without anyone noticing—unless, as in Harry's case, someone develops an interest in noticing. What you do not see, you need no name for. Harry is not a recluse: he is frequently outside his apartment. But as the film progresses he has less and less of any real life.

What is significant, then, is not so much that in the modern city intrusive surveillance may be more difficult to detect, but that the city offers far greater possibility of securing the personal self from human contact. Once Harry himself becomes someone else's target, however, he finds that he has no place to hide: it is those who are observing him who, he suspects, are able to make themselves and their bugging devices untraceable. At the end of the film Harry is convinced that his privacy has been invaded, but it is also the case that his privacy, his personal self, has not been opened up enough to exchange with the privacies of others, so that even before he himself becomes the target he has very little that he can call a private life. The more paranoid he becomes, the more other people are locked out. In this final scene he mimics genuine interaction when he plays the saxophone karaoke-style, accompanying a record. This activity suggests, it is true, a world in which the human has been replaced by simulacra: recordings and photographs. But the real problem is not that of modern technology—which after all only refines what we see in its traditional form in the scene in the confessional—but in Harry's belief that access to his own privacy constitutes not intimacy but invasion. Like Brecht's Mother Courage, Harry owes allegiance to precisely that system and set of values that is destroying him. Harry followed by the mime artist at the start of the film; Harry playing his saxophone to the accompaniment of a recording at the end of the film: both scenes suggest activities that mimic human interaction but that involve no genuine reciprocity.

The scene in the confessional occupies a pivotal place in the film. Harry is worried that people will die as a result of his surveillance activities, and he goes to confess his guilt. During this whole scene he is shot from side view, and the priest is never shown on screen except in very shadowy outline. We do not hear the priest's voice, or see his eyes. It suddenly strikes the viewer during this sequence that while Harry goes to the confessional as a refuge from the world of surveillance and spying, what he actually gets is an extension of this world. He is observed without observing, and his privacy is exposed to a hidden observer. That lack of personal interaction and mutual human self-confirmation that is absent from the world of his work is equally absent here—in a setting which is part not of a brave new world but of one that has not changed in centuries. The priest, like the cinematic viewer, sees Harry without being seen by him.

Harry is depicted as someone who simultaneously craves and fears intimacy, whose feelings for others can overcome his professional amorality but who is unable to interact in an exchange of mutual intimacy with another person. In the confessional, for once, Harry is able to a certain extent to open himself up to another, but another who is concealed, who does not reciprocate, and who confronts Harry not so much as an individual but more as an office. This scene represents a critical point in the film for another reason. Right from the start of the film Harry Caul is portrayed as secretive and obsessed with protecting his own privacy, and after the tape of the conversation has been stolen from him he becomes more and more threatened by the suspicion that his own privacy is being invaded—which it is. But in the confessional he is the one who gives up his private thoughts and worries to another. Ironically, though, he delivers them up to one of the few human beings unable to respond with genuine intimacy—a priest hearing his confession. His opening up is not primarily to another human being but to God, a God who apparently gives him no sign of responding in kind. In the confessional Harry can be looked at, but confined in this miniature panopticon he cannot return the priest's gaze. In the confessional Harry's delivery is awkward and halting, and his eyes waver and look down, suggesting that he finds the publication of privacies extremely difficult. The sins to which he confesses are of wildly varying levels of seriousness—ranging from taking newspapers without paying for them to endangering the lives of the couple on whom he is spying. And even his confession seems to involve an element of holding back: talking about a previous occasion on which his surveillance activity ended up hurting someone, he protests that "I was in no way responsible, I'm not responsible."

The only time in the film when Harry is portrayed freely talking about himself is in the initial dream sequence, a sequence which suggests that Harry feels a need to engage in a reciprocal sharing of privacies with another human being, but cannot do so in waking life precisely because the habits of his professional activities have seeped into the realm of his private life.

If the classic Hollywood plot is "A chasing B chasing C," then the opening of *The Conversation* exemplifies this to perfection in miniature while the film as a whole exemplifies it at length. Harry is pursuing the young couple—his target—for information, while he himself is being followed by the mime artist, imitated without his knowledge, having people's attention drawn exactly where he does not want it drawn—towards himself. But Harry himself resembles the mime artist to the extent that he is concerned with capturing revealing detail without any desire for human closeness. He wants to have as much to do with his targets as the mime artist has with his—to be able to profit from an unobserved familiarity with the externals of the behavior of others—and to be able to move from one uninvolved encounter to another just as the mime artist does. Harry tries to live like the mime artist, never casting a look back at the previous victim of his gaze, as impossible to read as is the mime artist's grease-painted face. But his powers of disengagement are not as effective as those of the mime artist.

Many commentators have drawn attention to the ironies surrounding Harry's transparent, plastic coat. The man most concerned with being invisible is merely transparent; the man who wishes his privacy to be invulnerable can (prophetically) be seen through. Coppola has reported that Harry's name was originally Call: it became Caul because the screenplay was dictated, and the secretary taking the dictation spelled it this way. Once the mistake was made, Coppola seems to have realized the appropriateness of the change: Harry's coat is like a caul, transparent and enclosing. He is like a man waiting to be fully born. And when, later on, we see Mr. C wrapped in clear plastic, we realize that, just like Harry, he is the predator who has become the victim; not waiting to kill, but waiting to be killed.

For most of the film Harry is obsessively working to establish exactly what Mark says to Ann in one comment made during the conversation recorded at the start of the film. Bit by bit this is reconstructed from the different tapes made at the time, so that what is initially heard just as " . . . he'd . . . chance . . . ", with the ellipses representing the sound of bongos that obscures the words uttered, eventually, by painstaking work on the tapes, is revealed to be "he'd kill us if he got the chance." Harry understands this to represent the couple's fear that Mr. C is plotting to kill them, but understands too late that the comment is made as justification for their own plot to kill him, which they eventually carry out. Coppola engages in a little trickery here, as when we first hear the full phrase the emphasis is on the word "kill," but when Harry finally understands the full force of the comment, in the playback the emphasis is on the word "us," thus radically shifting the meaning of the utterance so that it can be understood as a justification for what they are planning to do. Harry's initial failure to understand the comment is significant: it reminds the viewer that words are given meaning by the context—the human relationships—in which they are uttered. It is in part because Harry is a man who is unable to form—and thus to understand—relationships, that he fails to detect the ambiguous nature of the words uttered.

In chapter 5 I referred to Sidney Lumet's *Twelve Angry Men*, at the end of which the Henry Fonda character Mr. Davis walks out of the claustrophobic jury room into the bright sunshine in a scene possessed, I argued, of an obvious political symbolism. In stark contrast to this ending, the final scene of *The Conversation* has Harry Caul seemingly unable to leave his stripped-down apartment, sitting in the midst of desolation and playing his saxophone karaoke-style to the accompaniment of recorded music.

If the viewer of *Twelve Angry Men* can feel that in leaving the cinema he or she is emulating Mr. Davis's move from claustrophobic enclosure to the freedom of public space and liberated nation, the viewer of *The Conversation* goes out of the cinema with his head full of the image of Harry remaining in his locked room, descending into madness. We go out of the movie theater with Mr. Davis; we leave Harry behind inside when we walk through the door marked "Exit" after having watched *The Conversation.*

At the end of many novels or films there is typically a sense of liberation that comes as we lay the book down or leave the cinema. After a stretch of imagined but non-reciprocal relationships with fictional characters, observing them and becoming familiar with the intimate details of their lives but unable to receive any sense that they are intimate with us, we crave human interaction. We want to talk to others about what we have read or seen on the screen, to discuss with them, to have a real conversation. My feeling at the end of a cinematic experience of *Twelve Angry Men*, however, was that of wanting to share Mr. Davis's sense of individual freedom, to breathe in the fresh air, to feel that I had left behind problems that the film had resolved for me and to relax into a problem-free present. *The Conversation* does not leave the viewer in this frame of mind. As we leave the cinema we carry with us our own impotent pity for Harry, left behind in his lonely apartment. We thereby carry with us a critique of the non-reciprocity of the viewer's relationship to the characters whose lives he or she has followed. Artistic closure gives way immediately to the possibility of reciprocity in our relation to others. Rather than wishing to enjoy our solitude, we feel an urgent need for human interaction. This feeling, it may be countered, is located outside the filmic universe, but it is nonetheless a product of what the viewer has experienced inside that universe. As I will suggest in the conclusion that follows, all of the texts I have considered evoke some sense of claustrophobia or imprisonment, especially in their endings. But in *The Conversation* this sense is more comprehensive, stifling, and unrelieved by any vision of escape. If the viewer wishes to escape, he or she must leave Harry behind. For him there is no hope.

CONCLUSION

THERE IS A SHORT PASSAGE in George Eliot's *Middlemarch* (1988) which has fascinated me for many years, and on which I have commented a number of times. It comes in chapter 27 of the novel. Lydgate, the young, good-looking, unmarried doctor, is visiting his patient Fred Vincy in the Vincy family home. While there, he is frequently forced into contact with Fred's pretty but shallow and selfish sister Rosamond. Mrs. Vincy, the mother of Fred and Rosamond, never leaves her sick son. As a result,

Rosamond was in the unusual position of being much alone. Lydgate, naturally, never thought of staying long with her, yet it seemed that the brief impersonal conversations they had together were creating that peculiar intimacy which consists in shyness. They were obliged to look at each other in speaking, and somehow the looking could not be carried through as the matter of course which it really was. Lydgate began to feel this sort of consciousness unpleasant, and one day looked down, or anywhere, like an ill-worked puppet. But this turned out badly: the next day, Rosamond looked down, and the consequence was that when their eyes met again, both were more conscious than before. There was no help for this in science, and as Lydgate did not want to flirt, there seemed to be no help for it in folly. It was therefore a relief when neighbours no longer considered the house in quarantine, and when the chances of seeing Rosamond alone were very much reduced.

> But that intimacy of mutual embarrassment, in which each feels that
> the other is feeling something, having once existed, its effect is not to be
> done away with. Talk about the weather and other well-bred topics is apt
> to seem a hollow device, and behaviour can hardly become easy unless it
> frankly recognizes a mutual fascination—which of course need not mean
> anything deep or serious. (219)

As I have pointed out elsewhere (Hawthorn 2006, 508), this brief passage illustrates perfectly the inescapably reciprocal nature of person-to-person contact and communication. Alone with Rosamond, Lydgate cannot not convey the fact that he is aware of and responsive to her youth and attractiveness. When he attempts to communicate nothing by looking down, or anywhere, he of course exposes his wish to communicate nothing and thereby communicates something. As the narrator tells the reader, the two characters "were obliged to look at each other while speaking"; person-to-person conversation has its rules and conventions. These rules and conventions may vary from culture to culture, and according to divisions (gender, age, class) within a culture, but attempting to ignore them reveals as much as, if not more than, it conceals.

Moreover, as the narrator here also points out, interaction has a history, and the residue of this history may be as hard to remove as is the residue of the history of relations between nations. Once one person has betrayed his or her embarrassment to a conversational partner, the record cannot easily be erased. The effect of such an intimacy of shared embarrassment "is not to be done away with." Note that the passage informs the reader about nothing that the two characters actually said to each other; we merely learn that they engaged in "brief impersonal conversations." As in the passage from Jane Austen's *Sense and Sensibility* that I discussed in my introduction, nearly all the significant work here is done by the eyes. The eyes in such a situation do not just gather information, nor do they convey to an interlocutor only what we wish to convey. In many circumstances they reveal what we do not intend to reveal, and they may betray what we absolutely wish to conceal.

The passage, then, isolates what it is surely not too much to describe as a fundamental aspect of being human, that in conversation with another individual we naturally detect things about them through their body language—and particularly through their eyes. Moreover, while we are doing this we are naturally revealing similar things about ourselves—not least when we attempt not to do so. The word "intimacy" here is surely just right: it is attached to a process of mutual discovery and disclosure, as if the separate circles of identity that constitute the two individuals Lydgate and Rosamond start to overlap like the circles of a Venn diagram. There has not been much of this sort of intimacy in the texts considered in previous pages. In James's "In the Cage" the telegraphist believes that she experiences "intense intimacy" not when she is face-to-face with Captain Everard but when she reads his name on the list of occupants of his apartment building. However, as I argue in chapter 4 (p. 117), what she actually experiences better merits the term "pseudo intimacy." Perhaps the nearest we get to genuine intimacy between two characters is in Hitchcock's *Rear Window* when Jeff and Lisa start to share a common concern with what has gone on in the apartment over the courtyard, and to interact as they discuss this.

However, if Lydgate and Rosamond share a genuine (if awkward) intimacy here, George Eliot's narrator can hardly be said to enjoy a comparable relationship with her characters or readers. This narrator can, technically, be described as a non-character narrator, but she seems so consistently possessed of a specific personality that while reading the novel we think of her much as we think of a human individual. She is able to penetrate her characters' privacies, of course—so effectively that she can inform the reader of their secrets by means of the subtle hints effected by such words as "naturally" and "somehow," hints that mimic the thought processes of the two characters and convey their failure to understand both what is going on inside themselves and what is going on inside the other. If Lydgate is like "an ill-worked puppet," within the diegesis this can be attributed to his shyness and embarrassment, but the phrase also draws the reader's attention to the fact that both characters are the puppets not just of Eliot's narrator but of Eliot herself. The phrase stirs an uneasy sense of the world outside of the world of the novel in the mind of the reader, who for a moment is conscious of the artifice working the fiction. It is like a glimpse of cameras and backcloth in a film, and it reminds us that not only is the relationship between author and narrator, and characters, a non-reciprocal one, but so too is the relationship between the reader as member of the narrative audience, and narrator and characters. The tone in the passage is informal and familiar—an effect helped by such words as "naturally," which in addition to telling us what is going on inside Lydgate's mind imply that the narrator knows the reader well enough to be able to assess how much he or she needs to have explained. But somehow, the intimacy and embarrassment experienced by Lydgate and Rosamond are more convincing than the familiarity expressed by the narrator. Eliot's narrator addresses her reader as if the two of them shared an intimacy that made such assumptions straightforward, although in terms of technique it is the tone that is designed to inspire the sense of intimacy, not an intimacy that inspires a particular tone.

For all that this passage fascinates me, then, and for all that its portrayal of the rich, cumulative complexity of the intimacy that is engendered by person-to-person conversation is profound and insightful, it is as if there is a ghost at this feast of subtle observation. Like the ghost in Jean Rhys's "I Used to Live Here Once," this ghost is the fact of our non-reciprocal relationship with the characters and events that we observe in the novel and, in particular, with the narrator who tells us about them. We are perhaps especially conscious of this lack of reciprocity in our relationship with Eliot's narrator precisely because what we see of the relationship between Lydgate and Rosamond reminds us of the inescapable reciprocity of ordinary person-to-person contact. Observing Lydgate and Rosamond interact, we are made more aware of the impossibility of our interacting with them, or with George Eliot, or with her narrator. It is, again, as if we are trapped in a world within which we can look but not touch, hear but not converse, perceive but remain invisible to those whose lives we witness. We will never convey our own embarrassment to Eliot or to her narrator in the way that Lydgate and Rosamond convey their embarrassment to each another.

○

It is only right at the end of Jean Rhys's "I Used to Live Here Once" that the narrator realizes that she is a ghost, and it is typically at the end of fictional narratives that the reader or viewer experiences most strongly a sense of ontological separation from characters and events. In many of the texts at which I have looked in previous pages, the reader as member of the narrative audience may feel part of a community of characters, and even a sense of intimacy with the narrator of the literary fictions, through much of the work in question. But by the close of each text there is, typically, an impoverishing sense of isolation for the reader or viewer, one that is not altogether dissimilar from that experienced by characters in the different works. At the start of *The Conversation* Harry is, apart from his fellow spies, alone in a crowd of people. At the end of the film he is alone without a crowd, accompanying recorded music on his saxophone, sitting in the middle of the apartment that he has destroyed in his unsuccessful attempt to locate the bug that is allowing others to spy on him. Loneliness—or death—that is the fate of many of those characters on whom we have spied as they have spied on others. Arthur Dimmesdale in *The Scarlet Letter,* Fagin in *Oliver Twist,* and Mark in *Peeping Tom* are all dead at the end of the narratives in which they appear. In *Typee* Tommo leaves Fayaway and returns to America alone. The telegraphist of "In the Cage" has a married life to look forward to, but it is not one that excites her in the way that her fantasies about Captain Everard have, and there is a suggestion that marriage will replace one cage with another. L. B. Jefferies may also have a married life to look forward to, but if so it is one being planned by his future wife in secret, while he sleeps.

And what of the reader or viewer at the end of these fictions of nonreciprocity? Every single one of the texts with which I have been concerned induces, I would argue, an increasing sense of claustrophobia in the viewer or reader. Although it is only James's "In the Cage" whose title directly implies a form of imprisonment, each of these texts portrays forms of incarceration of one sort or another. Dimmesdale is trapped by fear, self-deception, and the dictates of an intolerant religion. Chillingworth is increasingly trapped by his pursuit of hidden knowledge and his desire to possess Dimmesdale. The world of *Oliver Twist* is a world full of observing eyes that seems to offer no place in which one can be seen only by those one sees, and it ends with Fagin facing thousands of hostile eyes in the courtroom and the prison death-cell. Tommo faces a literal prohibition on leaving the land of the Typee, a prohibition that turns the happy valley into a jail for him. The telegraphist will perhaps go from a physical cage to another, less material prison, and from a world in which she is cut off from the lives that she finds most full of life to a world in which marriage to Mr. Mudge will fix this separation for good. In *Rear Window* Jeff remains trapped in his apartment at the end of the film, facing the prospect of a life with Lisa that may promise the Himalayas but that actually may have more to do with the domesticity he perceives as confinement. Mark in *Peeping Tom* is trapped within a psyche distorted by his upbringing, from which death offers the only escape—as it does for Dimmesdale. And at the end of *The Conversation* Harry is even more trapped than is Jeff: alone in his stripped-down apartment, finding no trace of the bug (which some commentators have suggested may even be in his saxophone) but believing that he is fixed in the sights of those observing him.

Opening his discussion of *Rear Window,* John Fawell (2001) suggests that

> [t]he film is so highly charged with a sense of the significance of the hidden, with the mystery of the barely glimpsed and distantly heard, that it is difficult not to carry this same sense of mystery back to our own world. Hitchcock's cinema leaves us with a more highly charged sense of the mystery of the world.
>
> . . .
>
> *Rear Window* specifically heightens our attention to the barely glimpsed sights and distant sounds of hidden lives, to the mysterious presence of loneliness and alienation in our own world. (8)

I think that this is true. But I believe, too, that the sense of relief we get at the end not just of *Rear Window* but of all the texts at which I have looked in this book has to do with a "more highly charged sense" of the human need for communication, for mutual engagement, for reciprocity. We feel a hunger for human contact of a sort that may be portrayed in, but cannot be provided by, fiction. We have witnessed the life-denying nature of non-reciprocal forms of human interaction; we have experienced the non-reciprocal nature of reading a book or watching a film. We are ready for life. We want to talk to other, living people. If fictional narratives offer us the initially attractive prospect of escape into a world in which we can see but not be seen, they also typically conclude by making us happy to rejoin a world in which our relationships with others can be reciprocal, interactive, human. And if this is true to some degree of all fictional narratives, it is particularly so when these narratives have depicted a world dominated by relationships of non-reciprocity.

BIBLIOGRAPHY

Abrams, Robert E. 1982. "*Typee* and *Omoo*: Herman Melville and the Ungraspable Phantom of Identity." In Stern 1982, 201–10. (Repr.; orig. pub. in *Arizona Quarterly* 31 [Spring, 1975], 33–50.)

Allen, Jeanne. 1988. "Looking through 'Rear Window': Hitchcock's Traps and Lures of Heterosexual Romance." In *Female Spectators: Looking at Film and Television*, ed. E. Deirdre Pribam. London: Verso, 31–44.

Anderson, Charles Roberts. 1939. *Melville in the South Seas*. New York: Columbia University Press.

Argyle, Michael, and Mark Cook. 1976. *Gaze and Mutual Gaze*. Cambridge: Cambridge University Press.

Austen, Jane. 1995. *Sense and Sensibility*. Ed. Ros Ballaster. London: Penguin. (Orig. pub. 1811.)

Banfield, Ann. 1987. "Describing the Unobserved: Events Grouped around an Empty Centre." In *The Linguistics of Writing*, ed. Nigel Fabb, Derek Attridge, Alan Durant, and Colin MacCabe. Manchester: Manchester University Press, 265–85.

Barthes, Roland. 1991. *The Responsibility of Forms: Critical Essays on Music, Art, and Representation*. Trans. Richard Howard. Berkeley: University of California Press. (Orig. pub. English 1985; orig. pub. French as *L'obvie et l'obtus*, Editions du Seuil, 1982.)

Barthes, Roland. 1993. *Camera Lucida*. Trans. Richard Howard. London: Vintage. (Orig. pub. French 1980; English 1982.)

Bauer, Dale M., and Andrew Lakritz. 1987. "Language, Class, and Sexuality in Henry James's 'In the Cage.'" *New Orleans Review* 14: 61–69.

Beaver, Frank. 1994. *Dictionary of Film Terms: The Aesthetic Companion to Film Analysis*. Rev. ed. Boston: Twayne.

Bergman, Andrew. 1999. Brief comment cited in *Hitchcock,* a booklet attached to *Sight and Sound,* August 1999, 21.

Bhabha, Homi K. 1985. "Signs Taken for Wonders: Questions of Ambivalence and Authority Under a Tree Outside Delhi, May 1817." Repr. in *The Post-Colonial Studies Reader,* ed. Bill Ashcroft, Gareth Griffiths, and Helen Tiffin. London: Routledge, 29–35.

Bordwell, David. 1985. *Narration in the Fiction Film.* London: Methuen.

Božovič, Miran. 1992. "The Man Behind His Own Retina." In Žižek 1992, 161–77.

Brand, Dana. 1999. "Rear-View Mirror: Hitchcock, Poe, and the Flaneur in America." In *Hitchcock's America,* ed. Jonathan Freedman and Richard Millington. New York and Oxford: Oxford University Press, 123–34.

Bronfen, Elisabeth. 1996. "Killing Gazes, Killing in the Gaze: On Michael Powell's *Peeping Tom.*" In *Gaze and Voice as Love Objects,* ed. Renate Salecl and Slavoj Žižek. Durham and London: Duke University Press, 59–89.

Brookman, Philip. 2010. "A Window on the World: Street Photography and the Theater of Life." In *Voyeurism, Surveillance and the Camera,* ed. Sandra S. Phillips. London: Tate, 213–19.

Bryson, Norman. 1983. *Vision and Painting: The Logic of the Gaze.* New Haven, CT, and London: Yale University Press.

Buelens, Gert. 2006. "Imagining Telegraphic Joy in the Canny Cage of Metaphor, Metonymy, and Performativity." *The Henry James Review* 27(2): 126–39.

Burney, Frances. 2008. *Cecilia: or Memoirs of an Heiress.* Ed. Peter Sabor and Margaret Anne Doody. Oxford: Oxford University Press. (Orig. pub. 1782.)

Chatman, Seymour. 1990. *Coming to Terms: The Rhetoric of Narrative in Fiction and Film.* Ithaca, NY: Cornell University Press.

Chion, Michel. 1992. "The Fourth Side." In Žižek 1992, 155–60.

Christie, Ian. 1994. *Arrows of Desire: The Films of Michael Powell and Emeric Pressburger.* New ed. London and Boston: Faber and Faber. (Orig. pub. 1985.)

Clark, Michael. 1982. "Melville's *Typee:* Fact, Fiction, and Esthetics." In Stern 1982, 211–25. (Repr.; orig. pub in *Arizona Quarterly* 34 [1978]: 351–70.)

Clover, Carol J. 1992. *Men, Women, and Chainsaws: Gender in the Modern Horror Film.* London: BFI.

Cohn, Dorrit. 1999. *The Distinction of Fiction.* Baltimore and London: Johns Hopkins University Press.

Cole, Jonathan. 1998. *About Face.* Cambridge, MA: MIT Press.

Conrad, Joseph. 1990. *The Secret Agent.* Ed. Bruce Harkness and S. W. Reid. Cambridge Edition of the Works of Joseph Conrad. Cambridge: Cambridge University Press. (Orig. pub. 1907.)

Conrad, Joseph. 2003. *Under Western Eyes.* Ed. Jeremy Hawthorn. Oxford: Oxford University Press. (Orig. pub. 1911.)

Conrad, Joseph. 2008. "A Smile of Fortune." In *'Twixt Land and Sea,* Cambridge Edition of the Works of Joseph Conrad, ed. J. A. Berthoud, Laura L. Davis, and S. W. Reid. Cambridge: Cambridge University Press, 13–78. (Orig. pub. 1912.)

Conrad, Joseph. 2010a. "Geography and Some Explorers." In *Last Essays,* Cambridge Edition of the Works of Joseph Conrad, ed. Harold Ray Stevens and J. H. Stape. Cambridge: Cambridge University Press, 3–17. (Orig. pub. 1924.)

Conrad, Joseph. 2010b. *Youth, Heart of Darkness, The End of the Tether.* Cambridge Edition of the Works of Joseph Conrad. Cambridge: Cambridge University Press. (Orig. pub. as *Youth, A Narrative and Two Other Stories,* 1902.)

Conrad, Joseph. 2012. *Lord Jim.* Ed. J. H. Stape and Ernest W. Sullivan II. Cambridge Edition of the Works of Joseph Conrad. Cambridge: Cambridge University Press. (Orig. pub. 1900.)

Cook, David A. 1996. *A History of Narrative Film*. 3rd ed. New York and London: W. W. Norton.

Coppola, Francis Ford. 1999. "*The Conversation*." *Scenario: The Magazine of Screenwriting Art* 5(1): 11–59.

Corber, Robert J. 1993. *In the Name of National Security: Hitchcock, Homophobia, and the Political Construction of Gender in Postwar America*. Durham, NC, and London: Duke University Press.

Crawley, Budge, Fletcher Markle, and Gerald Pratley. 1972. "I Wish I Didn't Have to Shoot the Picture: An Interview with Alfred Hitchcock." In LaValley 1972, 22–27. (Repr.; orig. pub. in *Take One* 1.1 [1966].)

Denzin, Norman K. 1995. *The Cinematic Society: The Voyeur's Gaze*. London: Sage.

Dickens, Charles. 1965. *Great Expectations*. Ed. Angus Calder. Harmondsworth: Penguin. (Orig. pub. 1861.)

Dickens, Charles. 1985. *The Adventures of Oliver Twist*. Ed. Peter Fairclough. London: Penguin. (Orig. pub. 1838.)

Dixon, W. W. 1995. *The Returned Gaze of Cinema*. Albany: State University of New York Press.

Docherty, Thomas. 2012. *Confessions: The Philosophy of Transparency*. London: Bloomsbury Academic.

Dolar, Mladen. 1992. "A Father Who Is Not Quite Dead." In Žižek 1992, 143–50.

Donoghue, Daniel. 2003. *Lady Godiva: A Literary History of the Legend*. Oxford: Blackwell.

Ehrenburg, Ilya. 2005. *My Paris*. Facsimile ed. in Russian of orig. 1933 ed., with separate English trans. by Oliver Ready of the text in booklet form. Paris: Edition 7L.

Eliot, George. 1988. *Middlemarch*. Ed. David Carroll. Oxford: Oxford University Press. (Orig. pub. 1871–72.)

Fawell, John. 2001. *Hitchcock's "Rear Window": The Well-Made Film*. Carbondale and Edwardsville: Southern Illinois University Press.

Fetterley, Judith. 1978. *The Resisting Reader: A Feminist Approach to American Fiction*. Bloomington: Indiana University Press.

Findley, Timothy. 1993. *Headhunter*. Toronto: HarperCollins.

Foucault, Michel. 1979. *Discipline and Punish: The Birth of the Prison*. Trans. Alan Sheridan. Harmondsworth: Penguin. (Orig. pub. French 1975.)

Freedman, Jonathan, and Richard Millington, eds. 1999. *Hitchcock's America*. New York and Oxford: Oxford University Press.

Gargano, James W. 1979. "The 'Look' as a Major Event in James's Short Fiction." *The Arizona Quarterly* 25: 303–20.

Genette, Gérard. 1988. *Narrative Discourse Revisited*. Trans. Jane E. Lewin. Ithaca, NY: Cornell University Press.

Gottlieb, Sidney, ed. 1995. *Hitchcock on Hitchcock: Selected Writings and Interviews*. London: Faber.

Hansen, Per Krogh. 2012. "Formalizing the Study of Character: Traits, Profiles, Possibilities." In *Disputable Core Concepts of Narrative Theory*, ed. Göran Rossholm and Christer Johansson. Bern: Peter Lang, 99–118.

Hawthorn, Jeremy. 2006. "Theories of the Gaze." In *Literary Theory and Criticism: An Oxford Guide*, ed. Pat Waugh. Oxford: Oxford University Press, 508–18.

Hawthorn, Jeremy. 2013. "Reading Fiction: Voyeurism Without Shame?" In *Narrative Ethics*, ed. Jakob Lothe and Jeremy Hawthorn. Amsterdam and New York: Rodopi, 73–88.

Hawthorne, Nathaniel. 1972. *The American Notebooks*. Ed. Claude M. Simpson. Vol.

8 of *The Centenary Edition of the Works of Nathaniel Hawthorne*. Columbus: The Ohio State University Press.

Hawthorne, Nathaniel. 1983. *The Scarlet Letter: A Romance*. Introd. Nina Baym. Reprints text of the Centenary Edition, The Ohio State University Press, 1962. Harmondsworth: Penguin. (Orig. pub. 1850.)

Hazlitt, William. n.d. *Table Talk or Original Essays*. London: J. M. Dent.

Hecht, Michael L., Peter A. Andersen, and Sidney A. Ribeau. 1989. "The Cultural Dimensions of Nonverbal Communication." In *Handbook of International and Intercultural Communication*, ed. Molefi Kete Asante and William B. Gudykunst. Newbury Park, CA: Sage, 163–85.

Herbert, T. Walter Jr. 1980. *Marquesan Encounters: Melville and the Meaning of Civilization*. Cambridge, MA, and London: Harvard University Press.

Hinton, Laura. 1999. *The Perverse Gaze of Sympathy: Sadomasochistic Sentiments from "Clarissa" to "Rescue 911."* Albany: State University of New York Press.

Hitchcock, Alfred. 1972. "Rear Window." In LaValley 1972, 40–46. (Repr.; orig. pub. in *Take One 2*, November–December 1968, 18–20.)

Horton, Susan R. 1981. *The Reader in the Dickens World*. London: Macmillan.

Humphries, Reynold. 1979. "*Peeping Tom*: Voyeurism, the Camera, and the Spectator." In *Film Reader 4: "Point of View" and "Metahistory of Film,"* ed. Blaine Allen. Evanston, IL: Film Division, Northwestern University, 193–200.

Humphries, Reynold. 1995. "Caught in the Act of Looking: The Opening Sequence of Michael Powell's *Peeping Tom*." *Caliban* 32: 39–53.

James, Henry. 1972. *In the Cage and Other Stories*. Harmondsworth: Penguin.

James, Henry. 1984. *Literary Criticism: Essays on Literature; American Writers; English Writers*. Selected and With Notes by Leon Edel. New York: The Library of America.

James, Henry. 1999. *The Turn of the Screw*. Ed. Deborah Esch and Jonathan Warren. Norton Critical Edition. 2nd ed. New York and London: W. W. Norton.

Jay, Martin. 1993. *Downcast Eyes: The Denigration of Vision in Twentieth-Century French Thought*. Berkeley: University of California Press.

Kaplan, E. Ann. 1997. *Looking for the Other: Feminism, Film, and the Imperial Gaze*. London: Routledge.

Kendon, Adam. 1990. *Conducting Interaction: Patterns of Behavior in Focused Encounters*. Studies in Interactional Sociolinguistics 7. Cambridge: Cambridge University Press.

Lacan, Jacques. 1998. *The Four Fundamental Concepts of Psycho-analysis*. Trans. Alan Sheridan. London: Vintage. (Orig. pub. French 1973; English 1977.)

LaValley, Albert J., ed. 1972. *Focus on Hitchcock*. Englewood Cliffs, NJ: Prentice-Hall.

Lemire, Elise. 2000. "Voyeurism and the Postwar Crisis of Masculinity in *Rear Window*." In *Alfred Hitchcock's "Rear Window,"* ed. John Belton. Cambridge: Cambridge University Press, 57–90.

Lévinas, Emmanuel. 1987. *Collected Philosophical Papers*. Trans. Alphonoso Lingis. Dordrecht/Boston/Lancaster: Martinus Nijhoff.

Lewis, Paul and Rob Evans. 2013. *Undercover: The True Story of Britain's Secret Police*. London: Faber.

Lothe, Jakob. 2000. *Narrative in Fiction and Film: An Introduction*. Oxford: Oxford University Press.

Lyon, David. 2007. *Surveillance Studies: An Overview*. Cambridge: Polity.

MacLean, Robert M. 1979. *Narcissus and the Voyeur: Three Books and Two Films*. Mouton: The Hague.

Marks, Leo. 1998. *Peeping Tom*. With an interview of Leo Marks by Chris Rodley. London: Faber.

Marks, Leo. 1999. *Between Silk and Cyanide: A Codemaker's War, 1941–1945*. London: HarperCollins. (Orig. pub. 1998.)

Melville, Herman. 1996. *Typee*. Ed. Ruth Blair. The World's Classics. Oxford and New York: Oxford University Press. (Orig. pub. 1846.)

Menke, Richard. 2008. *Telegraphic Realism: Victorian Fiction and Other Information Systems*. Stanford, CA: Stanford University Press.

Merleau-Ponty, M. 1962. *Phenomenology of Perception*. Trans. Colin Smith. London: Routledge & Kegan Paul. (Orig. pub. French 1945.)

Miller, D. A. 1988. *The Novel and the Police*. Berkeley: University of California Press.

Modleski, Tania. 1988. *The Women Who Knew Too Much: Hitchcock and Feminist Theory*. London: Routledge.

Monaco, James. 2000. *How to Read a Film: The World of Movies, Media, and Multimedia: Language, History, Theory*. 3rd ed. New York and Oxford: Oxford University Press.

Moore, Lucy. 1997. *The Thieves' Opera: The Remarkable Lives and Deaths of Jonathan Wild, Thief-Taker, and Jack Shepherd, House-Breaker*. London: Viking.

Mulvey, Laura. 1989a. "Melodrama Inside and Outside the Home." In Mulvey 1989b, 63–77. (Orig. pub. 1986.)

Mulvey, Laura. 1989b. *Visual and Other Pleasures*. London: Macmillan.

Mulvey, Laura. 1989c. "Visual Pleasure and Narrative Cinema." In Mulvey 1989b, 14–26. (Orig. pub. 1975.)

Newton, Adam Zachary. 1995. *Narrative Ethics*. Cambridge, MA, and London: Harvard University Press.

Nocenti, Annie. 1999. "Writing and Directing *The Conversation*. A Talk with Francis Ford Coppola." Coppola interviewed by Annie Nocenti at his vineyard home in Napa Valley, California. *Scenario: The Magazine of Screenwriting Art* 5(1): 60–67, 185–88.

Partridge, Eric. 1984. *A Dictionary of Slang and Unconventional English*. Ed. Paul Beale. 8th ed. London: Routledge.

Pelko, Stojan. 1992. "*Punctum Caecum*, or, Of Insight and Blindness." In Žižek 1992, 106–21.

Phelan, James (1996). *Narrative as Rhetoric: Technique, Audiences, Ethics, Ideology*. Columbus: Ohio State University Press.

Pickering, Michael, and Kevin Robins. 1984. "The Making of a Working-Class Writer: An Interview with Sid Chaplin." In *The British Working-Class Novel in the Twentieth Century*, ed. Jeremy Hawthorn. London: Edward Arnold, 139–50.

Plato. 2002. *Phaedrus*. Trans. Robin Waterfield. Oxford: Oxford University Press.

Pollard, Tomas. 2001. "Telegraphing the Sentence and the Story: Iconicity in *In the Cage* by Henry James." *European Journal of English Studies* 5(1): 81–96.

Pomerance, Murray. 2013. *Alfred Hitchcock's America*. Cambridge and Malden, MA: Polity.

Rabinowitz, Peter J. 1998. *Before Reading: Narrative Conventions and the Politics of Interpretation*. Reissued with a Foreword by James Phelan. Columbus: The Ohio State University Press. (Orig. pub. by Cornell University Press, 1987.)

Rhys, Jean. 1979. "I Used to Live Here Once." In *Sleep It Off Lady*. Harmondsworth: Penguin, 175–76.

Rothman, William. 1982. *Hitchcock—The Murderous Gaze*. Cambridge, MA, and London: Harvard University Press.

Rothman, William. 1988. *The "I" of the Camera: Essays in Film Criticism, History, and Aesthetics*. Cambridge: Cambridge University Press.

Said, Edward W. 1979. *Orientalism*. New York: Vintage Books. (Orig. pub. 1978.)

Sanborn, Geoffrey. 1998. *The Sign of the Cannibal: Melville and the Making of a Postcolonial Reader*. Durham, NC, and London: Duke University Press.

Sartre, Jean-Paul. 1969. *Being and Nothingness: An Essay on Phenomenological Ontology*. Trans. Hazel E. Barnes. London: Methuen. (Orig. pub. French 1943; English 1958.)

Savoy, Eric. 1995. "'In the Cage' and the Queer Effects of Gay History." *Novel: A Forum on Fiction* 28(3): 284–307.

Schulz, Charles M. 1976. *Peanuts Jubilee*. London: Allen Lane.

Seltzer, Mark. 2000. "The Postal Unconscious." *The Henry James Review* 21(3): 197–206.

Silverman, Kaja. 1988. *The Acoustic Mirror: The Female Voice in Psychoanalysis and Cinema*. Bloomington and Indianapolis: Indiana University Press.

Spearing, A. C. 1993. *The Medieval Poet as Voyeur*. Cambridge: Cambridge University Press.

Spoto, Donald. 1983. *The Dark Side of Genius: The Life of Alfred Hitchcock*. Boston: Little, Brown.

Stam, Robert, and Roberta Pearson. 1986. "Hitchcock's *Rear Window*: Reflexivity and the Critique of Voyeurism." In *A Hitchcock Reader*, ed. Marshall Deutelbaum and Leland Poague. Ames: Iowa State University Press, 193–206. (Repr.; orig. pub. in *enclitic* 7.1 [1983].)

Stern, Milton R. 1982. *Critical Essays on Herman Melville's "Typee."* Boston: G. K. Hall.

Stevens, Hugh. 1998. "Queer Henry *In the Cage*." In *The Cambridge Companion to Henry James*, ed. Jonathan Freedman, ed. Cambridge: Cambridge University Press, 120–38.

Thomas, Kate. 2012. *Postal Pleasures. Sex, Scandal, and Victorian Letters*. New York: Oxford University Press.

Thompson, David, and Ian Christie, eds. 1996. *Scorsese on Scorsese*. London: Faber. (Repr.; orig. pub. 1989.)

Thomson, David. 1978. *America in the Dark: Hollywood and the Gift of Unreality*. London: Hutchinson.

Thurschwell, Pamela. 1999. "Henry James and Theodora Bosanquet: On the Typewriter, *In the Cage*, at the Ouija Board." *Textual Practice* 13(1): 5–23.

Truffaut, François, with the collaboration of Helen G. Scott. 1986. *Hitchcock*. Rev. ed. London: Paladin. (1st ed. 1968.)

Warhol, Robyn R. 2003. *Having a Good Cry: Effeminate Feelings and Pop-Culture Forms*. Columbus: The Ohio State University Press.

Waterhouse, Ruth. 1993. "The Inverted Gaze." In *Body Matters: Essays on the Sociology of the Body*, ed. Sue Scott and David Morgan. London: Falmer Press, 105–21.

Watzlawick, Paul, Janet Helmick Beavin, and Don D. Jackson. 1968. *Pragmatics of Human Communication: A Study of Interactional Patterns, Pathologies and Paradoxes*. London: Faber.

Weis, Elisabeth. 1982. *The Silent Scream: Alfred Hitchcock's Sound Track*. Rutherford/Madison/Teaneck, NJ: Farleigh Dickinson University Press.

Wilde, Oscar. 1992. *The Importance of Being Earnest and Related Writings*. Ed. Joseph Bristow. London: Routledge. (Play orig. performed 1895.)

Williams, Keith. 2007. *H. G. Wells, Modernity and the Movies*. Liverpool: Liverpool University Press.

Williams, Linda. 1984. "When the Woman Looks." In *Re-Vision: Essays in Feminist Film Criticism*, ed. Mary Anne Doane, Patricia Mellencamp, and Linda Williams. Frederick, MD: University Publications of America, 83–99.

Wood, Robin. 1969. *Hitchcock's Films*. 2nd ed. London: Zwemmer. (1st ed. 1965.)

Wood, Robin. 1989. *Hitchcock's Films Revisited*. New York: Columbia University Press.

Woolrich, Cornell. 1998. *The Cornell Woolrich Omnibus*. Harmondsworth: Penguin.

Žižek, Slavoj. 1991. *Looking Awry: An Introduction to Jacques Lacan through Popular Culture*. Cambridge, MA: MIT Press.

Žižek, Slavoj, ed. 1992. *Everything You Always Wanted to Know About Lacan (But Were Afraid to Ask Hitchcock)*. London: Verso.

Zunshine, Lisa. 2008. "Theory of Mind and Fictions of Embodied Transparency." *Narrative* 16(1): 65–92.

INDEX

THEORY AND INTERPRETATION OF NARRATIVE

James Phelan, Peter J. Rabinowitz, and Robyn Warhol, Series Editors

Because the series editors believe that the most significant work in narrative studies today contributes both to our knowledge of specific narratives and to our understanding of narrative in general, studies in the series typically offer interpretations of individual narratives and address significant theoretical issues underlying those interpretations. The series does not privilege one critical perspective but is open to work from any strong theoretical position.